Self-Defense

Self-Defense

A Philosophy of Violence

Elsa Dorlin

Translated by Kieran Aarons

VERSO

London • New York

This English-language edition first published by Verso 2022
Originally published in French as *Se défendre:
Une philosophie de la violence*
© Editions LA DÉCOUVERTE, Paris, France, 2017
Translation © Kieran Aarons 2022

The publisher gratefully acknowledges the support
of the Centre national du livre in France.

All rights reserved

The moral rights of the author have been asserted

1 3 5 7 9 10 8 6 4 2

Verso
UK: 6 Meard Street, London W1F 0EG
US: 388 Atlantic Avenue, Brooklyn, NY 11217
versobooks.com

Verso is the imprint of New Left Books
ISBN-13: 978-1-83976-105-8
ISBN-13: 978-1-83976-107-2 (UK EBK)
ISBN-13: 978-1-83976-108-9 (US EBK)

British Library Cataloguing in Publication Data
A catalogue record for this book is available from the British Library

Library of Congress Cataloging-in-Publication Data
A catalog record for this book is available from the Library of Congress

Typeset in Sabon by Hewer Text UK Ltd, Edinburgh
Printed and bound by CPI Group (UK) Ltd, Croydon CR0 4YY

Contents

Prologue: What a Body Can Do — vii

The Production of Disarmed Bodies — 1
Defense of Self, Defense of the Nation — 27
Testaments of Self-Defense — 53
The State, or the Non-monopoly on Legitimate Defense — 73
White Justice — 97
Self-Defense: Power to the People! — 111
Self-Defense and Safety — 133
Reprisals — 153

Acknowledgments — 181
Notes — 183

Prologue: What a Body Can Do

On Brumaire 11, Year XI [November 2, 1803], a Guadeloupe tribunal sentences Millet de la Girardière to be placed in an iron cage in the square at Pointe-à-Pitre and left there until dead. The cage employed for this public torture is eight feet tall. The person confined therein straddles a sharp blade. His feet are shackled and he must keep his legs straight to avoid being wounded by the blade. A table is placed within his reach containing provisions and drinks to quench his thirst, but a guard is there night and day to prevent him from touching them. When the victim weakens, he falls on the edge of the blade, which inflicts deep and cruel wounds. The wretch pulls himself upright from the pain, only to again fall on the cutting blade, wounding himself horribly. This torture lasts three or four days.[1]

In this type of apparatus, the convict dies because he resists—because he tries, desperately, to escape death. The atrocity of the torture lies in the way it transforms every movement by the body to protect itself from pain into a new agony. The slightest reflex of preservation becomes the impetus for the most unbearable suffering: this is what defines such modes of annihilation. What is remarkable is not the novelty of the torture, over which the modern colonial system certainly had no monopoly. The scene, along with the rhetorical device used to re-create its horror, resonates with another torture narrative, namely, the story of Damiens as described by Michel Foucault at the outset of *Discipline and Punish*.[2] However, the two cases are entirely different. As Foucault shows, the wounds inflicted on Damiens's body are not aimed at him as an individual but instead intended to restore the all-powerful will of the sovereign and the subjugation of the community, which the crime had jeopardized. Mutilations by pliers and shears, scalding hot lead, boiling oil, and molten wax, and finally dismemberment by horse . . . throughout this atrocious ordeal, Damiens remains tied up, and there is nothing to suggest that he could do anything. In other words, minimal as it may be, his power is in no way taken into account, precisely because it does not count. Damiens's body is reduced to nothingness; it is already nothing other than a theater where a vengeful community can act out cohesion and ritualize the sovereignty of its king. It is a display of the complete absence of power, the better to express the magnificence of absolute sovereign power.

In the case of the torture of the iron cage, the public is still present looking on. However, there is something else happening in the public exhibition of the victim's suffering. The technique appears to target the subject's capacity to (re)act, the better to dominate it. The repressive apparatus provokes the condemned person's bodily reactions while exhibiting them, constituting them as both the power *and* weakness of the subject. Repressive authority is no longer obliged to cast its victims as absolutely impotent in order to affirm itself. On the contrary, the more their subjective power drives its repeated and desperate efforts to survive, the more repressive authority succeeds in governing it, while disappearing behind the passive and puppet-like figure of the executioner. This deadly governance of the body is carried out with such an economy of means that the condemned appears to perish by his own hand alone. The situation is designed so that he will resist the sharp blade that threatens to fatally mutilate him: he must stand up straight in his stirrups, inside his cage. The apparatus makes the condemned man think his life depends on his strength, not only muscular and physical, but also mental: he must strain to stay alive, if he does not wish to suffer worse or die. At the same time, the sole purpose of this technology of torture is to kill him, but in such a fashion that *the more he defends himself, the worse he will suffer.* The cruel comedy of the food placed around him attests to the fact that the torture plays on the efficacy of vital actions so as to control them totally, the better to annihilate them. Just as exhaustion will cause him to collapse onto the edge of the blade, his unbearable need to eat and drink will likewise become fatal. In addition, the initial impact point on the body will almost certainly be the genitals. It is almost as if power's work of encoding gender reaches its completion here, given that the genitals, far more than any other part of the body, have become the ultimate site in which the subject's power of action lurks. When we defend them, we defend *ourselves.* That the apparatus strikes them first indicates that it seeks to destroy that by which the subject—not the legal subject, but the *capable* subject—was established.

This system of execution regards those subjected to it as *capable of doing something,* and it targets, stimulates, and encourages every last vital impulse, however slight, so as to interpellate them as *in*-efficacy, to transmute them into impotence. It is a technology of the powerful that produces a *subject* whose power of action has been aroused in order that it may be seized upon, in all its heteronomy. In spite of being entirely directed toward the preservation of life, the victim's power of action is reduced to nothing but a mechanism of death in the colonial penance machine. Here we see how an apparatus of domination can persecute the very movement of *life*, targeting vital impulses in their most muscular forms. The slightest gesture of defense or protection, the slightest movement of self-preservation, is enlisted in the annihilation of the body. By targeting the *subjects' power* as it is expressed in the impulse to defend themselves and their life, this form of power constitutes self-defense as the very expression of corporeal life, as what a subject is, and as an answer to the question "What is a life?"[3]

From the iron cage to certain modern and contemporary torture techniques, it is entirely possible to identify a common framework, a repertoire of techniques of power that can be distilled into the following adage: "The more you defend yourself, the more you'll suffer, the more certain you are to die."[4] In certain circumstances, for certain bodies, to defend oneself is equivalent to dying from ego depletion: there is no sense fighting back; to resist is to be defeated. Such an *unhappy* mechanics of action has implications at the level of political mythology (what will our resistance accomplish?), as well as for our representations of the world and of ourselves (if every effort to save myself only leads to my ruin, what can I do?). Our sense of our own power becomes just an awareness of its insufficiency, its limits, and its repercussions, leaving us to feel doubt, anxiety, and fear. The lived experience of these emotions becomes foundational, in that such experiences no longer seem to be caused by an exogenous enemy or threat of danger, however terrible, but by a projection of ourselves and our own actions and reactions. The originality of such techniques lies in the way they force us to ceaselessly work to incorporate this deadly dimension of *the subject's power*, the suspension of which becomes the only way to stay alive, since every movement of self-defense becomes at the same time a threat, a promise of death.

This economy of means, which transforms the body of the condemned (and of the violated more generally) into its own hangman, presents an outline of the modern subject in negative relief. It is certainly the case that this subject was defined by its capacity to defend itself (more on this below); however, this capacity for self-defense also became a criterion for distinguishing between those accorded full subjectivity and everyone else. The latter included all those whose capacity for self-defense needed to be either diminished or annihilated, corrupted or delegitimated, and whose unwilling bodies were exposed to the risk of death, the better to instill in them their incapacity to defend themselves, their radical *impotence*.

Here, it is less the body itself than its power of action that the apparatus seeks both to target and to mobilize. This *defensive governance* exhausts, conserves, cares for, arouses, and kills, following a complex mechanism. It decides whom to defend and whom to leave defenseless, according to a carefully graduated scale. Here, to be *defenseless* does not mean that one is "no longer able to exercise one's power"; rather, it is to be affected by a power of action that is no longer a polarized movement.[5] There is no greater danger of death than in situations like this, in which our power of action becomes twisted into an autoimmune reflex. It is no longer a question of directly obstructing the action of minorities, as in the case of sovereign repression, nor of simply leaving them to die, defenseless, as in the framework of biopower. It is a matter of *conducting certain subjects to annihilate themselves as subjects*, arousing their power of action to better guide them toward their own ruin. It is a matter of producing beings who in defending themselves destroy themselves.

March 3, 1991, Los Angeles. Rodney King, a twenty-six-year-old African American taxi driver, is pursued by three police cruisers and a helicopter over a speeding violation. When he refuses to exit his vehicle, a police officer points a gun at his face. A few seconds later, he complies and lies down on the pavement; he is then shocked with Tasers, and as he tries to get up and protect himself from a police officer's blows, he is brutally beaten, receiving dozens of baton strikes on his face and body. He is tied up and left unconscious—his skull and jaw fractured in several places, open lacerations on his mouth and face, and a broken ankle—until an ambulance arrives some minutes later to take him to the hospital.

Such a detailed account of Rodney King's attempted lynching is possible thanks to amateur footage recorded by a witness named George Holliday from his balcony overlooking the freeway, producing a genuine document of contemporary domination.[6] The video aired on television the same night and quickly circulated around the globe. One year later, a trial began of the four police officers most directly involved in King's beating (there were more than twenty at the scene of the arrest) on charges of excessive use of force. It took place before a jury from which defense lawyers had struck every single African American (there were ten white jurors, one Latin American and one Chinese American). After nearly two months, the jury opted to acquit the officers. As soon as the verdict was announced, the famous 1992 Los Angeles riots began: six days of urban revolt in which clashes with police and the army—veritable scenes of civil war—would leave 63 dead and more than 2,000 demonstrators injured.[7]

Beyond the verdict exonerating the police officers and whitewashing their acts, what is instructive here are the arguments that succeeded in convincing the jury to absolve the four accused, as well as the reasons they gave for doing so.[8] The strategy of the defense was to convince the jury that the officers were in danger. According to them, they felt they were being attacked and had no choice but to defend themselves against this "giant" (King was over six feet tall) who was striking them even while down on the ground, and who seemed to be under the influence of a drug that made him "impervious to pain." During the second trial some months later, King would state that he was "just trying to stay alive."[9] This inversion of responsibility proved to be the decisive issue. In the first trial, lawyers for the police produced and relied on a single primary piece of evidence, namely, George Holliday's video. The same video that the public regarded as proof of police brutality was called upon as evidence that, on the contrary, it was the police who were "threatened" by Rodney King. In the courtroom, the video—as seen by the jurors and narrated by the police's legal team—was interpreted as showing legitimate defense, attesting to the "vulnerability" of the police. How can such an interpretive gap be explained? How can the same images engender two versions of events, each with a radically distinct victim, depending on whether you happen to be a white juror in a courtroom or an *ordinary* spectator?[10]

This is the question posed by Judith Butler in a text composed just days after the announcement of the verdict. Rather than focusing on the divergent interpretations of who the victim is, Butler draws our attention to the conditions under which certain viewings of the video predispose individuals to judge that Rodney King is the victim of attempted lynching, *or* that the police are victims of an assault. In accordance with the Fanonian perspective she adopts, Butler contends that the proper object of critique is not the arguments of the contradictory opinions but the framework of intelligibility of perceptions that are themselves never immediate. The video should not be treated as a brute datum used to produce interpretations but as the manifestation of a "racially saturated field of visibility."[11] In other words, the racial schematization of perception defines both the production of the perceived and what it means to perceive:

> How do we account for this reversal of gesture and intention in terms of a racial schematization of the visible field? Is this a specific transvaluation of agency proper to a racialized episteme? And does the possibility of such a reversal call into question whether what is "seen" is not always already in part a question of what a certain racist episteme produces as the visible?[12]

What must be examined, then, is the process of the social construction of perceptions by a corpus that continues to constrain any possible act of knowledge.[13]

Independently of his distressed posture and signs of vulnerability, Rodney King's body was seen as the aggressor, feeding into "the phantasm of white racist aggression."[14] In the courtroom and in the eyes of the white jurors, Rodney King could be seen *only* as an "agent of violence." The same was true of male former slaves (or descendants of slaves) throughout the entire segregationist period who, unjustly accused of sexual assault, were hunted down in the streets, dragged out of prison cells or their homes, tortured, and executed. And the same remains true today for African American youths and young adults, who continue to be beaten and murdered in the streets. The perception of Rodney King's body as the aggressor is both a condition and an ongoing effect of the projection of "white paranoia."[15]

Images never speak for themselves, particularly in a world in which the representation of violence has become such a central feature of visual culture.[16] At the very beginning of Holliday's video, Rodney King is seen standing with his arms outstretched toward a police officer who is trying to hit him. This protective gesture will be consistently regarded as a threatening posture, a blatant aggression. As Kimberlé Crenshaw and Gary Peller observe, the police's legal team's tactic of *making* evidence out of the video by sequencing it into a multitude of still images, disconnected one from another, made room for endless interpretations. By proliferating contradictory narratives about a scene that had been fragmented and isolated from the social context in which it took place, police lawyers succeeded in blurring or "disaggregating" the meaning of the sequence as a whole.[17] Whereas certain citizens (Black as well as white) saw in the video overwhelming evidence of police brutality, lawyers in the courtroom were able to claim that it offered no evidence of excessive use of force: the officers' use of violence was "reasonable." The moment when the police brutality reaches its peak, at the eighty-first second of the recording, was depicted as legitimate defense against a maniac.

The perception of police violence is not exclusively based on a framework of intelligibility drawn from the past. This framework is continually updated with material and discursive techniques of power that serve (among other things) to disassociate the perception of events from the very social and political struggles that situate them historically, and craft alternative frameworks for the apprehension and intelligibility of lived reality.

By defending himself against police violence, Rodney King became indefensible. In other words, the more he defended himself, the more he was beaten and the more he came to be perceived as the aggressor. This reversal of attack and defense, aggression and protection, within a framework that allows their terms and legitimate agents to be structurally assigned irrespective of the efficacy of their gestures, tends to transform such actions into anthropological markers, delineating a color line that discriminates against the bodies and social groups that it forms thereby. This dividing line is never solely about distinguishing threatening/aggressive bodies from defensive bodies. Rather, it separates those who are agents (agents of their own defense) from those whose power of action has an entirely negative form, in the sense that they can only ever be agents of pure violence. Like any African American man arrested by a racist police force, Rodney King is recognized as an agent, but only as an agent of violence, as a violent subject, to the exclusion of any other sort of action. Black men are always made responsible for this sort of violence: they are its cause and effect, its beginning and its end.[18] From this point of view, Rodney King's protective reflexes, the disorderly movements by which he struggled to stay alive (he flaps his arms, staggers, tries to get up, stands on his knees) were described as being under his "total control" and as evidence of "dangerous intent," as if violence were the sole voluntary action possible for a Black body, effectively excluding the very possibility of legitimate self-defense.[19] Social groups constructed as "at risk" are attributed an exclusively negative power of action, as well as violent actions that are both disqualified and disqualifying, and this serves an important function, since it prevents police violence from being seen as an attack. Since bodies that have been made into minorities represent a threat, since they are a source of danger as the agents of every conceivable violence, the violence that is continuously enacted on them (beginning with that of the police and the state) need never appear as the filthy violence that it is: it is secondary, protective, defensive—it is a reaction, a response that is always already legitimate.

In the case of the iron cage torture, we have seen how targeting a body's power of action permits a certain technology of power to transform it into impotence (the more we struggle to escape suffering, the more we are wounded), with the result that the subject's defensive efforts to survive insidiously become the very mechanism of his negation. Self-defense is thus rendered irremediably impracticable for the resisting body. In the case of Rodney King, another element also comes into view. Here it is no longer simply about the power of action, but interpellation, the moral and political qualifications by which "subjects of law"—or better, subjects with the right to defend themselves—can be recognized. Rodney King cannot be perceived as a body defending itself; he is seen a priori as an agent of violence. The very possibility of defending oneself is the exclusive privilege of a dominant minority. In the case of the beating of Rodney King, the state (through the intermediary of its armed representatives) was not regarded as violent but as reacting to violence: *it defended itself against violence*. Conversely, for Rodney King, as for every other body victimized by this rhetoric of self-defense, the more he defended himself, the more *indefensible* he became.

Millet de la Girardière could have defended himself, but by defending himself he became defenseless. Rodney King defended himself, but by defending himself he became indefensible. These two logics of subjection converge upon an unhappy subjectivation, which is the focus of this book—and this at a time when technologies of power have never relied so heavily on this defensive logic to ensure their own perpetuation.

With this point of departure, we may begin to trace the outline of a certain apparatus of power, which I will call the defensive apparatus. How does it function? By targeting anything that expresses a force, an impulse, a polarized movement of self-defense, and then, for some, marking out its trajectory and encouraging it with legitimating structures, or else, for others, obstructing its realization, its very possibility, making these impulses awkward and faltering, or dangerous and threatening, for oneself and others alike.

This double-edged defensive apparatus traces a line of demarcation between subjects who deserve to be defended and to defend themselves, and bodies forced to use defensive tactics. For these bodies, vulnerable and violable, only unarmed subjectivities remain. Kept in check through violence, they live or survive only to the extent that they manage to equip themselves with defensive tactics. These subaltern practices constitute what I call *self-defense* in the proper sense of the term, by contrast with the juridical concept of legitimate defense. Unlike the latter, self-defense paradoxically has no subject—by which I mean that the subject being defended does not preexist the movement to resist the violence directed at it. In this sense, self-defense is part of what I propose to call the "martial ethics of the self."

Tracing this system back to its colonial origins makes it possible to question the monopolistic capture of violence by states laying claim to the legitimate use of physical force. Instead of a tendency toward monopoly, we hypothesize an imperial economy of violence that paradoxically defends individuals whose self-defense has always already been recognized as legitimate. This economy maintains the legitimacy of the use of physical force for certain subjects, granting them powers of preservation and jurisdiction (vigilantism) that amount to a license to kill.

However, what is at issue is not merely the distinction, fundamental though it may be, between "defended subjects" and "defenseless subjects," between subjects who may defend themselves legitimately and those for whom self-defense is illegitimate (and who are therefore indefensible). There is an even subtler threshold, since this government of the body intervenes at the level of the muscles. There is an art of governance that acts on nerve impulses, muscular contractions, tensions of the kinesthetic body, and the discharge of hormonal fluids. It operates upon whatever stimulates or inhibits our muscles, whatever allows them to act or that counters them, whatever restrains or provokes them, reassures them or makes them tremble, whatever causes them to strike or not strike.

To begin from muscle rather than from law: this is certain to change the way in which violence is theorized in political thought. The focus of *Self-Defense* is on the moment violent defensive action is taken, and I do not believe such moments could be rendered intelligible by subjecting them to a political and moral analysis centered around questions of legitimacy. At each of these moments, the stakes of defensive violence are nothing other than life itself: to not be cut down where you stand. Physical violence is thus understood as a vital necessity, a praxis of resistance.

The history of self-defense is polarized, marked by the continuous opposition of two antagonistic expressions of the defense of the "self." On the one hand, there is the dominant juridical-political tradition of legitimate defense, linked to myriad practices of power with various modalities of brutality. On the other hand, there is the hidden history of a "martial ethics of self" that cuts across contemporary political movements and counter-conducts, testifying to a surprising continuity of defensive resistance that makes them strong.

I propose to map out a constellational history of self-defense. I did not choose my route by picking out the most illustrative examples but by exploring the memory of struggles for which the dominated body constitutes the principal archive: the syncretic knowledge and cultures of slave self-defense, feminist self-defense practices, the fighting techniques developed in Eastern Europe by Jewish organizations against pogroms, and so on.

By opening this archive, which includes many other stories as well, my aim is not to produce a work of history, but to contribute to a genealogy. In our darkening sky, this constellation sparkles with echoes, addresses, testimonies, and citational relationships that connect its various stars in a tenuous and subjective way. The major texts that form the philosophical backbone of the Black Panther Party for Self-Defense pay homage to the insurgents of the Warsaw ghetto; queer self-defense patrols are in a citational relationship with Black self-defense movements; the jujitsu practiced by English internationalist anarchist suffragists was accessible to them in part due to an imperial policy of capturing the wisdom and skill of the colonized, through their disarmament.

My own history and bodily experience served as the prism through which I listened, saw, and read this archive. My theoretical and political culture has instilled in me a foundational idea, namely, that relations of power in situ can never be fully reduced to collective standoffs, as they always involve lived experiences of domination that occur in the intimacy of bedrooms, in subway station corridors, beneath the surface of family reunions, and so on. In other words, for some, the question of defense does not disappear when the moment of overt political mobilization ends but is part of a continuous experience, a phenomenology of violence. This feminist approach seizes upon something in the fabric of power relations that was traditionally seen as being either pre- or extra-political. Having made this shift, I intend to work not at the scale of constituted political subjects but on that of the politicization of subjectivities: in everyday life, in the intimacy of the enraged affects trapped within us, in the solitude of lived experiences of violence, where we continuously practice self-defense without calling it such. From one day to the next, what does violence do to our lives, to our bodies, to our muscles? And what can our bodies both do and not do, in and through this violence?

The Production of Disarmed Bodies

A Brief History of Bearing Arms

Who has the right to defend themselves by having access to weapons? Conversely, who is excluded from this privilege?

Historically, the act of carrying weapons has been strictly codified and controlled. Such regulations classify weapons based on complex scales of their dangerousness and the technical skill they require. They are also intended to create hierarchies based on status, to distinguish between conditions, and to solidify social positions by creating a system of differentiated access to the resources necessary to *defend oneself*. This access is determined by rights of possession and rights of use; however, juridical opinion has always had a hard time establishing clear distinctions. Martial practices take innumerable forms. Objects that can be used as weapons may not be recognized as such (this is the case for items of all kinds, not only pitchforks, sickles, staffs, scythes, and pickaxes, but also knitting needles, hair pins, rolling pins, scissors, lamp stands, knickknacks, belts and laces, forks, keys, spray paint, gas canisters, or even the body itself—the hands, feet, and elbows). Herein lies the difficulty in the idea of *use*, which can never be fully anticipated, circumscribed, or prevented. Everything can be used in thousands of ways: any object can become an *improvised weapon*.[1]

With this qualification in mind, in Europe, with the exception of the armed forces and the police, the right to bear arms has traditionally been a privilege reserved for the nobility, bound up in their exclusive hunting rights.[2] In France, poachers were severely punished in accordance with a 1601 edict (lashing or, in the case of repeat offenders, the galleys or the death penalty), not only because they were stealing game, but primarily because they had given themselves the right to carry a weapon. This right would expand and become more complex as urbanization and industrialization progressed, notably in order to protect the urban bourgeoisie and their interests. The monarchic state regulated the carrying of weapons more and more strictly throughout the 1660s, although individual or collective ownership of weapons remained common up to the French Revolution.

In the Middle Ages everyone was armed. Certain populations were even encouraged to remain armed (such as those located in strategic areas), and military units were made of conscripted civilians who brought their own weapons. In this context, the emergence of clearly distinguished social groupings made up of armed individuals was due to progressive layers of regulation rather than any kind of systematic code.[3] There is thus no real contradiction between banning weapons and maintaining armed populations. The distinction between the possession and carrying of weapons is part of the judicial arsenal designed to control *armed bodies*. It is also based on a division between public and private spheres, the first legal expression of which, spelled out alongside permission for honest merchants to defend their cities, concerned the right to be armed in "public space," which referred to the king's roads and all spaces dedicated to the circulation of goods. The development of cities and large urban neighborhoods transformed the *hexis chevaleresque*.[4] By the early fourteenth century, it led to a ban not on the possession of weapons outright but rather on the carrying of weapons *outside the home*. Since disarming groups of people on the king's roads and public roadways was a necessary condition to allow the king to travel in peace and safety, public space is thus defined in reference to the safety of the king.[5] This ban occurred alongside a positive measure instituting a system of "weapons carry permits," the first recorded instance of which is from 1265. These permits specify the purely defensive purpose of the weapon and its type (sword, knife, or crossbow, for example) as well as the geographic area of authorization.[6] Until the fifteenth century, regulations relating to the carrying of weapons were collectively intended to control seditious currents among the nobility. "In France, the turning point was marked by the failure of the Fronde, the last manifestation of local armed forces standing outside the king's power. Henceforth the possession of weapons of war was reserved exclusively to the state."[7] This "monopolistic" tendency is linked to the state's control over the production, trade, and storage of weapons.[8]

In the fifteenth century, the legal framework around carrying weapons was upended by the formation of a professional army to protect the kingdom, which was to be the only force authorized to use weapons of war. Henceforth, there needed to be some kind of visible distinction between *military personnel* and *civilians*. Notably, this distinction was made on the basis of the kinds of weapons carried (combat weapons or purely defensive ones), which in turn had an impact on what kinds of personal weapons were accepted.[9] Romain Wenz shows that in this context, the categories of offensive and defensive weapons were not drawn along the same lines as they would be today: shields and armor were considered offensive weapons because "they demonstrate an intention to fight, whereas blades worn at the waist were considered defensive."[10] Men ready for combat gradually came to be seen as criminal, their weapons marking them as "disloyal." Confrontations were being increasingly policed, on their way to becoming a civilized, bourgeois form of intersubjectivity, and armed men upset the balance of this process. "Beyond coercion, the invention of 'prohibited weapons' teaches subjects to avoid violence by turning to the justice system."[11]

A distinction was also made between bearing arms and taking up arms: the former was restricted, with only a minority of individuals legitimately accorded this right, while the latter was forbidden in order to criminalize armed rebellion. Regulations around the carrying of weapons mutated, allowing for the externalization of protective force (the justice system), while still legitimating the right to self-defense for some by making it legal for them to carry weapons at all times.

Starting in the sixteenth century, this legislation was applied to the aristocracy, but the law could not eliminate certain chivalrous practices among the waning nobility of the sword, who refused to resolve affairs of honor in court, and laws criminalizing duels with increasing severity were of limited effect.[12] This legislation also represents a shift. Henceforth, the justice system's instrument for disciplining the use of weapons and martial practices came to focus on *the defense of persons and property*. The serious punishments handed down to aristocratic men who participated in duels show the lengths being taken to make them turn to the justice system to resolve conflicts among peers.[13] At the same time, however, they were ensured by law the right to carry and use "defensive" weapons to protect themselves from men belonging to other social classes. The nobility's privilege of personally defending themselves and their belongings still implies an aristocratic culture of combat. When it comes to defense, the law isn't everything—you still need to know how *to do it properly*.[14] In order that the nobility be allowed to maintain their martial superiority, the legislation guaranteed their right to self-defense by codifying as licit or illicit not only various kinds of weapons but also access to martial knowledge and the culture of "military" training. Arquebuses and pistols were thus reserved exclusively for gentlemen.[15]

Nobles also frequently carried a rapier, which is easy to carry and handle and is used for thrusting more than slashing, distinguishing it from the swords generally used in military campaigns. A civilian sword, the rapier is meant for self-defense. Specifically, it can be wielded *in the city,* which is at once a perpetual site of crime and the primary stage for, if not a civilizing process, then at least "the pacification of manners" in what was coming to be known as "public space" in the modern sense of the term.[16] In such a space, the conditions necessary for commercial exchange, such as the safety of honest people, had to be ensured. In practice, the separation between private space and public (civil) space was increasingly marked by whether one *sets out armed* or *sets down one's weapons* upon entry.

Throughout modernity, the spread and the technical sophistication of firearms, alongside the gradual commercialization of civilian weaponry of all kinds, changed the very definition of "self-defense." The legal framework concerning carried weapons and self-defense practices influenced the bearing of arms but not the acquisition of attitudes, abilities, and martial skills, which were enmeshed in social antagonism. These antagonisms are visible throughout the Renaissance and the early modern period. In regard to fencing, the Italian school, dominant in Europe during the fifteenth and early sixteenth centuries, promoted an "art of fencing," quicker, more technical, and requiring less physical force than the handling of a war sword.[17] This style of "street" fencing, intended for self-defense, was made up of feints and ruses, dodges and surprise attacks (the famous *botta,* which means "strike" in Italian, a secret thrust), and it made the sword an even more offensive weapon than before.[18] It involved teaching how to wield a sword while dressed in city clothes and training in combinations that made use of the cape or coat. The development of "training," a genuine didactic self-defense practice, also led to the parallel development of symbolic or euphemistic combat, as exemplified by the appearance of weapons deliberately rendered harmless and intended for drills.[19] In the nineteenth century, in a treatise on the history of fencing, the author mocked this fledgling art as having "no system."[20] The remark is interesting because it shows how a set of pragmatic practices gradually reached an excessive level of formalization, losing in the process any effectiveness it had as a realistic art of self-defense. Combat had become codified, making it a marker of distinction, and fencing became a "science" and then a "sport" reserved for the elite. This was in opposition to the rabble's messy techniques, at a time when the values of noblemen were no longer shaping the dominant norms of "modern" masculinity. The tradeoff signaled a loss of effective martial skill and a crisis of virility among the declining aristocracy. Norbert Elias defines this process as one of "sportization," based on the experience of English sports during the Victorian era. For Elias, such codification is the mark of a ritualized activity that has adapted the affective experience of confrontation (pleasure, fear, anger) into a form that dramatically reduces its cost in injuries and long-term physical consequences.[21] In combat arenas where their bodies were safe, men from the most privileged classes kept their distance from the anarchy of street fighting. They fought among equals in specific time frames with agreed-upon moves, and so became sport fighters. As a self-defense strategy, this was not based on training your body for physical self-defense but on avoiding situations of "real" combat at all cost, as these risk being sites where class struggle is literally given flesh.

Disarming Slaves and Natives: The Right to Kill versus "Unarmed" Subjectivities

In 1685, Article 15 of the *Code noir*, or the Black Code (the law legalizing slavery in French colonies) forbade "slaves from carrying any offensive weapon or large stick," under penalty of lashing.[22] The corresponding Spanish law, the 1768 *Ordenanzas* signed in Santo Domingo, similarly forbade Black people "the use of weapons of any kind, under penalty of fifty strokes with the lash"; the machete was permitted for agricultural work, but its total length had to be less than a half cubit.[23] The law's 1784 version, the *Código Negro carolino*, or the Caroline Code, renewed this ban and added that machetes should be replaced by more "practical" tools, ones less "liable to upset the public's tranquility and repose on the island," reserving their use for quadroons and mixed-race, "or greater."[24]

The ban on carrying and on traveling in possession of weapons demonstrates the anxiety settlers felt about successful practices of slave resistance. Everything that gave slaves the chance to prepare or train for revolt was banned. In the nineteenth century, in the context of slavery in the United States, Elijah Green, a former slave born in 1843 in Louisiana, stated that Black people were strictly forbidden to own a pencil or pen on pain of hanging for attempted murder.[25] Contrast this with the right granted to settlers in most colonial and imperial contexts to carry and use weapons.

In the context of the colonial French state in Algeria, a decree issued on December 12, 1851, outlawed the sale of weapons to natives. By contrast, a decree issued on December 11, 1872, in response to a Kabyle uprising in 1871, granted the right to "French settlers of European origin" to buy, sell, possess, carry, and use weapons if they lived in isolated areas or in areas not protected by a garrison.[26] This meant they could "continue, on their request, to be authorized, in any area where it is needed, to possess such weapons and munitions of war deemed necessary by the territorial authority to defend themselves and their families and assure the safety of their home."[27] The fact is, the colonial state could not function without militias capable of doing the occupation's dirty work.

The Black Code had already granted policing powers to residents of the colonies, and it specified that any slaves found outside of their home without a "pass" (a detailed note written by their owner) would be punished by flogging and branded with the fleur-de-lys.[28] Any royal subject who saw an illegal gathering or meeting had the right to arrest the guilty parties "and take them to prison, though they be officers not yet subject to any decree" (Article 16).[29] Despite such drastic measures, the colonial government was faced with permanent crisis, as criminalizing the slaves' activities in this way required costly surveillance. On the heels of the Seven Years' War against the English, the French were unable to stop "criminality" among the slaves once they returned to Martinique. In a letter to Governor Fénélon, the Count of Elva wrote, "I have received many complaints of maroon Negros ravaging homesteads, traveling armed, gathering and insulting Whites, or selling all kinds of things publicly in town without the signed permission of their masters."[30] The governor's response blamed a lack of resources and men for police work but promised a new regulation (which came into effect the following month) increasing the punishment for gatherings and free movement by slaves.[31]

Throughout the era of slavery, the disarmament of slaves was accompanied by a veritable discipline of the body to keep them defenseless, which meant punishing the slightest use of martial practices. The philosophy behind this process gets at the essence of the condition of servitude: a slave is someone who does not have the right or the duty to preserve themselves. Disarmament should be understood as a measure for the security of the free population, but more fundamentally it traces a dividing line between subjects, who own themselves and are responsible for their own preservation, and slaves, who do not own themselves and whose preservation depends entirely on the goodwill of their masters. There are two different ideas of *self*-preservation at play here: preservation as it relates to the preservation of *one's own life,* and preservation as it relates to the capitalization of one's own value. These two ideas of preservation collide any time human beings are turned into objects, when the preservation of their lives becomes dependent on their owner and on the market that sets their price and allows them to be exchanged.

At the peaks of slave revolutions in Martinique, it was customary to execute "maroons" in front of their mothers, and to force these women to watch the torments inflicted on their children.[32] This was considered an "educational" practice by the administrators, but it was also a form of entertainment for settlers, many of whom enjoyed attending such punishments. Its true aim, of course, was to make fugitive slaves understand that, in attempting to preserve their lives, they were in fact "robbing their masters of their value"; by creating a new kind of crime in this way, the colonial justice system taught slaves that they possessed no right of self-preservation.[33] They were not authorized to preserve themselves or those to whom they gave life: this was the sole prerogative of their masters and only they were to decide it. Slaves did not have lives, only value.[34] As Joseph Elzéar Morénas wrote in his argument for abolition: "The right of preservation belongs wholly to the master." Any attempt at preserving one's life was thus transformed into a crime, and any act of self-defense by slaves was construed as an assault on the masters.

In the same way that slaves were stripped of their natural right to self-preservation, they were also denied access to the courts, a privilege reserved for settlers. Concerning the exercise of justice, a royal ordinance on December 30, 1712, forbade whites to torture their slaves while interrogating them, punishable by a £500 fine. Black people were to be tried in private sessions by a lone judge, without a lawyer or the chance to call witnesses. They were truly defenseless.[35] There was also a principle of impunity at work. Article 43 of the Black Code "absolves masters who kill slaves under their authority," and although the murder of a slave belonging to a different master was punishable by death, in most cases the killer was acquitted.[36] Notably, this was the case in the murder of a slave named Colas, twenty-five years old and pregnant, who was shot to death by a planter, M. Ravenne-Desforges, while she was crossing his coffee plantation in Marie-Galante on October 5, 1821. In the initial ruling, the court refused to apply Article 43, because the settler was carrying a weapon with the intention of going hunting and that "the shot fired by M. Ravenne cannot be considered a thoughtless act of anger intended to kill, but rather was fired with the goal of marking the Negro woman with some lead so that he would be able to recognize her."[37] He was sentenced to ten months' exile and the confiscation of his gun; should the offense be repeated, he would be stripped of his right to carry weapons in the colony. A second ruling also declined to apply Article 43 of the Black Code, citing a royal letter from 1744. In the end, the minister ordered a new trial in the case, and Ravenne-Desforges chose to defend himself by making his slave Cajou stand trial in his stead, as the slave was carrying his master's rifle. Cajou was sentenced to ten years' forced labor, since he was still a minor. This practice of "guilt by substitution" was widespread in the colonies, although in this case it was ultimately rejected by the Royal Court of Justice, in a ruling that also found Ravenne-Desforges not guilty.[38] The slave could be used as a sort of *legal replica* of the master, able to be judged, sentenced, and punished in the master's place, making slaves the best defense.[39]

The colonial order's systematic disarmament of slaves, natives, and subalterns benefited the white minority, who enjoyed an absolute right to carry weapons and to use them with impunity. The "old" rights of preservation and access to the courts were adapted into a set of derogatory exceptions granting settlers policing and jurisdictional powers while disarming other individuals and rendering them *in essence* "killable" and "condemnable." This privilege was codified as legitimate defense.

But that isn't all. The colonial definition of legitimate defense included a slew of specious "exceptions," which established that only a select group of people could demand that *justice be done*.[40] Isabelle Merle cites a decree from December 23, 1887, that lists infractions specific to the natives of New Caledonia that included "the carrying of Kanak weapons in areas inhabited by Europeans, as well as traveling outside of areas delimited by the administration, disobedience, entering cabarets or bars, and nudity on the roads." The list was expanded in 1888, 1892, and 1915 to include "refusal to pay the head tax," "missing an appointment at the office of Native Affairs," refusing to provide requested information or to collaborate with the authorities, "disrespectful acts," and "public speaking with the goal of undermining respect for the French authorities."[41] The fast-growing list of special crimes and infractions reveals a racial, anthropological categorization of criminality: actions *became* criminal when they were committed by a slave or by an Indigenous, colonized, or Black person.[42] The justice system becomes a process of incriminating a class of persons *always presumed* guilty—meaning the only agency they were ascribed was the product of phantasmic aggression—for the benefit of the class of persons always entitled to demand justice.

The history of apparatuses of disarmament points to the production and maintenance of a defenseless social group. These measures came along with regulations designed to repress counter-conduct of all kinds, by restricting access to both weapons and defensive techniques. Throughout the modern era, conflict was increasingly judicialized, with social antagonism and conflict "between peers" sharply delimited in order to push individuals to resort to the justice system and the law. This process also produced a space outside of the rights of citizenship. Because they were considered "dangerous," some subjects were excluded from the right of self-defense, and this despite all the efforts to make them powerless to defend themselves. They thus become indefensible, exposed to violence and *always already guilty*.[43]

Martial Asceticism: Cultures of Self-Defense among Slaves

Transgressive, informal, indirect martial techniques: there is a whole underground genealogy of defensive practices of self. Our goal here is not to retrace the political and legal history of legitimate defense but to evoke its combative flip side. From this perspective, the history of "unarmed" martial cultures among slaves reveals forms of subjectivation involving forms of resistance that do not fit within a traditional temporality of confrontation, meaning confrontation can be said to be *differentiated*.

In *The Wretched of the Earth*, Frantz Fanon describes how colonization causes time to coagulate by dividing up space (the urban space is divided into two zones: a bright, rich, proper one for the settlers, and one in which the natives "swarm" like rats), by hemming in colonized people and keeping them at a respectful distance. In the colonial world, colonized bodies are obstructed at every turn: it is completely impossible to defend yourself physically and mentally from violence. Colonized people are thus outside their body, seeing their body experience violence, their body made unrecognizable and uninhabitable, caught in the inertia of an endless cycle of brutality. The body of the colonized person can only be reanimated by and in a dreamlike temporality. Outside of time in their dreams, natives can finally use their strength:

> The first thing the colonial learns is to remain in his place and not overstep its limits. Hence the dreams of the colonial subject are muscular dreams, dreams of action, dreams of aggressive vitality ... During colonization the colonized subject frees himself night after night between nine in the evening and six in the morning.[44]

Dreaming of their bodies in motion, colonized people run, jump, swim, and strike. Their relationship to time, their relationship to space, their lived experience—all of these are distorted by their phantasmic selves. Caught in "hallucinatory dreams" as a way of trying to survive in the colonial system, the colonized remain passive in their daily life.[45] However, this passivity is also subject to a constant muscular tension, the implacable promise of vengeance:

> The muscles of the colonized are always tensed ... The symbols of society such as the police force, bugle calls in the barracks, military parades, and the flag flying aloft serve not only as inhibitors but also as stimulants. They do not signify: "Stay where you are." But rather "Get ready to do the right thing."[46]

The phantasmic body is hyperbolic, its muscular existence extending to infinity, and it is a crucible for pathogenic subjectivity, one stripped of any real capacity. The alienated, colonized subject is no more than a witness to the anguish of dematerialization, the derealization of their bodies and agency. But it's this very process of derealization that initiates a liberatory dynamic involving rebellious sensuality, or rather *rampant* sensuality, inexorably violent. If the brutality of colonization lets up for so much as a second, the people who are not yet subjects will explode. Self-defense becomes ecstatic: it is both in and through this violent labor, when the colonized are *outside of themselves*, that they get free and become subjects.[47] Being enclosed in a spectral body that comes to life again each night is a form of damnation. However, it is also a position that gives rise to a form of martial resentment, a rumination in the muscles in preparation for combat: the colonized "patiently waits for the colonist to let his guard down and then pounces on him."[48] Colonial violence has a paralyzing effect—it inhibits, and it produces a body petrified in terror. Although this paralysis is an effect of constant repression, of being controlled, it is also an attribute of tense bodies that are visualizing the confrontation to come, bodies ready to leap forth: "a constant muscular tonus."[49] According to Fanon, although this muscular tension is first released through fratricidal conflict, and although it exhausts and domesticates itself in "terrifying myths" (part of a "magical superstructure") and through "the ecstasy of dance," the act of entering a struggle for liberation will transform, *reorient*, this violence—frustrated, fantastic, projected—into real violence.[50] It is also possible that this new orientation brought about by the liberation struggle—in which futile violence becomes total, historic violence—is in fact simply a way of following through on promises made, as Fanon describes it. If we suppose that simulated experiences by spectral bodies are also a form of study in preparation for confrontation, then it follows that imagined combat is not only a form of mental self-defense but also a form of physical training anticipating and visualizing the move to defensive violence.

In a certain way, the settlers were not mistaken. For instance, at the end of the seventeenth century, Article 16 of the Black Code forbade all gatherings, assemblies, or meetings of slaves belonging to different masters, by day and by night, even those festive in nature.[51] Any activity involving dancing, singing, or music that required participants to be arranged combatively in a circle contributed to the "unarmed" martial culture that created such *white panic*.[52] Jean-Baptiste Labat wrote:

> Laws have been passed in the islands to prevent these *calendas* not only because of the indecent and lascivious postures of this dance, but also to avoid overly large congregations of slaves who, finding themselves so joyfully thrown together, usually under the influence of brandy, could stage a revolt, an uprising, or thieving raids. However, in spite of these laws and all the precautions their masters can take, it is practically impossible to prevent them.[53]

Dance steps were suspected of being a way of engaging in combat. At the end of the eighteenth century in the Antilles and Guyana, there were many rules forbidding gatherings and martial dances such as calendas, a term found in almost all creole dialects, from occurring at night.[54] Only *bamboulas* were authorized, slave dances set to the beat of a drum (the bamboula) where a king and queen are elected—often with white approval.[55] Calendas continued to be held in secret at night up in the hills, away from the white gaze. These dances are made up of pugilistic movements to the rhythm of percussion and are accompanied by magical rituals. They combine wrestling, stick fighting, striking (with hands and feet), leg sweeps, and acrobatics, a legacy of the transatlantic martial skills that developed in the context of the slave trade (incorporating notably African, Indigenous, and European combat techniques).[56] They can thus be interpreted as preparatory classes for confrontation. In the Francophone Caribbean, Madagascar, and the Mascarene Islands, other such practices include the *sové vayan,* the *bèrnaden,* and the *maloyè* (stick) in Guadeloupe; the *kokoyé* and notably the *danmyé ladja* (involving broad movements, dance steps, and hand or foot strikes) in Martinique, as well as the *wolo* or *libo* (aquatic combat techniques where fighters could attach blades to their feet); and finally the *moringue* in Réunion and Madagascar.[57]

Because our knowledge of self-defense practices among the enslaved relies entirely on the records of the dominant, it is difficult to get a full picture.[58] It is clear, however, that these martial dances were part of a suite of codified oppositional cultural forms in the Caribbean and Americas that disappeared in the late nineteenth and early twentieth centuries.[59] They have since been revived in a different mode as part of "Creole culture," which dilutes their violence in a certain way, in order to make them a more "perfect legacy," part of the memory and historiography of Afro-descendants.[60]

That being said, these cultures all share that they were created through colonization: they were criminalized, surveilled, appropriated, disciplined, instrumentalized, and exhibited, notably during fights to the death between slaves organized by settlers.[61] These diasporic martial and musical cultures were "creolized" in diverse and locally specific ways.[62] Following Christine Chivallon's analysis, "creolization" means, on the cultural level, "the development of ways of coming to terms with the powerful," and we use it in this way here.[63] These self-defense practices are at once a way of training for combat *and also* codified forms in the context of hierarchical social relations internal to slave societies. Their martial practices develop both in and through a phenomenology of the dancing body and a mythology expressed in magic rituals, Voodoo, celebrations, and ceremonies (notably wakes) and in its own cosmogonies. Furthermore, they are all characterized by skillful tactics and the importance of ruses and hybrid forms of combat. These martial practices have no rules, and the fighters, in perpetual polyrhythmic motion, use any technique while feinting, dodging, tricking, attacking. As a form of self-defense, these practices cannot be reduced to a collection of effective strikes, but rather they are based in an acute sense of the opportunities made possible in real combat by the ceaseless dancing movement. This confuses the adversary, clouds their perception, and interferes with their ability to anticipate the blow.[64] Fighting becomes a matter of setting the pace, by either following or defying the drumbeat that holds together the circle of initiated fighters. All of these aspects contributed to the creation of a syncretic self-defense system for the enslaved, combining many traditions, techniques, and cultures—both of combat and of choreography. It drew on physical techniques and rhythm, as well as a philosophy and mysticism of combat, in order to create a self-defense system capable of ensuring survival.[65]

Moreau de Saint-Méry described this syncretic culture of slave self-defense as it existed on Hispaniola:

> The *calenda* and the *chica* are not the only dances brought from Africa to the colony. There is another we have been aware of for some time, mostly in the western part of the island, that is known as *vaudoux*. The *vaudoux* should not be thought of as only a dance, or rather the dance is accompanied by activities that should cause it to be classed among those institutions made up in large part of superstitions and bizarre practices. According to the Negro laborers, who are the true spectators of *vaudoux* in the colony and who are also responsible for its rules and principles, *vaudoux* refers to an all-powerful supernatural being on whom everything that happens in the world depends.[66]

The reference to Voodoo in the colonial historiography allows us to better discern the diversity and intricacy of slave combat techniques that involved invoking, harnessing, and incarnating natural and spiritual forces in order to defend themselves against the system of slavery.[67] In the colonies, the settlers, soldiers, and missionaries perceived esoteric knowledge of self-defense held by slaves and colonized people to be a formidable threat, believing the magical rituals could grant invincibility.[68] They considered slave martial practices aggressive, otherworldly, and demonic, and targeted them for repression accordingly.[69]

When organized revolts broke out all across Saint-Domingue in 1791, they bore the trace of these nocturnal rituals so often repeated in the hills. The insurrection was described as a bloody dance:

> In all the multitude, there were hardly sixty guns. They were armed with knives, hoes, iron-tipped sticks, and slings. At three in the morning, they attacked the whites, who stood ready for battle around the city, with prodigious determination. The Blacks, put into a frenzy by their witches, ran joyfully to their deaths, believing they would be reborn in Africa. Hyacinthe carried a bull's tail as he walked through the ranks, saying it would protect them from bullets. While keeping the white cavalry at bay on one side, on the other, he launched an attack on the national guard. The young settlers from Port-au-Prince who made up this corps, though brave, proud, and magnificently equipped, could not resist the insurgents' impetuousness. They were losing ground when Philibert came with his African troops and restored the balance. Both sides were fighting with equal furor. With rapid volleys of coordinated fire, the Artois and Norman regiments mowed down whole lines of Blacks as they charged chaotically toward the bayonets. From time to time, the cavalry would mount an impressive charge, but they were quickly pushed back to the city by the insurgents, who furiously clung to the horses and, despite the saber blows, would drag the rider from the saddle. The most hideous carnage occurred near where the Praloto's artillery was set up. The Blacks charged the cannons audaciously, only to be crushed by the deadly shelling. They seemed to

falter, but Hyacinthe, waving his bull's tail all the while, reignited their ardor with these words: "Forward, forward! The cannonballs are dust!" And he led the charge into the bullets and shelling himself. We saw insurgents grab hold of artillery and cling to them tightly, refusing to let go even while they were being killed, and we saw others reaching their arms into the cannons to pull out the ammunition, and yelling to their fellows: "Come on! We've got them!" The guns fired, carrying their limbs into the distance.[70]

The emergence of martial asceticism as a clandestine, polysemic practice also speaks in part to the enormously unequal nature of any possible synchronic confrontation. The colonial context forced slaves to arrange indirect, displaced, and figurative confrontations. Combat was moved elsewhere or delayed, and so it became an imagined duel between peers.[71] James Scott theorizes the opposition between the "hidden transcript" and the "public transcript" of resistance as follows:

> For most bondsmen throughout history, whether untouchables, slaves, serfs, captives, minorities held in contempt, the trick to survival, not always mastered by any means, has been to swallow one's bile, choke back one's rage, and conquer the impulse to physical violence. It is this systematic *frustration of reciprocal action* in relations of domination which, I believe, helps us understand much of the content of the hidden transcript. At its most elementary level, the hidden transcript represents an acting out in fantasy—and occasionally in secretive practice—of the anger and reciprocal aggression denied by the presence of domination.[72]

Scott refuses to accept that "reciprocal action" is impossible, which means taking the time to prepare the ideal or partial conditions for such action, but these could also be said to be toxic conditions. When combat against the oppressor is deferred, it can turn back against the oppressed and their loved ones—bloodletting occurs out of a cathartic need to experience and manifest the phantasm of repressed struggle. This modality of domination perpetuates itself by preventing or deferring confrontation, and its effect is twofold: keeping the dominated in line also means keeping them under constant tension, which contributes to self-destructive conflicts. However, tension is also a form of training under "real" conditions (not at all symbolically), which leads to the growth of extreme, explosive violence and radical forms of martial sociability. Thus, this approach by the dominant is doubly polarizing, bringing about a form of self-defense that lacks any modality of self-preservation, meaning that when defensive struggle is engaged, fear of death will be neither a limitation nor even a dialectical problem.[73]

The Empire's Black Force: "Long Live Patriarchy! Long Live France!"

While slaves and natives were being systematically disarmed and kept defenselessness, they were also subject to national defense policies to enroll them in the armed forces. Although their units were armed, they were also the first to be sent to their deaths. The empire's subjects were tasked with doing the "dirty work" in the colonies, and with "taking care" of the national army, protecting both by sparing the lives of citizens, of French soldiers, while also allowing them to keep their consciences clean. The French army could conquer without needing to personally commit atrocities in the name of colonial paternalism.[74] In the eyes of European commanders, their ragtag native troops did "fine work." In the early twentieth century, West African infantry developed a good reputation in metropolitan France, where they were seen as courageous, loyal, and docile. In 1910, Lieutenant-Colonel Charles Mangin wrote the emblematic work in this vein, *La Force noire* (The black force).[75] In it, he develops a racial classification system of the qualities of a good soldier, then uses it to advocate for the massive use of colonized people, especially those from West Africa, in the military.[76] "The West African races," Mangin writes, "are not only warlike, they have a fundamentally military disposition. They not only love danger and lives of adventure, but are fundamentally open to discipline."[77] In a military take on the "civilizing mission," Mangin bases his argument on the idea that African men have an innate need to be under someone's command: they are, in his opinion, made for obedience.[78] Evoking the virtues of animism, this high-ranking officer praises the "primitive patriarchy" existing in some Black nations, where the head of the family commanded his sons, wives, and captives and had them work for him.[79] He maintains that unlike Arabs and Berbers, who are quick to "betray" the flag, whether because of their commitment to Islam or their nomadic lifestyle, the men of sub-Saharan Africa need leaders and have no difficulty recognizing the authority of white officers due to their innate sense of hierarchy.

The deference attributed to Black soldiers is linked to a whole racist dogma around how work is supposedly organized in "primitive patriarchies." Mangin even states that the ease of training African soldiers for the military is due to their bodies and minds being untainted by agricultural work, as this is traditionally left to women.[80] Although they have not been civilized by labor, military service can offer colonized peoples the chance for a beneficial metamorphosis, allowing them to enter the course of history. Here we see once again a classic theme of colonial rhetoric: the blank slate. Considered to be outside the sphere of productive relations, colonized peoples were portrayed as governed by nature's cyclical time, an immature time, reproductive rather than accumulative, that left them on the doorstep of history. They were thus seen as being without experience of any kind, without any knowledge or skills to capitalize on. Mangin goes even a step further by making reference to a supposed mental atavism: "The recruits learn by imitation, by suggestion. They thought little before deciding to serve, and we can reach their unconscious mind while hardly engaging with their consciousness."[81] Like people under hypnosis, their minds stripped of socialization, Black men were considered nearly perfect soldiers, *unthinking weapons*.

Some critics felt that natives serving in the military deprived the French Empire of the agricultural laborers needed to profitably cultivate its territories, as these were so environmentally and socially inhospitable that only local laborers could endure the conditions. Mangin responded to this argument, saying:

> But for this, you would need to establish that the conditions of agricultural labor are different between the Black and white races, that for instance work was done only by Black men, without the support from their wives and children that European farmers receive.[82]

Rather, the author concludes, not only is the land on the African continent worked by family units, but also, unlike under European patriarchy, among some "polygamous peoples" men *never* work in the fields and instead remain idle, their role limited to commanding the household. A military imperative thus led to the invention from whole cloth of a discourse justifying racial hierarchy and the sexual and racial division of labor under Empire. Taking polygamy as a premise, alongside the male idleness it results in, provided a moral justification for colonization and constituted the condition of possibility for the mass conscription (compulsory, but supposedly not "forced") of colonized men. Their "civilizing mission" to impose the norms and values of bourgeois patriarchy failed to conceal the economic and military interests European nations had in building an armed force of natives. As they were supposedly without a productive role, colonized men could be employed full-time in military "care" work as though it was their "natural" function.

Other characteristics that made the "Black race" natural soldiers included their adaptability to different climates and to new types of armed conflict.[83] The colonies provided a decisive numerical advantage in the face of an imminent need to mobilize as quickly as possible a considerable mass of men between the ages of sixteen and thirty-five.[84] The psychology of the "Black race" specifically made them a valuable military weapon. The deference, ignorance, and fatalism shown by Black soldiers were considered the martial qualities most needed in modern warfare. Mangin argues that the colonies held human resources that, if enrolled in the army, would be its secret thrust, the only solution in the increasingly likely event of war with Germany: "In Europe's present state, the Black force would make us a formidable adversary."[85]

Finally, Mangin evokes the major problem with incorporating the "Black race" into the French armed forces: the inextricable link between civil rights and military duties. The Empire's soldiers "consider themselves French. French and Black, but very French."[86] Nonetheless, they did not have the same rights as their brothers in arms and were accorded a status of immaturity. These *sons of France*, as the high command liked to call them, fought for the motherland without the benefits of the "republican solidarity" that binds citizens together "fraternally." In reading Mangin, the variability in how rights relating to conscription and citizenship are applied is obvious.[87] Mangin concludes:

> We believe that, in Senegal as in Algeria, the issues of political rights and compulsory military service should not be linked. It

is no more necessary to impose military service on Senegalese voters than it is to grant voting rights to the Arabs made to serve in our regiments. For the success of our enterprise, we would happily sacrifice ten thousand Senegalese voters, a negligible number in the scheme of things.[88]

He would rather have subjugated militiamen than citizen soldiers. Here we see the creation in law of imperial militias to take the place of an army of citizens. The law is fully on the side of the flag rather than on the side of those who defend it, and they will have the right to die without having the right to vote. "(A) nation has the right to call all of her children to her defense," Mangin states, "even her adoptive children, *regardless of race*."[89]

Racism was not only on the side of those advocating to massively conscript soldiers from outside of metropolitan France. In the eyes of other military men, anthropologists, and ideologues opposed to Mangin, using African troops was seen as a handicap, a sign of "decadence." Some military theorists believed the defense of the nation could not be left to foreign armies, "defeated peoples," or "mercenaries."[90] In other words, troops from outside the nation would always sooner or later choose their own survival over the orders of a foreign chain of command sending them to their deaths.[91] Mangin responds that these troops would only be a supplementary force and never the whole of the French army. The battalions of colonized people were subjects at the Empire's disposal, and if the slogan of mercenaries is "The world is our country," that of the colonial soldiers might be "The Empire is our grave.[92]

How could the loyalty of these troops be assured? This issue was long a key consideration for the African army's upper echelons. One effective solution was to intensify existing racism among colonized people themselves. After all, as Mangin observed, "You are always a barbarian to someone."[93] By using colonized, vanquished men as soldiers to subjugate and exterminate other "natives," the French Empire bolstered one form of racism with another.[94] This created a repressive *and* emotional apparatus for different degrees of nonrecognition: the imperial militiamen, *native soldiers*, stood halfway between *French citizens* and *barbarians*, not fully the former while no longer quite being the latter.

Defense of Self, Defense of the Nation

To Die for One's Country

The process of regulating the legal use of armed force is closely connected to modern interpretations of the law of peoples (*jus gentium*), which forms the theoretical groundwork for debates about the legitimacy or illegitimacy of violence per se. Legitimate defense was once a principle shared, to a certain extent, by both private law and by public and international law (in the latter case, it was related to the right of states to legitimately use violence on their own territories or in international conflicts).[1] Grotius lays out the theory behind this overlap in *The Rights of War and Peace*, and it was amply discussed by his contemporaries as well as by many authors in the tradition of natural law (*jus naturalis*). Building on Cicero, Grotius defines war as "the state or situation of those ... who dispute by force of arms," and includes in this definition both "private war" (defined as a conflict between individuals) and "public war," in addition to various mixed forms.[2] This definition means the principle of "just defense of oneself" applies to *both* individuals and states, and provides a basis for regulating its legality (effective dissuasion, establishment of courts of justice, failure of the sovereign protecting authority). However, in the order of reasons, how the principle of just defense was interpreted gradually shifted, from being without distinction (referring to both individuals *and* states) to starting from the individual and building toward the state. "If there is law in war, it is not based on the justness of the cause, but rather on the rights of the ones who make it, and these rights are primarily the natural rights of individuals. They can then be transferred to states."[3] In Grotius's formulation, the relationship between states and individuals is a bilateral one, which means that the *sovereign subject* can be seen as a "microstate." This signals a theoretical shift in debates about just war and the legitimate use of force.[4] Rather than considering the cause of a conflict, what is at issue is the anthropological status of the defending party and the *rights of the individual*. It is then a matter of determining who is entitled to legal personhood, and who will thus have a legitimate right to defend themselves or to be defended (that is, to delegate this natural right to a regulatory body).

Throughout the twelfth and thirteenth centuries, the just defense of individuals steadily lost importance relative to the right of states to legitimate defense. Behind this lay the goal of circumscribing the private use of violence, which involved limiting individuals' ability to legally use violence or to bear arms. Weapons could be used not only to defend one's person, but also as part of rebellious movements, revolts, challenges to authority, or revolutions seeking to overturn the existing power structure. The right to be armed—whether to practice a martial art, to carry a weapon, or to take up arms—came to be defined in theory and in law relative to the role of citizens in defending the nation, and it was often restricted to this defense, with varying levels of strictness.

Historically, the issue of an armed populace has been dealt with in two separate ways: in the first model, broadly Anglo-Saxon, the defense of the nation is understood as an *extension* of the natural right to defend one's person, of self-defense. In the second model, associated with "the Continent" in general and France specifically, the defensive resources of citizens are drawn on differentially and for specific reasons: participation in collective defense is framed as a condition of membership in the national community.

DEFENSE OF SELF, DEFENSE OF THE NATION

In the latter political tradition, defense of the nation takes the place of self-defense. During the French Revolution, granting all males the right to bear arms was part of the project of building a republican armed force. No longer framed as an aristocratic privilege, bearing arms was *a right and a duty of citizenship*. If you're armed, this is not in order to defend *yourself* but rather to defend the *homeland*. At the core of the social contract, dedication to the military defense of the nation ("serving your country") forms the condition of possibility for incorporating the individual defender *into the civil body*. The first attempts at organizing "citizen militias" are best understood as an effort to make national defense a public service provided to citizens *by* citizens.

The military conscription bill put forward on 2 Thermidor, year 6 (July 20, 1798), perfectly illustrates the republican idea of national defense.[5] It was framed in opposition to the existing practice, random selection, which had been intended to make conscription more equal, but it was significantly distorted. In practice, the better-off among those selected could simply pay mercenaries to replace them in fighting for the flag. By establishing the principle of voluntary enrollment by *civilian citizens*, rather than forced conscription, honor replaced money as the core value of the new Jacobin civil order. This "democratic" conception of military service kept the military hierarchy and its chain of command in place, but it still represented the spirit of the "soldier-patriots of the Revolution."[6] Although the law ultimately adopted by the Directory, the governing committee of the First Republic, reinstated the old principles and instituted mandatory conscription for all French men between the ages of twenty and twenty-five, it nonetheless also reaffirmed the military conception of citizenship: "All Frenchmen are soldiers and must defend their country."[7] And yet, the text abandoned the idea that if defense is a duty, it is also a right. The founding principle of male citizenship, elaborated throughout the

Revolution and linking *the duty to defend* with *the right of defense*, was cast aside.[8] A century after the French Revolution, France adopted a bastardized system midway between a professional army and a citizens' militia, while still requiring all French men to fight for their flag *in order to become fully French*. This meant that the army acted as a sort of imperial civil incubator, indelibly marked by antagonisms along the lines of class, sex, and race.[9]

Making military service a right *for all Frenchmen* had a performative dimension: its aim was *to forge* a people, a community of citizen-soldiers, whose civil rights stemmed from their military commitments.[10] However, the political incarnation of *self-defense by substitution* was never applied in its pure form. The freed slaves who participated in the Revolution, the Senegalese infantry deployed to Verdun, and the residents of shantytowns sent off to Indochina could all testify to this.[11] The human shield could never fully cover the national body.[12] The more privileged (bourgeois white men) found ways of avoiding the so-called voluntary conscription—or at least the most dangerous or degrading posts—and this was generally tolerated. At the same time, the right to become a conscripted defender of the nation was a unique privilege denied to a large part of the civilian community (women, as well as men who were deemed unfit). National defense glorified the republican ideal of citizenship, but this ideal could not hide the relations of domination involved in that defense, or the creation of what were effectively second-class citizens.

In spite of, or because of, this paradox, it is easy to understand why the right and the duty to participate in the defense of the nation have historically been central to the political demands of social movements and marginalized subjects, notably post-slavery abolitionists and feminists. These movements tended to adopt a strategy either of refusing conscription (refusing to die for a country that trampled their rights and freedoms, while the blood and tears of citizens with full rights went unshed) or else of demanding to be incorporated into the military as a way of denouncing the privileges reserved for a minority and as a step on the path toward real citizenship. In both cases, they tend to reject the civil double standard around the risk of death among so-called passive citizens.

"Women, Arm Yourselves": The Amazon Battalions

In the Republic, the right to bear arms was an important factor in being recognized as a citizen. Efforts to de-gender or de-racialize the civic heroism promoted by the Revolution's ideals opened the door to denouncing the norms that oppressed women, male slaves, and free people of color. Although for the excluded, one of the issues at play in gaining access to weapons is inclusion as active citizens, it is not the only one. It also represents a chance to access the martial training necessary for social struggle. From this point of view, the problem is that not having the duty of defending your country means not having the ability to defend *yourself,* and continuing the struggle for equality unarmed. We can therefore also approach the issue from the other direction and say that inclusion in the military allows access to weapons skills and martial knowledge.

In this respect, rather than a "monopoly on legitimate violence," it might be more accurate to describe the situation as a *social management of martiality*. This phrase, modeled on "social management of reproduction," coined by the feminist anthropologist Paola Tabet, emphasizes the idea of a *continuum* of armed practices, beyond simply the codified and monopolistic uses of weapons.[13] These practices are subject to a discriminatory social management, notably along lines of class, race, and sex, that deserves historical attention. The phrase also makes obvious the division of martial labor, with tasks divided *both* by sex *and* race.[14] What discriminatory technologies did the powerful use to categorize people and regulate their access to certain weapons and defensive resources? What discourses and practices contested this division? What forms of *détournement*—what transgressive uses—of objects not considered dangerous did the disarmed need to develop in their struggles?[15]

A paradigmatic example from the French Revolution can be found in those women who—barely permitted to listen to the debates during revolutionary assemblies—sat knitting as orators argued over the limits of universal rights:

> The activity indicated by the word *tricoteuse*, the activity of a peaceful mother, of a family, is positive. Upon leaving the foyer to pass into the public scene, displaced, *tricoteuse* develops a negative meaning. And in the imagination needles are always symbolic of this sort of disloyalty; they can become dangerous; weapons without names; tools for labor tinged with bloody tips.[16]

As the historian Dominique Godineau points out in regard to the petitions made by women in 1792, the issue of bearing arms was central to mobilizations by women and working-class people calling for the abolition of the distinction between active and passive citizens.[17] Revolutionary women were at the forefront of those citizens labeled passive in demanding inclusion in the National Guard, which they justified in terms of their natural right to defend themselves and their country.[18] "On March 6, 1792, Pauline Léon, at the head of a delegation of female citizens, read at the bar of the Legislative Assembly a petition signed by more than 319 women who demanded permission to organize a female national guard."[19] This marked the birth of the famous Parisian "*tricoteuses*," or knitters: revolutionary women claiming their natural rights, but constantly denigrated as crazy, unnatural, and bloodthirsty. Their petition, called the *Adresse*, opens with a clear affirmation of the natural right to self-defense:

> We are women patriots, and we stand before you to claim the right all individuals have to see to the defense of their lives and their liberty ... We seek only to be able to defend ourselves; you cannot deny us [Sirs], and society cannot strip us of a right given to us by nature; unless you are to claim that the declaration of rights does not apply to women and that we must let ourselves have our throats slit like lambs, without any right to defend ourselves.[20]

The text called for women to have the right to bear arms (pikes, sabers, pistols, and rifles) and also for them to receive weapons training from former soldiers. Technically, the women of Paris were not excluded from National Guard units in the city. The law stated that "people over 60 years of age, the infirm, clergy, widows, and unmarried women are required to serve by having a substitute replace them," but this simply meant paying a tax.[21] Women were thus forced to pay for not serving—not only were they *passive citizens*, they were also paying to be *infirm patriots*.

The deputies' reactions were harshly mocking and scornful but were also accompanied by panicked suspicion and constant police surveillance. The arming of women was almost never raised as an ethical dilemma in the political realm, nor in philosophical considerations of what conditions would exist at the Revolution's end. And yet, armed women were seen as threatening *in themselves*. A police report from May 18 and 19, 1793, states:

> A crowd of women claiming to be with the Fraternal Society descended on the Jacobins to demand of the patriotic deputies that the Convention abolish reserved seating in the gallery.

Most of these women were armed with hidden daggers or pistols, and our chief worry was that there would be bloodshed, provoked by aristocrats disguised as women hidden among them. Our assumption is that a malicious person used the language of patriotism to rile up these heroines of the revolution, inciting them to form a mob and take up arms in order to dissolve the Convention and spill their patriotic blood.[22]

Throughout the seventeenth and eighteenth centuries, feminist demands and women's movements (especially mass uprisings of women) were considered monstrous "gender mutations"—lower-class women in particular were called *viragos*, virile women at odds with the sexual and social order.[23] It was as though any demand for rights was a form of virilization, of cross-dressing, sex change, or sexual inversion.[24] Yet in this police report, the old idea of women as heteronomous beings resurfaces, an anthropological description laid out in classical philosophy that has turned up in countless forms.[25] In its political iteration, this doctrine holds that women must have been *possessed* and that movements of women must have been *infiltrated*. The revolutionary women citizens must have been manipulated by an antipatriotic and counterrevolutionary current; worse still, their movement is porous, riddled with traitors, aristocrats, and foreign spies crossdressing as women (the scheming, effeminate, and treacherous aristocrat was cast as a foil to revolutionary masculinity). By claiming the right to defend the nation and the Revolution, rights that are theirs by both nature and reason, women were simply the dupes of foreign powers, whose occult manipulations were using this feminine masquerade as an opportunity to overthrow the Convention. Essentially, this is a way of saying that women engaging in self-defense are *ridiculous*, that they are playing at being soldiers just as the *précieuses* played at being scholars in their aristocratic salons before the Revolution.

Faced with the stubborn refusal of male citizens to recognize the rights of women, the petitioners developed the rhetorical strategy of supporting their claims with a complementary framing of *sexual difference*, stripping it of the pejorative dimension used to justify social injustice. In promoting a sexual division within the revolutionary armed forces, they argued that women would be able to "guard the interior" of the country "while [their] brothers are defending the borders."[26] The metonymy between women citizens and the homeland meant the territorial integrity of the nation could be understood as a woman's honor, the defense of which fell "naturally" to women themselves. Defending herself, defending her children, and defending her country's lands and cities were all actually just a singular expression of her natural right to self-defense. Patriotic self-defense by women was presented as the counterpart to men's duty of military service that had them stationed on the external borders, facing threatening foreign armies. Framed as an army mobilizing on a second front, women citizens sought the ability to defend their country in the name of their right to defend themselves (to defend their physical integrity, their honor, and their children, but also their streets, their shops, and their subsistence).

Just a few days after Pauline Léon read out her petition, on March 25, 1792, another revolutionary woman, Théroigne de Méricourt, gave a speech at the Fraternal Society's Minimes Club (part of the Place-Royale section) in which she called for the creation of an Amazon battalion of French women.[27] She stirred up the women, urging them to rise up as citizens and to *become citizens*. She said:

> Nature, as well as the law, gives us the right to arm. Let us show men that we are not inferior to them in either virtue or in courage. Let us show Europe that Frenchwomen know their rights, and are amongst the most enlightened of eighteenth-century people.[28]

Théroigne de Méricourt played on their patriotic feelings, claiming that arming women was simply a corollary of the laws of reason and nature governing their fledgling revolutionary nation. Anyone who would forbid women to arm themselves or to distinguish themselves through their courage and strength was nothing but a counterrevolutionary. She encouraged women who doubted their own physical ability and warrior courage to trust in enlightened reason. In her framing, the arming of women by other women was not only a right, but a civic *duty*:

> Frenchwomen, I say to you once more, let us rise to the utmost height of our destiny, let us break our chains; it is time at last that women should throw aside their shameful inactivity in which ignorance, pride, and the injustice of men have kept them bound for so long ... *Citoyennes*, why do we not enter into rivalry with men? They pretend that they alone have rights to glory. No, indeed no ... We also wish to merit a civic crown, to sue for the honor of dying for a liberty which is perhaps dearer to us than to them, because the effects of despotism weigh still more heavily on our heads than on theirs.[29]

In the first part of her speech, she ties the arming of women to the national cause and argues that women's battalions were sorely needed to counter the threats and despotism of the other European empires. However, in the second part, she denationalizes the armed emancipation of women, presenting it as a universal struggle transcending national boundaries. Théroigne de Méricourt does not conceal the fact that women would be able to compete with men on an even footing and could even turn their guns against those who refused to accept equality.

To die for the country is to die to stay free, or rather to become free: it is to die *for yourself*.

Army of Citizens or Defense of Capital?

In 1911, one of the major texts on contemporary political thought dealing with the arming of citizens was published: Jean Jaurès's *L'Armée nouvelle* (The new army).[30] In it, Jaurès returns to a long-running debate in socialist thought.[31] Although its primary focus is still on how to prevent the army from crushing social movements, the book is also preoccupied with defense, as part of a broader anxiety around the imminent threat from Germany. *L'Armée nouvelle* is a compromise between the tenets of patriotism on the one hand (while remaining critical of permanent standing armies) and, on the other, those of pacifist and antimilitarist socialists, who had always warned that there was a contradiction between the priorities of the military and those of the working class.

Within the French high command there were two opposing military strategies about how to organize French troops in preparation for a conflict with Germany. Each had its own corresponding ethical and political conception of the responsibilities of "virile," *white* citizens. One strategy involved an experienced armed vanguard that emphasized speed, supported by a lightly trained reserve; the other called for a massive, steadfast deployment along the borders made up of indefinitely replaceable men. The latter option was, of course, supported by officers of the colonial army, who bragged of the incredible boon represented by their colonized territories, since *subjects of the Empire* could be mobilized without compensation.

These two strategies would obviously determine the kind of conscription and mobilization that would occur, but they also had consequences in terms of the moral and martial education received by *French citizens*. Jaurès writes that the "preparation of the nation" associated with each strategy would focus either on the qualities of audacity and aggression, on the one hand, or of patience, sacrifice, and abnegation on the other.[32]

Further, the strategy chosen would help shape policies for maintaining order and the management of the population using the police and military, particularly in the event of revolts or mobilizations by workers. Military concerns were closely linked to policing when it came to providing arms and martial training to masses of people in metropolitan France. In his view, the people were capable of transcending class interests in order to defend the nation. To others, though, they were not capable, and so the nation had to move ahead with training and arming a select elite, prepared to defend France militarily on an international scale but devoted to capital and used repressively within the national territory.

Jaurès argues that France's real problem is that the military high command has not decided which strategy to apply to the country:

> I am absolutely convinced that the choice between a proper offense and a proper defense has not yet been made, that the high command, in its decisions about mobilization, the concentration of forces, and the general conducting of the war, has accepted hybrid strategies, combinations with two goals.[33]

An offensive military strategy would be sure to lose against the hardened, battle-ready German troops, but the French high command had not excluded it. They claimed to be following Clausewitz's adage to avoid basing your own movements on the movements of your enemy and to avoid falling into a negative and reactive posture of strategic heteronomy: "Do not submit to the enemy's will."[34]

Jaurès therefore proposes a novel defensive strategy: it would be truly original to respond to a German offensive with a French defense. He presents himself as having a better interpretation of Clausewitz than high-ranking members of the French military leadership, such as Captain Gilbert, who was in charge of redefining France's strategy.[35] Don't be fooled by the title of Gilbert's manifesto, *La Défense de la France* ("Defending France")—in it he advocates for an offensive to be carried out by a relatively small permanent army. Jaurès takes aim at Gilbert as the standard-bearer of an elitist professional force that he claims would be best suited to the French temperament. In Gilbert's text, this reference to the temperaments of peoples is supported by a military psychology analysis arguing that the French are best suited to a quick, agile offensive.

Beneath the discussion of the merits of a defensive or offensive French strategy, there lies a larger question about the very definition of a military corps. One of Jaurès's major contributions in his critique was to highlight how uncomfortable the thought of an armed nation made the French high command. The commanders were far more comfortable with a military elite backed by an unqualified army of reservists who would not have the military experience and weapons training to use against the state and the bourgeoisie during social conflicts. And yet the French high command was unable to make do without an "armed nation"; it knew "neither how to do without massive numbers nor how to organize them."[36] This contradiction prevented military thinkers from developing a viable defensive strategy.[37]

However, Jaurès is caught in his own untenable contradictions. In his vision, the "armed nation" is a defensive army, a tool "implacable in defense and unusable for external aggression."[38] Arming the people is then just another way of considering how to form a citizen's army whose duty is the collective defense of the nation. This issue contains several major challenges. There is, on the one hand, the inescapable paradox of taking up arms to defend the peace, of the need for states of exception to defend the rule of law, of using violent repression to defend nonviolence, and so on. Then, on the other hand, forming a people's army—or arming the people and calling it a "national army"—is inextricably tied to the management of social movements by means of both police and politics. There is in fact a risk that replacing a professional army with a citizens' militia will mean turning comrades into enemies.

In an article published in 1911, Rosa Luxemburg provided a lucid analysis of the aphorisms into which *L'Armée nouvelle* led the working class, as well as the radical departure from the militias advocated by German social democrats that this vision of a national army represented.[39] Luxemburg considers Jaurès guilty of "overzealous" patriotism, resulting from a "legal fanaticism" incompatible with socialism ("an obstinate petit bourgeois and democratic belief" in the power of legislation) and unable to conceal the excessively large concessions Jaurès makes to French warmongers and to capitalism.[40] The proof of this is his argument for "defensive war," the only kind of war he would consider "just" and therefore the only kind deserving of the participation of the French working class—even if it were against their German comrades. To Luxemburg, the distinction between offensive and defensive war is a legalistic abstraction: Who decides if a given conflict is defensive? And what of the European diplomats who incite "weak adversaries to attack" in order to be able to send troops to the border?[41] No warring state has "right on its side," because "modern wars can't be understood in terms of 'justice' or neatly broken down in terms of defense and aggression ... It won't be the material might of capitalist development caught in this tangled logic and potentially distorted by it, but the strength of socialist action."[42]

Jaurès's text was poorly received and even ridiculed by many socialists, and it provoked a sharp rupture with the antimilitarist positions held by anarchist and pacifist strains of syndicalism. Under pressure from radicals and French socialists, the CGT union had put critiques of patriotism and the military front and center. These critiques are notably summarized in Georges Yvetot's *The New Soldier's Guide*, published in 1902.[43] At play beneath the surface of these debates is the crucial issue of internationalism. Such debates about the army and national defense, about patriotism and the democratization of law enforcement all eventually lead to placing limits on the internationalization of struggles and working-class mobilizations. They also make invisible the violence caused by capitalist modes of production by emphasizing militaristic and nationalistic issues:

> Does defending a nation mean being killed for the interests of a few? Is it only a matter of defense if the primary condition that makes defense necessary is attack? Who then is attacking us? Why would we be attacked? To take our wealth? Well we have none.[44]

Paraphrasing Rousseau's *Social Contract* as well as the *Communist Manifesto*, Yvetot denounces militarism as the "religion of violence" and the armed wing of capitalism.[45] Over three years of service, the army makes people into fearful, submissive brutes:

> Soldiers are sent to picket lines with loaded guns, bayonets fixed to the barrel. It is they who gallop and charge through the streets, when workers, having been driven from the workplace by the bosses' greed, rightly believe their place is in the streets. And the army doesn't only come to the aid of capital with its guns. Soldiers also replace workers during strikes. The nation's army, made up of sons of the people, stands against the people in service of the bosses . . . While waiting to serve in foreign wars, soldiers serve first and foremost in the *social war*.[46]

Democratizing the armed forces is thus no solution to the use of military repression by the elite in the service of capital. Rather, it would only fan the flames of fratricidal conflicts and further crush the workers' movement. Working-class people betray their own as soon as they put on the uniform: "The proletarian soldier is a common man trained to defend the rich and powerful, armed and equipped to fight his brothers."[47]

Yvetot's antimilitarism is tied to his anti-Semitic politics as well, though, and he does not shy away from invoking a foul corpus of texts. In denouncing the depravity of conscripts, he quotes conservative politicians and intellectuals, as well as nationalists, anti-Dreyfus partisans, and racists (Édouard Drumont, Charles de Freycinet, Jules Delafosse, François Coppée) in order to drive home the idea that the army is a veritable "school of vice": it uproots and deforms the nation's vital force, the young men from the countryside, sons of the land, who return from the barracks with syphilis after a life of alcoholism and prostitution, having lost all respect for women.[48] He does write, though, that "most terrifying of all are the acts of militarism in the colonies."[49] He does not refer to any specific episodes, however, and quickly moves on to the abuse young French recruits face if they do not submit to military rules: thumbscrews (torture devices made to squeeze and crush the fingers or thumbs); the pear of anguish, or the gag (a tent spike or large stone placed lengthwise in the mouth and held in place by a handkerchief, often soaked in excrement); hog-tying (the hands and feet tied together behind the back, forcing the body to arch); correctional cells (the soldier is stripped, thrown into an isolated cell, and starved); irons (enclosing the legs of a naked soldier), the tomb (a 40 cm–high tent in which a bound, naked soldier is placed and exposed to the heat of the day and the cold of the night), pack drills (either barefoot or in boots, the soldier is made to wear a heavy pack and to stand immobile or perform exhausting drills). "Three years in the barracks will either make a man into a conscious rebel or a passive brute."[50]

Yvetot urges soldiers to desert and to maintain their political consciousness, to form unions, to participate in popular education centers, and to not fire on their *brothers*: "Let those who would arm you against your brothers tremble, because your only enemy is the one who exploits you, oppresses you, commands you, and lies to you."[51] Patriotism is the biggest obstacle to internationalizing the struggle, and the idea of a people's army ready to defend its borders is just a myth in the service of capital.

Suffragette Jujitsu: Close Combat and Anti-Nationalism

In the constellational history of modern self-defense, the suffrage movement in England in the early twentieth century serves as a privileged point of reference. One section of this movement has become emblematic due to its anti-nationalist theoretical and political positions and its willingness to resort to the law. To an extent, it allows us to identify a tendency in the modern feminist movement that considers *turning to violence* a logical consequence of understanding that the state is structurally responsible for the oppression of women and for keeping them in a status of immaturity. "Turning to violence"—the violence of direct action and uncompromising demands—is based on the premise that demands for civil equality cannot be made to the state peacefully, since it is the primary cause of inequalities. It is useless to ask the state for justice because it is most responsible for institutionalizing social injustice. It is an illusion that the state could *offer us* protection, since it produces and supports the same apparatuses that *make us* vulnerable, and it is delusional even to trust it to defend us, since it is arming our attackers. Our goal here is to understand how a small number of feminist suffragists, revolutionaries inspired by anarchism and communist internationalism, put the above premise not only into practice but also into *motion*, incarnating their analytical position within the English feminist movement.

In the late nineteenth century, self-defense techniques in England were experiencing a revival due to the development and spread of hybrid bodily martial practices. These brought together European and Japanese combat styles to create something pragmatic and effective in a society where carrying firearms was very strictly regulated. In the 1890s, Edward William Barton-Wright, a British engineer, spent three years in Japan, during which time he learned judo and jujitsu at Jigoro Kano's school.[52] A lover of the art of self-defense, he developed his own technique, which he called Bartitsu. Upon returning to Europe in 1899, he opened a club in London and brought in many instructors, including the Japanese jujitsu masters Sadakazu Uyenishi and Yukio Tani, and Pierre Vigny, a Swiss trainer in defensive stick fighting.[53] By combining several techniques, Barton-Wright sought to make Bartitsu into a "real," or total, self-defense practice incorporating feet, hands, and sticks into both offensive and defensive techniques for distance, close, and hand-to-hand combat.[54]

From the beginning, the Bartitsu Club was open to women. Among Sadakazu Uyenishi's and Yukio Tani's students were William Garrud and Edith Margaret Garrud.[55] In 1908, the couple took over Sadakazu Uyenishi's London dojo, the School of Japanese Self-Defence, and began giving jujitsu-inspired self-defense courses, including to women and children. In this pioneering experiment, the important point is that self-defense was presented as a useful technique against multidimensional violence, and involved defensive techniques for use when a person—notably a woman—is alone with an aggressor (whether in the public or domestic sphere). These techniques were soon adapted to political struggle by practitioners who were also engaged in the women's suffrage movement, primarily to defend against police brutality.

The Garruds held numerous public demonstrations and appeared in short films depicting their "unisex" self-defense practice and promoting its effectiveness and accessibility.[56]

Soon, feminist associations were reaching out to the instructors for training. In 1909, Emmeline Goulden-Pankhurst, founder of the Women's Social and Political Union (WSPU), invited William Garrud to give a demonstration at an assembly, but it ended up being Edith Garrud who came.[57] The WSPU was impressed by both the effectiveness of the techniques and by the fact that a woman could be so skilled in combat. Soon after, they began organizing workshops and trainings. Edith Garrud became a leading figure in the WSPU and, in late 1909, she opened the Suffragettes Self-Defense Club in London's Kensington neighborhood (in a space that also offered sculpture, painting, and singing lessons), where she offered self-defense classes every Tuesday and Thursday night.[58] Self-defense was effectively becoming a total art, due not only to its wide range of pragmatic, effective martial techniques, but also to how it contributed to new practices of self that entailed transformations at once political, bodily, and intimate: by freeing the body's motions from cumbersome clothing, by unfurling in movement, by appropriating familiar objects and turning them to different uses (umbrellas, pins, broaches, coats, heels), and by bringing muscles to life. By training bodies that inhabit and occupy the streets, that move from place to place and find their balance, feminist self-defense opened up a new relationship to the world, a different way of being. By learning to defend themselves, these activists created and modified their corporeal schemas, making them the crucible for the development of political consciousness.

Garrud set up a secret team of marshals for the WSPU, directed by Gertrude Harding, called the Bodyguard Society, or the Amazons. It was made up of thirty or so trained militants who would protect other activists during meetings and actions and prevent their arrest.[59] They combined close-combat techniques for hand-to-hand combat (parries, arm bars, using the adversary's momentum, etc.) to develop strategies against police, activists, or even passersby opposed to the women's cause. They also developed ruses that played on the sexist stereotypes that women are incapable of defending themselves. These techniques depended on the element of surprise and social astonishment, taking advantage of the adversary's disorientation after his prejudices caused him to let down his guard: cutting a policeman's suspenders so he has to hold up his pants, blinding police by opening an army of umbrellas, attacking horses during mounted charges, and so on. Their feminist direct action stemmed from genuine *feminist self-defense tactics*, including political objectives, physical training, plans for action and withdrawal, hiding arms under clothing, cross-dressing and disguise techniques, support networks, arms caches, hideouts, and the like. These tactics speak to a well-developed urban guerrilla strategy that did not merely make use of direct action tactics but literally incorporated them as a *means* of building feminist political consciousness. Their practice of direct action did not involve throwing bombs but rather becoming "human bombs."[60] In other words, the WSPU activists' self-defense was not simply one type of action selected from among others in their repertoire to advance their cause and get women the vote. Rather, it was what allowed them to struggle together, for themselves and by themselves, and to avoid any nationalistic instrumentalization of their cause. Self-defense was not a means to an end, allowing them to gain a certain political status and recognition—it politicized their bodies, without mediation, delegation, or representation.

Other feminist figures practiced self-defense at that time, but the WSPU's militants stand out because of Edith Garrud's incredible contribution to modern feminist self-defense. In her text *The World We Live In: Self-Defense!*, published on March 4, 1910, she lays out a pragmatic philosophy for feminist self-defense. Her starting point is that men and women are imbalanced in terms of physical strength, but the self-defense techniques developed in jujitsu are powerfully effective tools for the weak against the strong. Asian martial arts are traditionally understood as techniques for turning an attacker's force back against him, but here they take on a political dimension, since they were being promoted to women in order to even the playing field. Edith Garrud's jujitsu-inspired defensive techniques have three basic principles: awareness of balance, movements, and forces; the art of trickery and surprise; and an economy of strikes. And so she teaches evasive movements and how to use the attacker's momentum to throw him off balance, block strikes, and send him quickly to the ground. The element of surprise involves using the opponent's momentum to change his course and safely get close to his body to apply holds and bars or to land effective strikes. The essence of *mixed self-defense* is the blending of defense and attack. In terms of strikes properly speaking, the key word is *economy*: regardless of the attacker's strength, size, or skill, the body's vulnerable points remain the same: the face, joints, and organs. Edith Garrud's vision is of self-defense becoming like second nature—it is not the means by which equality is gained, but rather an ongoing process of embodying equality and putting it into practice.

From this perspective, her teachings are a radical departure from other jujitsu texts and manuals aimed at women. The best-known author was Irving Hancock, though he presented almost no combat techniques and reduced "feminine" jujitsu to a physical practice more like Swedish gymnastics, the main virtue of which was that it avoided calling into question dominant gender norms. Dr. Fernand Lagrange authored the preface and was the book's main promoter in France.[61] He praised the anatomy of Japanese women: while respecting the standards of "feminine grace," they are the physical equals of men "of their race."[62] As is typical of polemics about women's sport, physical exercise is only seen as acceptable for women as long as it does not diminish their sexual characteristics.[63] This is also true of Charles Pherdac's text published in 1912.[64]

In it, self-defense techniques are counterbalanced by reminders of the rules of decency spelled out in a preface by the Countess d'Abzac: "Worry not, Sirs! Learning to defend herself does not mean a woman will refuse to give herself."[65] Self-defense as it was taught by male instructors (whether military or sporting) was mostly restricted to basic techniques, described with a succinctness that made them difficult to embody. However, these texts also had a positive effect, making it possible to consider that in hand-to-hand assaults, women are not overcome due to their physical strength but because of the ignorance they are consigned to, although they are the primary victims of such attacks. Women can then learn to defend themselves, and although the debate continued about the ability of "the weaker sex" to learn self-defense, the quantity of articles written at this time, including critical or sarcastic ones, demonstrates a real fascination with martial arts capable of changing the balance of power.[66] Some publications praised the social utility of women's self-defense more openly, emphasizing its real defensive uses and not just its health benefits.[67] In contrast with feminist self-defense, these guides and manuals for *womanly self-defense* reveal a different politics of the body, one in which the effectiveness of martial arts is counteracted by another imperative: women should be able to access physical training and benefit from prophylactic measures to maintain their health, and even learn a few techniques for their protection, but on the condition that they remain "women," meaning bodies that are fundamentally defenseless.

As in Europe, the United States was also fascinated by jujitsu in the early 1920s, particularly following the publication of *The Secrets of Jujitsu: A Complete Course in Self-Defense*. Its author, Captain A.C. Smith, was the first American citizen to be awarded a black belt in Japan (1916) and was the instructor for unarmed close combat at the Fort Benning Infantry School in Columbus, Georgia. In 1942, William E.

Fairbairn published two manuals on women's self-defense, one of which, *Hands Off*, was very successful.[68] He had served as an officer in the English army and commanded crowd-control forces in Shanghai before joining the British secret service during the Second World War.[69] His self-defense techniques were thus primarily developed within repressive colonial armed forces. Self-defense techniques learned from jujitsu masters were turned against the colonized themselves as part of colonial repression—a perfect example of colonizers capturing knowledge held by the colonized. These practices then circulated among civilians back home, where they were considered exotic. Since they originated among subalterns, they were of lower value, which made it possible to consider teaching them to white women. However, they were also seen as new knowledge, with benefits still unknown, that had been improved through their discovery and reinterpretation by colonizers who adapted them to Western masculinity.

William Fairbairn is considered one of the twentieth century's greatest theoreticians of close combat. His manuals describe effective techniques adapted to situations that women are particularly likely to experience: attempted groping, theft, and strangling that might occur while in a waiting room, on a first date, or in a hallway or other out-of-the-way place. He is focused on effectiveness, but this is only meaningful if there is a corresponding attention to choosing realistic situations that truly require those effects—this is the very principle of self-defense. And yet, William Fairbairn's analysis is necessarily limited: from whose point of view is realism defined? His martial knowledge comes from experience with small-group operations intended to maintain the colonial order, and it forms the basis of his defensive system. First popularized under the name Defendo (or Defendu), it is based on hand-to-hand techniques drawn from several different martial arts. Fairbairn was also a specialist in offensive and defensive knife techniques and is considered the "inventor" of the commando knife. Yet one of his system's principles is to avoid at all costs being taken down and having to defend yourself on the ground. This principle does not take into account the reality of sexual assaults, meaning the system is unrealistic for most of the violence women face, and the same is true for other social groups consigned to immaturity for their failure to conform to dominant gender norms. In other words, this defensive system does not match the reality of the violence experienced by these marginalized groups.

Although the First World War put a stop to most feminist mobilizing in Europe, and so interrupted the development of feminist self-defense, during the Second World War, on the other hand, women's self-defense flourished.[70] Women were targeted by a massive propaganda campaign encouraging them to enter the factories en masse to support the war effort. They were interpellated as strong, brave, and capable of doing *their* men's work. But this interpellation did not fit with the dominant values of "defenseless femininity." There were also public campaigns teaching women to fight, to strike back if coarse men who hadn't been mobilized tried to take advantage of vulnerable girls, women, and wives left to fend for themselves. As the nationalist context wills it, so shall it be: self-defense and pride were not only permitted for women; they became values expressing the strength and unity of the nation. One example is the image known as *Rosie the Riveter*, widely recirculated and creatively reappropriated during the 1980s, with its accompanying slogan "We can do it!" In fact, this conflates two different images.[71] The original "We Can Do It!" image was created by J. Howard Miller in 1942 for the Westinghouse Company's War Production Coordinating Committee and depicted a determined-looking female worker wearing makeup, blue overalls, and a red bandana, proudly showing her bicep (the model was Geraldine Hoff, a seventeen-year-old woman working in a metallurgy factory). This poster did not actually circulate widely at the time and was just one of a series of posters encouraging women to work in metallurgy factories and be more productive. *Rosie the Riveter* is the title of a work by Norman Rockwell, published in the *Saturday Evening Post* in May 1943, showing a muscular, red-headed American woman worker in overalls sitting and eating a sandwich on her lunch break. Her rivet gun is in her lap, and under her feet is a copy of *Mein Kampf*. Rockwell had his model (Mary Doyle, a nineteen-year-old telephone company worker) pose in such a way as to imitate the posture of the prophet Isaiah in the Sistine Chapel, painted by Michelangelo in 1509.[72] Patriotic iconography of this kind, depicting American women of supposedly dubious femininity, was accompanied by a wave of encouragement for women to learn to defend themselves and of self-defense guides for women and girls. Let us keep in mind, though, that this push for women's self-defense was tailored to serve a nationalist and capitalist agenda that had its own reasons for valorizing a young, muscular, industrious form of femininity. However, these standards of workers' femininity soon fell out of favor and were replaced by the bourgeois ideal of "the lady of the house," who was by definition a white woman.

Testaments of Self-Defense

Going Down Fighting: The Warsaw Ghetto Uprising

The occupier proceeds to the second phase of your extermination.
Don't go blindly to your death.
Defend yourself.
Pick up an axe, a crowbar, a knife, and barricade your home.
Don't just let yourself be captured!
By fighting, you stand a chance at survival.
Resist.[1]

The topographical configuration of the Warsaw Ghetto—its walls rising as high as the second or third floors of buildings and encircling the whole ghetto—was designed to stifle anything happening inside.

> And already from the third floor one could see the *other* street. We could see a merry-go-round, people, we could hear music, and we were terribly afraid that this music would drown us out and that those people would never notice a thing, that nobody in the world would notice a thing: us, the struggle, the dead ... That this wall was so huge that nothing, no message about us, would ever make it out.[2]

In the ghetto, the Nazis used a special device to detect the sound of voices, in particular when looking for people who had fled and might be hiding in a basement. Resisting this device meant staying quiet. Silence was of vital importance if one was to survive the constant searches, but it also contributed to a form of death beyond the world, a *worldless death*.[3]

Concretely, preparing for self-defense in the ghetto involved collecting weapons, hiding them, and arming all the survivors. This was accomplished by buying weapons; by reaching out to the Polish resistance and getting them to smuggle pistols, grenades, and ammunition into the ghetto; by organizing ambushes to capture uniforms and weapons from SS patrols; by crafting homemade weapons (mostly explosives); by building barricades, stashes, tunnels, and bunkers; and by training bodies for combat.[4] As a space-time outside of the world, the ghetto had become an anteroom of death, where those who had escaped the raids faced certain death and became defenseless ghosts—it would need to be turned into a battlefield.

In September 1942, Menachem Kirszenbaum managed to get the following message out of the ghetto: "We declare war on Germany. This is the declaration of the most desperate war that has ever been waged. Let us see if Jews can earn the right to go down fighting."[5] The Polish police, the SS, and their allies were made to carry fear in their bodies whenever they entered the ghetto, knowing that they were risking their lives and that every one of the living dead they encountered, whether man, woman, or child, was a potential source of armed resistance.[6]

Calls for self-defense (and the language of battlefields, war, and armed resistance that underpinned them) contributed to a process of rehumanization and stand as an homage to the lives of those in the ghetto: by embracing violence, the survivors wrote their own eulogy. There is no doubt that the decision to embrace violence was a tragic one, leading to a parody of war: the fighters had no chance, the imbalance was insurmountable. However, to act as though it was combat, as though the outcome was yet to be determined, meant dispelling the passive acceptance of death, along with the abyss from which it had come.[7]

In late October 1942, several meetings were held between members of the different resistance organizations active in the ghetto. The Jewish Combat Organization (Żydowska Organizacja Bojowa, or ZOB) was formed in order to "prepare for the defense of the Warsaw Ghetto."[8] In January 1943, its members posted texts throughout the ghetto, reading: "We are ready to die to be human."[9] In the most tragic situation imaginable, human dignity required dying with a weapon in hand—to fight, and perhaps survive, but to become, above all, the heralds of life against death.

Two different vocabularies existed in the ghetto, embedded in the discourse and narratives of the residents and fighters involved in the insurrection. On the one hand, there was the language of resistance, of a counterattack, and of open conflict; on the other hand, there was the language of *self*-defense: defending their choice of death, defending their humanity, defending selves that were already partially condemned, and always defending the vital principle immanent in the combative reflex.[10]

"It was always death that was at stake, not life. You see, maybe there was no drama at all there. Drama is when you make a decision, when something depends on you, whereas here, everything had been predetermined."[11] What conditions are required for there to once again be choices beyond those related to survival? If it is even meaningful to speak of choice in such conditions, moving from a choice between life and death to one between types of deaths entails adopting an ethical position in defense of the value of life itself. "Choosing" your death means to die as a fighter rather than be exterminated. In describing the long consultation involved in the formation of the ZOB, notably between Zionist and Communist groups, Marek Edelman wrote:

> The majority of us favored an uprising. After all, humanity had agreed that dying with arms was more beautiful than

without arms. Therefore we followed this consensus. In the Jewish Combat Organization there were only two hundred twenty of us left. Can you even call that an uprising? All it was about, finally, was that we not just let them slaughter us when our turn came. It was only a choice as to the manner of dying.[12]

They ultimately chose to defend *themselves,* not a cause, a territory, or a people, not even a hope. They took up weapons to defend *their deaths*, and so what was at stake in self-defense was first and foremost another modality of the politicization of life. They decided to choose combat over suicide: most of the resistance fighters considered suicide a waste of bullets that should be saved for the Nazis.[13]

The idea was omnipresent that it was better to die with a weapon in hand, or at least in combat, even barehanded, than to be gassed or executed by a bullet to the head.[14] "We must not think so much of saving our lives, which seems to be a very problematic affair, but rather of dying an honorable death, dying with weapons in our hands."[15] Thus, we can speak of an opposition between *thanato-ethics* and Nazi biopolitics, which involved the death of entire populations—an organized, industrial, mass extermination of millions of people. Thanato-ethics may be defined as the set of practices wherein death serves as an agent for restoring life's value.[16] Death then becomes a means by which the body, destined to be murdered, regains its humanity. On April 19, 1943, the Nazis entered the ghetto to carry out an "action" intended to fully liquidate the last survivors: they were met by a thousand men and woman ready for combat who put up a fierce struggle. A clandestine Polish newspaper circulated in Warsaw in April and May 1943 reads:

The Jews are fighting. Not for their lives, since their war against the Germans is one of desperation and despair; their war is about the value of life. Not in order to rescue themselves from death, but over the manner of death—to die like men and not like worms. For the first time in eighteen centuries, they have risen from their humiliation . . . The Warsaw ghetto may not be an end but a beginning; whoever dies as a human being has not perished in vain.[17]

However, Marek Edelman is also critical of the mythology of armed struggle, which he refers to as "symbolic death."[18] Hanna Krall conveys Edelman's anger:

> He screams that I probably consider the people who were surging into the train cars to have been worse than the ones who were shooting. Of course, I do, absolutely, everybody does. Even that American, the professor who recently visited Marek and told him, "You were going like sheep to your deaths." . . .
> He tried to explain . . . several things—how to die in a gas chamber is by no means worse than to die in battle, and that the only undignified death is when one attempts to survive at the expense of somebody else . . .
> My dear, Edelman says, you have to understand this once and for all. It is a horrendous thing, when one is going so quietly to one's death. It is infinitely more difficult than to go out shooting. After all, it is much easier to die firing—for us it was much easier to die than it was for someone who first boarded a train car, then rode the train, then dug a hole, then undressed naked . . . Do you understand now? he asks.
> Yes, I say. I see. Because it is indeed easier, even for us, to look at their death when they are shooting than when they are digging a hole for themselves . . .[19]

Léon Feiner was a member and contact of the Bund who survived outside the ghetto by passing himself off as "Aryan" in Warsaw. Regarding the indifference with which their situation was viewed internationally, he said, "We are preparing to defend the ghetto not because we believe the ghetto is defensible, but so that the world will take the desperation of our struggle as a reproach."[20] Léon Feiner repeatedly alerted the Polish resistance and the Allies to the extermination of the Polish Jews and the situation of the fighters in the ghetto. He was the one who transmitted information to the Bund's representative in the Polish government-in-exile in London, Artur Zygielbojm, who in turn tried every means to incite the British and American governments to act during a conference in Bermuda from April 19 to 30, 1943, while the Warsaw Ghetto uprising raged. On May 12, 1943, Zygielbojm committed suicide in London:

> By looking on passively upon this murder of defenseless millions, tortured children, women and men, they have become partners to its responsibility ... I cannot continue to live and to be silent while the remnants of Polish Jewry, whose representative I am, are being murdered. My comrades in the Warsaw ghetto fell with arms in their hands in the last heroic battle. I was not permitted to fall like them, together with them, but I belong with them, to their mass grave.
>
> By my death, I wish to give expression to my most profound protest against the inaction in which the world watches and permits the destruction of the Jewish people.[21]

The Warsaw Ghetto Uprising and its thanato-ethics produced a form of negative heroism that, although resembling fatalism, is marked by the ardent desire for an "us" to survive the horror and annihilation, as well as the world's obscene indifference. Marek Edelman emphasizes that to go down fighting was primarily an example set for "others," for his companions: the sight of people ready to die with weapons in hand could pull the terrified residents of the ghetto from their daze.[22] To die fighting was the only way for the community to outlive its members.

Self-Defense as National Doctrine

The political history of self-defense by Jewish movements is profoundly tied to their struggles against pogroms, primarily in Russia, in the late nineteenth and early twentieth centuries (1881–83, 1903–7, 1917–21). One of the first self-defense groups was formed in Odessa in 1881 on the initiative of a student committee, following the pogroms that occurred after the assassination of Alexander II. The group called itself *Yevreyskaya Druzhina* (the Jewish militia) and was made up of some 150 men—workers, shopkeepers, and students—who used clubs and iron bars as their weapons.[23] After the Bund's creation in 1897, it became the primary force organizing groups for self-defense against the pogroms. The Bund's political line was set by revolutionary socialist Jews, and it advocated for defensive violence to protect the Jewish population and their neighborhoods, as well as for measures to educate and organize the proletariat internationally, denouncing anti-Semitism as a counterrevolutionary ideology that divides the working class. Even before the tragic pogrom in Kishinev (in the Bessarabia region of the Russian Empire), the police and army were actively complicit in anti-Semitic violence, arming and protecting the pogromists against whom the Bund was preparing for armed self-defense. Socialist Jewish workers were the driving force behind the self-defense strategy, though it was also supported by non-Jewish workers and organizations, who participated in significant numbers. In August 1902, following the Czestochowa pogrom, the Bund initiated a program to establish self-defense groups everywhere it was active. A few weeks later, a newspaper close to the Bund, *Di Arbeter Shtime* (no. 30, October 1902) published a text that could be considered the organization's self-defense manifesto—*answer force with force*: "We must come out with arms in hand, organize ourselves and fight to the last drop of blood."[24] The analytical framework underpinning these actions was also very clear: "We should do everything we can to spread socialist ideas, specifically that of general liberation, among the Christian masses. This will transform today's enemies into tomorrow's friends, creating comrades in the struggle for our ideas."[25] The groups organized by the Bund trained for both armed and unarmed self-defense: one widely practiced fighting style at that time was an ultraviolent form of bare-knuckle boxing, without rules or referees, known as *kulachnyi boi*.[26] The groups were armed with clubs, stakes, axes, iron bars, and knives. They also trained with firearms, practiced making explosives, and even carried out assassinations against infiltrators from the czar's police, the Okhrana.[27] To be ready in the event of a pogrom, they formed protection and intervention squads, drawing on skills gained serving as marshals during demonstrations and large strikes during the same period.

Self-defense groups were also formed by Zionist workers' organizations. Their members were mostly craftsmen or residents of semi-industrialized areas where the Bund was not as present, such as southern Russia and Ukraine, parts of Poland, and Crimea. Existing alongside—or in opposition to—the Bund and international socialism, socialist Zionist currents merged to form the Poale Zion in 1901. They developed their own idea of self-defense, oriented toward the defense of their communities and less interested in struggling against anti-Semitic propaganda circulating within the working class.[28]

The Kishinev pogroms were a turning point.[29] On April 6 and 7, 1903, Passover was held in the context of a relentless anti-Semitic campaign around the supposed ritual murder of infants by Jews. With police encouragement, armed groups led a crowd of 2,000 people into Kishinev, home to 50,000 Jews.[30] Police prevented a 150-person self-defense group from intervening, arresting many of them and forcing them to disperse.[31] Thirty-four men, seven women, and two babies were massacred, while hundreds of others were injured and more than 1,500 homes and businesses were ransacked. Many women and girls were raped and some were tortured, including by having their breasts cut off, and some children were horribly mutilated.[32] The outcry from Jewish parties and organizations in Russia was fierce, and they were joined by intellectuals and the international press, but despite this, none of the killers were ever punished.[33] All the investigations were botched, and the prosecutions went nowhere, in spite of the commissions formed by Jewish organizations to collect evidence. As part of one such commission based in Saint Petersburg, the poet Hayyim Nahman Bialik spent over a month collecting testimonials and photos and compiling them in a 200-page document for publication. Inspired by this experience, in 1904 he wrote the poem "The City of Slaughter":

> Unto the attic mount, upon thy feet and hands;
> Behold the shadow of death among the shadows stands.
> There in the dismal corner, there in the shadowy nook,
> Multitudinous eyes will look
> Upon thee from the somber silence—
> The spirits of the martyrs are these souls,
> Gathered together, at long last,
> Beneath these rafters and in these ignoble holes.
> The hatchet found them here, and hither do they come
> To seal with a last look, as with their final breath,
> The agony of their lives, the terror of their death.
> Tumbling and stumbling wraiths, they come, and cower there
> Their silence whimpers, and it is their eyes which cry
> Wherefore, O Lord, and why?[34]

This long poem became a symbol of the victims' passive acceptance:

> For great is the anguish, great the shame on the brow;
> But which of these is greater, son of man, say thou.

The poem was widely read after being translated into Russian and Yiddish, and it has had an enduring legacy. Despite—or perhaps because of—its tone, it marked a shift from horrified despair to cries for revolt, which breathed new life into the drive for self-defense. In Vilnius, Michael Helpern, a prominent member of Poale Zion, recruited and trained self-defense groups under the rallying cry "Remember the shame!"[35]

Between 1903 and 1905, the Bund and Poale Zion initiated a clandestine program of active cooperation. The two organizations collaborated in the formation of dozens of self-defense groups, called BO (*Boevi Otriadi*, or combat detachments):

> Military and paramilitary training sessions were conducted in safe locations, such as on islands in the Dnieper ... When we anticipated a pogrom, the groups were contacted by telephone so they could gather and prepare to counterattack. And so it was in Vilna, Warsaw, Rostov, Minsk, Gomel, and Dvinsk [modern Daugavpils]. The self-defense groups were made up of young factory workers, carpenters, locksmiths, butchers, and other trades, and they also fought against the police, managing to free their arrested comrades on several occasions.[36]

By 1905, there were self-defense groups active in forty-two cities.[37] They faced intense brutality, but the Jewish organizations' defensive strategy allowed them to resist anti-Semitic violence and to prevent or hinder some pogroms.[38] However, police persecution, the imprisonment and deportation of activists, the repression of union activities, increasingly difficult social conditions, and the revolutionary context led to the gradual disbanding of self-defense groups. The murderous pogroms from 1903 to 1905 triggered a major wave of immigration (sometimes called the second Aliyah) to the United States and, to a lesser extent, Palestine, where many Zionist militants with experience in self-defense groups in Russia put their knowledge to use.

This moment makes the distinction between two different ideas of self-defense very clear: that of the Bund (which tried to maintain its activities in Russia in spite of the repression) and that of the Zionist parties. This split also occurred within the Zionist movement more broadly. There was a conflict between the socialist and cultural strains of Zionism and those that were ultraconservative, nationalistic, or even fascistic. The former lost the ideological struggle, which saw the rise of a militarized and terroristic form of colonial Zionism.

The translation into Russian from Hebrew of Bialik's poem cited above was done by Ze'ev Vladimir Jabotinsky, then a young writer and journalist.[39] Jabotinsky was very active in the Zionist movement and participated in self-defense groups in Odessa in the 1900s. During the First World War, he advocated for an alliance with the British and launched a paramilitary organization, the Jewish Legion, whose goal was to conquer Palestine. During the rioting in April 1920, he was once again at the head of self-defense groups, this time in Jerusalem—these groups had trained at the Maccabi Jerusalem sports club. He was sentenced to fifteen years in prison by the British but was freed the following year.[40] He left for London, then traveled to Paris.[41] In 1925, Jabotinsky created *Hatzohar*, the Revisionist Zionist Party, representing the far-right, fascistic current in the Zionist movement, with its headquarters in Paris.[42] He was one of the great theorists of a nationalist and authoritarian vision of self-defense that became dominant in Israel, a vision he continued to practice and promote throughout his life, as spelled out in his text *The Iron Wall*.[43] Jabotinsky's Zionism involved building an offensive Jewish armed force that "the native population cannot breach" and that would be capable of imposing an asymmetrical power structure on "the Arabs" in order to force them to accept the new borders of a Jewish state. His ideas would become dominant through the Haganah (The defense), an organization he cofounded with Eliyahou Golomb in 1920 as an outgrowth of the Hashomer (The guardian) that was dissolved that same year. The Hashomer had been a small, composite force founded by Israel Shohat in 1909 to defend the Yishuv—which from 1880 referred to Jewish immigrants who arrived in Palestine as part of the Zionist project—and had been targeted for repression by the Ottoman authorities. Its replacement by the Haganah in the 1920s signaled a shift: the Haganah's mission was no longer "defending" the Jewish population, but ensuring the Yishuv's growth, leading the Haganah to gradually become an offensive militia, a paramilitary force that targeted armed groups and the Arab resistance. The Haganah had no legal existence (the British forbade both Jewish and Arab residents of Palestine to organize autonomous armed groups). Still, many Jews of the Yishuv were involved in the British auxiliary police force (the Notrim, a Jewish police force founded by the British in 1936) and so had access to training in hand-to-hand combat (jujitsu). They also learned the basics of military counterinsurgency and offensive combat in the Special Night Squads, which were created in 1938 during the Arab Revolt as special forces under the command of a pro-Zionist British officer, Orde Charles Wingate.[44]

In 1931, a split within the Haganah led to the creation of the Irgun Tsvai Leumi (National Military Organization), known as the Irgun. This split was the product of a conflict over the ethical principle of "restraint" (*havalga*) that existed within the Haganah, whereby any "response" against the Arab population must be strictly defensive.[45] From 1937, the Irgun followed an increasingly radical path, carrying out deadly terror attacks against Arab civilians.[46] The Stern Gang emerged from far-right, nationalist currents of Zionism close to Jabotinsky and the Betar movement, but in its actions it went far beyond Jabotinsky, who had chosen to stand down his troops, both to avoid putting the backs of the British against the wall, and for strategic reasons. In

Jabotinsky's vision, offensive self-defense should not indulge in blind attacks, which disperse energy, wasting it on anarchic, spectacular actions that in practice do little to neutralize "the enemy."

And so the foundations of Israeli close combat were laid: the civil sphere was to be considered a continuous space of imminent violence. Jabotinsky conflated the situation of Jewish communities in Russia, threatened by pogroms, with that of Jewish militias and soldiers in Israel and their concerns about the Palestinian population and so-called Arab terrorists. Self-defense was, in his view, a way of being: the world is a violent place; this violence traverses every person and they will inevitably enact it; and combat techniques allow for effective and prompt control of the intensity of this violence.[47] In the context of a colonial conflict presented as a war on terrorism, you are always exposed to danger with no chance of retreat (close combat) and so must be ready to react to sudden attacks.[48] You must always make use of all your physical, sensorial, emotional, and environmental resources to neutralize any possible exogenous source of violence, while adapting to any context or situation, to any kind of threat or enemy.[49] On the scale of the nation, one still being established, such a politics of self-defense comes along with a set of *defensive practices of self*, which force you to live in the immanence of reflex reactions, muscular tension, and emotional connection, to suspend your discernment in regard to complex social relations, historical situations, intentions, meanings, and contexts. This impoverished world gives rise to a "cosmology of terror and total war" that encloses the defensive individual in a hand-to-hand phenomenology of lethal bodies.[50] Self-defense becomes a politics, literally a way of governing—at the scale of our bodies—the intensity of violence.

Genealogy of Krav Maga

Imi Lichtenfeld, the inventor of krav maga, a self-defense technique currently enjoying prolific success, was born in 1910 in Budapest, then a part of the Austro-Hungarian Empire. His family moved to Bratislava, Slovakia, where he grew up. His father, Samuel Lichtenfeld, had joined a traveling circus at age thirteen, where he learned a number of gymnastic and combat techniques. He spent nearly twenty years with the troupe, performing feats of strength (including weightlifting) and wrestling. When he returned to Bratislava, he founded Hercules, the city's first wrestling and weight lifting club, and became the lead detective of the local police force. There, he trained the police in self-defense techniques for immobilizing suspects during arrests. In 1928, Imi Lichtenfeld won the Slovakian junior wrestling championship, and the following year he won the adult title. He also competed internationally in wrestling, boxing, and gymnastics. Alongside this, he taught gymnastics to major theater troupes—notably in Czechoslovakia—and even acted in several plays. In response to the rise of anti-Semitic groups in the 1930s, Lichtenfeld participated in the defense of Jewish neighborhoods during pogroms and became the leader of a self-defense group in Bratislava. He gained experience in unarmed combat in fights against fascist militias. This trajectory is an example of "desportization," as the boxing and wrestling techniques he had learned were transported from the realm of sports to that of self-defense, from the ring to the street.[51]

In 1940, Imi Lichtenfeld left Slovakia aboard the *Pentcho*, the last ship to depart for Palestine, along with 400 other Slovakian Jewish refugees, on a trip paid for by the main right-wing nationalist Zionist party.[52] It would take Lichtenfeld two years to reach Palestine. On the way, the boat was repeatedly stopped and quarantined, before sinking off the coast of

Greece. Lichtenfeld was rescued by a British ship and spent several months recovering in a Jewish hospital in Alexandria, Egypt. He then enlisted in the Czech foreign legion, which had been placed under British command, and fought on various fronts in the Middle East, including Libya, Egypt, Syria, and Lebanon. In 1942, he received a permit to enter Palestine, where he proceeded to join the Haganah.

This is how the story of krav maga begins, and it is something of a founding myth for the Jewish state. Imi Lichtenfeld is a perfect narrative subject for the history of the self-defense system he developed in the units that would go on to become the Israeli army. The mythic biography of this one man linked the resistance of European Jewish youth to the rise of fascism, and the suffering it inflicted on their communities, to the providential birth of a nation that portrays itself as beset on all sides by attackers but that has managed to establish its existence, its authority, and its borders solely through the strength of its people. This new people, fully engaged in the military, celebrated the heroism represented by their shift from defense to offense. *Self-defense* in this context meant advancing, gaining ground, striking at the heart of the adversary, with an economy of means necessitating quick, efficient, and incapacitating attacks. Our hypothesis in this section is that a specific tactical understanding of close combat served as the foundation for a large-scale political and military strategy, or at the very least inspired the vocabulary of its propaganda. Krav maga symbolizes the national ideology of offensive defense, of a war of conquest waged in a context where an army came to define itself as a nation engaged in self-defense, against everyone, in order to survive.

In 1941, an elite, professional unit was formed within the Haganah. Known as the Palmach (an acronym for Plugot Mahatz, the strike force), it carried out targeted terrorist attacks, which were termed offensive self-defense. Due to a lack of logistical resources (wooden weapons were often used during training), this emerging force focused on techniques for hand-to-hand combat and developed its own training program. The same year, *kapap* groups (an acronym for *krav panim el panim*, "face-to-face combat") were established in both the Haganah and the Palmach. They were led by Gershon Kopler (jujitsu and boxing), Yehuda Markus (jujitsu and judo), and Maishel Horowitz (stick and knife fighting), nearly all of whom had served in the Special Night Squads.[53] The following year, Imi Lichtenfeld was recruited to the Palmach by Musa Zohar and became their *kapap* instructor—he taught jujitsu, boxing, and knife-fighting techniques. During this time, a particular strategic vision of offensive self-defense was coalescing among the leaders of what would become the IDF (Tsva ha-Hagana le-Yisra'el, the Israel Defense Forces), which would be founded in 1948 by merging all the existing paramilitary forces.[54]

Rather than a more traditional static defense along a front line, the IDF excelled in lightning attacks intended to stun the enemy and throw them into disarray, and in concentrated offensive actions to neutralize the enemy's center using (exclusively male) units with intensive training in hand-to-hand combat.[55] Despite its reputation as being ragtag and improvised, the IDF developed a novel self-defense strategy as part of its broader policy of colonization that would go on to be exported and recognized as one of the most effective counter-insurgency strategies in the world. Whether applied to an individual, a group, a militia, or an army, to civilians or to soldiers, whether it is termed sexual violence, criminality, or terrorism, the principle remains the same. Israel thus became a working model of a "security society," in which participation in paramilitary self-defense practices would soon lay the bedrock for a securitarian civility.[56]

The term *krav maga* (close combat) appeared in 1949 and was used alongside *kapap*. In 1953, Imi Lichtenfeld was part of a group that began codifying an unarmed combat system based on thirty-five core techniques that were constantly renewed, tested, and adapted to the current situation. In 1958, he became the military's lead krav maga instructor. *Krav maga* became the official name for the defensive combat system used by the IDF, and soon it was a profitable military export. In 1964, Lichtenfeld left the army and founded the first civilian krav maga club in Netanya, where he continued developing its core practices, based on four main precepts: adaptability (to situation and context), effectiveness (in defense), universality (usable by everyone), and spreadability (in the national culture).[57] Since the 1980s, krav maga has been promoted around the world as the most "realistic" unarmed self-defense system, and also as one of the most profitable "Made in Israel" products. But krav maga is also so much more than this: it is a practice of self, a civic practice, and a national culture, in a context where its generalization helps maintain a world in which krav maga is the only possible way of being. Its *reputation* as the most practical technique, the most realistic, for self-defense is not the only reason for its success: its spread coincides with the generalization of a culture of defense. This has transformed civil society itself, along with each individual's experience of the world. Krav maga is a realistic combat technique insofar as it produces a reality in which it can be presented as the only viable approach to life.

Krav maga has also been used to produce a set of derivative techniques that are marketed to the public police forces around the world. These techniques complement—or in some cases upend—older counterinsurgency practices in two important ways.

Firstly, offensive-defensive close combat can conceal the fact that deadly weapons are being used, which can incite public outrage should it gain media attention. This is achieved by transforming the body itself into a deadly weapon, capable of using a small number of techniques to immobilize another body using anatomical "pressure points," producing paralysis, unconsciousness, or suffocation. It can also involve supplementing the lethal body with extensions (such as *tonfas*, Tasers, Flash-Balls, or dogs) that are supposedly nonlethal. Mathieu Rigouste showed that equipping police with these "less than lethal" weapons constitutes a decision to legalize murder, under the pretense of expanding the police's right to self-defense.[58]

Secondly, the spread of close-combat techniques changed the traditional practice of *creating distance* between police and disorderly situations. Creating distance involves principles of "defensive passivity" (such as police lines or filter cordons during demonstrations), the imposition of self-restraint (including dispersal techniques), or delegating the force of strikes to an instrument (for instance, a water cannon).[59] The spread and promotion of a public order strategy emphasizing hand-to-hand techniques contributed to a renewal of virile norms privileging deadly contact, shock, intrusion, infiltration, provocation, humiliation, and disorganization, thereby transforming the police officer's body into an offensive body.[60]

This creation of offensive bodies also results from a chemical transformation of the fear that inhabits the police, and which they help to spread, into a repressive dynamic that lays the groundwork for a new dominant virility.[61] As a value, fear has long been tied to effeminate, cowardly forms of masculinity, but here it has morphed into a source of virility, constructing bodies ready to defend themselves at the slightest of chemical signals, transforming the instinct to freeze into a trigger for attack.

The generalization of krav maga in Israeli civil society alongside the theory of offensive defense, in which *any good defense is also an attack*, has elevated the spirit and letter of techniques for self-defense in real situations—a core principle of the Israeli state's military strategy—to the level of national motto. Its spread also carries with it a macho, bellicose vision of citizenship, which invokes the principle of *defense of self* to legitimize its right to violence and colonization.

More broadly, modern Israel is a political model, both civic and civil, of how governance can transform in response to a force that typically leads to crisis or failure for the security state: a terrorist menace.[62] Terrorism provokes widespread fear, but when this becomes a *virtù*, it favors policies that can control fear by means of fueling the feeling of insecurity in civil society, and therefore also in its individual members, rather than providing defense or protection. Such policies are quite economical, since individuals become responsible for *defending themselves*, for embodying the use of violence and becoming defensive bodies. They can then be usefully transformed into deadly martial units, atomized and tasked with vigilance against a faceless enemy, willing to be governed by fear in the name of security.

The State, or the Non-monopoly on Legitimate Defense

Hobbes or Locke: Two Philosophies of Self-Defense

Social contract theory is where modern self-defense was first conceptualized. The defense of oneself by oneself is typically framed in terms of liberty and the natural right to *self-preservation*. Self-defense is at the heart of Thomas Hobbes's philosophical anthropology. Although his primary goal is to eradicate violence by *force* of sovereign right, Hobbes consistently frames this violence present in man in positive terms, as a necessity that no juridical artifice will be able to fully neutralize.

In *Leviathan*, one is free to use any means necessary to preserve oneself, and this is a "right of nature." Reciprocally, self-preservation is a "law of nature" that no one can escape: "a man is forbidden to do, that, which is destructive of his life, or taketh away the means of preserving the same; and to omit, that, by which he thinketh it may be best preserved."[1] The freedom and imperative of self-preservation result in absolute equality among people in a state of nature. Equality here is wholly the effect of the relative and commensurate nature of each person's resources (such as strength, cunning, intelligence, teamwork) and how they are used to *defend one's life*. "From this equality of ability, ariseth equality of hope in the attaining of our ends."[2] Everyone, then, is defending their life, using their body to defend their body, and this, rather than providing security, maintains a form of equality that is simply equality before the risk of death. Defending yourself is expressed concretely through your ability to effectively harm others.

Everyone seeks to preserve their lives, and this fact gives rise to an infinite variety of practices for the defense of self: from this common nature emerges an art with multiple expressions. All of these practices are legitimate in that they arise of necessity. In this way, Hobbes dismisses the question of the legitimate or illegitimate use of defensive violence.[3] Yet this condition of each defending against all results in an insecurity that is quite *unlivable*. The *condition of war* described in chapter 13 of *Leviathan* is not simply "the act of fighting" but a disposition toward combat that defines that time "wherein men live without other security, than what their own strength, their own invention shall furnish them withall."[4]

In such a context, we can speak of a *cunning disposition toward combat*, one that is not overconfident in the outcome of any fight, that represents a focused motion toward the "self" in such a way that the "self" does not preexist the defensive motion but rather emerges as an ongoing effect of it. This motion orients all other practices of the self—whether bodily, intellectual, imaginative, emotional, or linguistic—toward defense against others. Therefore, the disposition toward combat can be understood as creating the subject—a subject *in motion*—and also as a loss of momentum due to the ceaseless defensive efforts it demands.

Hobbes's political anthropology is far from considering defensive violence a "blind" tendency (which could anachronistically be called an instinctive tendency). The condition of mankind in a state of nature is more closely related to the *reasonable exercise of self-defense*, which could just as easily take the shape of the pursuit of peace (which Hobbes defines as a "duty") as the pursuit of an infinite arsenal: "by all means we can, to defend ourselves."[5] In other words, the ceaseless, reasonable effort to preserve our lives can be transformed into the freedom to do whatever we want and are capable of by means of a right of nature, but this right is at once impossible and imprescriptible. It is impossible to exercise it without interference *or* to relinquish it without also becoming prey and denying the essence of our nature, our humanity.[6]

Starting from this contradiction, Hobbes lays out the contract's condition of possibility: everyone's lives can only be efficiently and effectively assured when everyone gives up their own right of nature (and with it the freedom to use any means to suitably defend themselves) and submits to a singular authority. Yet delegating power to the Leviathan cannot fully extinguish the focused motion in defense of one's self: "When people are being led out to punishment (whether capital or not), they are held in chains or escorted by guards; that is the clearest indication that they are not seen as sufficiently obligated by an agreement not to resist."[7] In his *De Cive*, "the right to resist," as Hobbes terms it, cannot be considered a privilege: it is a right, rooted in a disposition both irrepressible *and* irreproachable, an impulsion that cannot be restrained. In the same text, in addition to the famous example of the prisoner resisting the jailers, Hobbes considers the question of slavery. He invokes the classical argument that the right of slavery is linked to the right of war: by convention, prisoners of war can have their lives spared in exchange for consenting to serve their conquerors. But Hobbes adds an important detail: "Slaves of the sort that are held in prisons, workhouses, or bonds are not included in the definition of slaves given above."[8] This is because they do not serve by convention, but by force: "hence, if they run away, or kill their Master, they are not acting against the natural laws."[9] Take note of the carte blanche Hobbes provides here. In Hobbes's time, slavery was usually understood in terms of just war and the fate of the vanquished, and only rarely in reference to the contemporary "embarrassing institution" of transatlantic slavery.[10] He is far from legitimating any right to resistance properly speaking here, but he does take account of the invincibility—or rather the *incivility*—of the disposition toward self-defense. Hobbes is not philosophizing over the legitimacy or illegitimacy of the institution of slavery but simply observing that violent practices of resistance and liberation among slaves are inevitable.

Hobbes's materialist anthropology considers the right of nature to self-preservation as a disposition, acting equally in everyone, and not just as an original right over one's self, enjoyed by some but not others. Throughout the twelfth and thirteenth centuries, the state of nature was typically invoked to criticize bad institutions, and so it is in Hobbes. However, in his view, bad institutions are not those that "denature" people but rather those that maintain "relics" of nature. In other terms, political institutions fail because they have not made a clean, definitive break with the state of nature (if that is even possible), which leads them to fail and in turn contributes to civil unrest, allowing violence to persist. At this point in his argument, Hobbes directly addresses his readers, whom he understandably suspects might be skeptical of such a tragic portrayal of the state of nature. Any incredulous person may

> therefore consider with himself, when taking a journey, he arms himself, and seeks to go well accompanied; when going to sleep, he locks his doors; when even in his house he locks his chests; and this when he knows there be laws and public officers, armed, to revenge all injuries shall be done him.[11]

Hobbes's critique of English society and its institutions hinges on the omnipresent *concern for defense*. He takes aim at dysfunctional political authorities in terms of their effect—or rather their non-effect—on social antagonisms. Habits of caution, suspicion, warlike ingenuity, and permanent vigilance, as well as fatigue of the body and of the calculating mind, are symptoms of a larger problem. They are signs of a subjectivation—a paranoiac self-becoming—that has not yet been subjugated by a state truly capable of exerting (by force) and expressing (by inspiring fear) the coercive power necessary for the security of society. All of Hobbes's philosophy is focused on theorizing a legitimate, absolute sovereign power (instituted by contract), which is the only way of bringing peace to the intrinsically violent relationships between individuals. However, this violence can never be fully eradicated from civic life. Maintaining the security of society requires everyone's *consent* and the *subjection* of their wills, but violence cannot be totally and definitively placed *outside of politics*.

Through this reading of Hobbes's anthropology, our goal is to show how self-defense can be considered a manifestation—perhaps the simplest—of a relationship with oneself immanent in vital impulses and bodily movements, particularly in the way they perpetuate over time. Subjectivity is made up of both bodily defensive tactics—skillful acts of resistance—against real and imagined interpersonal challenges, and material conditions that are unable to eliminate or conceal the establishment of a Subject of law who must be kept in line by the state. John Locke, however, provides an entirely different interpretation. His position is in striking contrast to Hobbes in terms of who he defines as the subject of self-defense: what is this "self" that *I* preserve?

Like Hobbes, Locke posits a state of nature in which all people are understood to be naturally equal. However, this equality is conceived as the equal distribution of the power to dispose of one's person, meaning *of one's possessions*. This is a limited right. It is to be exercised "within the bounds of the law of nature" unless "the Lord and master of them all" has given some the right to dominate, and others the duty to obey.[12] There are thus those who properly possess their bodies, and those who are by nature dispossessed, and this fundamental distinction determines who is granted freedom. Although Locke declares that everyone has an equal right to liberty, he goes on to introduce numerous discriminatory clauses.

Fundamentally, the freedom to dispose of one's person is subordinated to the duty of preserving oneself and, by extension, of contributing to the preservation of humankind. The freedom to dispose of oneself and one's goods is a right of enjoyment, insofar as humans remain the creatures of "one infinite, and infinitely wise Maker."[13] The right of enjoyment allows the free and reasonable use of one's own body and one's own property in order to preserve them. Self-preservation refers, then, to the body proper, which is defined as the subject's property, at once *relatively* (in that God alone fully possesses your person and therefore your self) and *originally*. The body proper is the foundation of all other property: by allowing you to transform nature, it lets you take ownership of other goods. The body is a property, and its use establishes a subject of law capable of extending its right to other things. This is because "every man has a property to his own person. This nobody has any right to but himself. The labour of his body and the work of his hands, we may say, are properly his."[14]

In addition to the power to dispose of oneself for the purpose of self-preservation, Locke introduces a power of jurisdiction that further solidifies the philosophical-juridical nature of Lockean subjectivity. His understanding of the freedom and the duty of self-preservation is radically different from Hobbes's, in that Locke reduces the preservation of one's person to the legality or illegality of *taking the law into your own hands*, whereas Hobbes defines it as a disposition immanent in the body. In Hobbes, self-defense always goes beyond the question of legality (whether natural or positive), since it is the expression of a material reality that constantly unravels the legal artifice, or at minimum places it in crisis.

To Locke, on the contrary, it is completely inconceivable that any defense could occur outside the framework imposed by the original right to self-ownership. Any manifestation of self-defense is considered through the lens of legality, reducing it to what is always already considered a right of legitimate defense. The question then is simply whether or not a given subject can legitimately engage in self-defense, meaning the issue hinges not on the type of defensive action taken, but on the status of the one taking it. Only "Subjects," subjects of law who are by definition free (in other words, only owners) can legitimately claim power of jurisdiction, and thus only they have a right to *defend themselves* and each other against damage to any of their property.[15]

In Locke's state of nature, power of jurisdiction allows you to take justice into your own hands (meaning to judge and punish) if your property—or that of another person—is violated (or threatened). God grants us a right of enjoyment over our own bodies proper, making us their owners, and in the same way He proclaims us judges and gives us permission to punish, or even to kill. People can then reasonably and legitimately inflict punishments on anyone who damages their property, since their acts are against the laws of nature.

Continuing in this line, Locke specifies that the right to punish should respect a principle of proportionality between crime and punishment. However, he argues that because damaging others' property (whether this means violence to their bodies or the theft of their goods) is a crime against the laws of nature and therefore against God, it is tantamount to excluding yourself from humanity. It goes without saying that this is not an argument for moderating the use of the right to punish. Locke sets up an opposition between, on the one hand, the right to preserve one's belongings and the legitimate right of all property owners to exact justice, and on the other, the "unjust Violence and Slaughter" of criminals. By their acts, criminals have "declared war against all mankind, and therefore may be destroyed as a lion or a tiger, one of those wild savage beasts with whom men can have no society nor security."[16] In a single sentence, Locke presents theft as a declaration of war—a social war if ever there was one—and then transforms this inexorable war into a "hunt": rather than a battle between property owners and thieves, he is describing a hunt for destitute, heteronomous, subjugated bodies.

Those who make themselves guilty of theft can, then, be legitimately punished by anyone else and treated like animals. Concretely, any offense against property owners' property authorizes them to make legitimate use of violence. And this violence should not be understood as strictly defensive (legitimate because immediate and proportional); it is also exemplary violence, whose purpose is prevention. As the schema for the dominant form of modern subjectivity, the right to property contains two inextricably linked privileges: the right of preservation and the right of jurisdiction. In this framing, *punishment is self-preservation.*

In Locke's philosophy, "I am defending myself" means "I am defending *my* belongings, *my* property," which also means "my body." The body proper establishes and defines the person; it is therefore the object of any act of justice carried out by a subject of law. The subject in self-defense is an "I" endowed with rights, the first of which is ownership of one's body. The establishment and constitution of such subjects occur through the property relation, which *therefore preexists the act of self-preservation.* The status of property owner—and of judge, its logical extension—is the condition of legitimacy (and also of efficacy) of self-defense.

The whole issue comes down to the following question: who will be recognized as a subject of law, able to engage in legitimate self-defense? Locke makes a radical distinction between free subjects (individuals who own themselves and who are therefore subjects of law) and others, for whom theft is a condition of their existence. These thieves of all kinds are not defended, because they are seen as not (or no longer) having a body proper, any rights, or *any self*: they have ceased to be people. They are bodies that must steal themselves if they are to survive: for them, *self-defense is just another theft.*

The "self" in "self-preservation" has its roots in the way the self is understood in the particular conception of consciousness that underpins modern subjectivity. In Locke's framing, the "self" in "self-defense" echoes his conceptualization of consciousness as a personal identity, as an "I" that turns back on itself because it is engaged in a continuous and unlimited process of appropriation—of its actions, its memories, its thoughts, its desires, right down to the smallest of its movements and gestures. For the others—Indians who enjoy the gifts of nature, slaves, servants, women and children, the destitute, criminals and scoundrels—there is no one inside their bodies, dispossessed as they are of themselves. Their existence is one of being *radically outside of themselves*.[17]

Locke's state of nature can transform into a state of war because of the intense violence of the conflicts resulting from the division between subjects—that is, between those who own themselves and are their own judges, who enjoy the privileges of preservation and jurisdiction, and the *others*. It is for this reason that political society's primary goal is to preserve each person's property and to guarantee that all (all property owners) are able to enjoy their body and their goods. To this end, judicial authorities are established to rule on conflicts and decide punishments. Once political society is able to assure respect for property rights and the provision of common justice, property owners are to give up their basic right of jurisdiction. But they never do fully give it up. Rather, they delegate this right and are always able to demand accountability, even though Locke limits the possibility of breaking the contract, since this would undermine any possibility of community.[18] Still, though, should political society fail in its foundational mission and become unable to protect property, every subject is able to reclaim the right of jurisdiction and exercise it there and then. This privilege forms the basis of the theory of possessive individualism, in which, partially contradicting Locke himself, the right to defend oneself is considered an inalienable right of legitimate defense, one that the individual shares with, rather than delegates to, the public authority.

Building on the idea of delegation, we can invert the usual terms of the debate: rather than the delegation of the individual right to self-defense to the state, it is a question of keeping the right to do violence or of transferring it in the opposite direction, from the state to the citizens. This counter-transfer has two main modalities. The first process involves delegating *security powers*. The public authority might rely on a militia made up of armed citizens rather than on an army, or it might supplement the one with the other—the paradigmatic example is repressive paramilitary formations or private police. The second process, still in reference to sovereign power, deals with the delegation of *juridical powers*: the authorities discharge themselves of their responsibility to punish by extending it to certain subjects. The paradigmatic example in this case is national legislation relating to the right to bear arms and to parajudicial structures. In both cases, the logic of delegation speaks to an economy of means that complicates the thesis of the state's monopoly on the legitimate use of violence. We might be tempted to see it is a sign of weakness or breakdown when states offload their responsibilities in this way, but that is not necessarily the case. By externalizing some of its prerogatives, the state can maintain order at a lower cost—this delegation of power occurs by interpellating citizens (or at least certain citizens) as *legitimate vigilantes*.

Taking the Law into Your Own Hands: Militias and "Judicial Cooperatives"

The natural right to self-preservation, as it is defined in the Lockean tradition, is materialized in the legal arsenal relating to the right to armed self-defense. This right is an essential element of Anglo-Saxon legal culture, but it has taken very different shapes in response to political concerns that are crucial for historicizing the concept of self-defense.

The right to armed self-defense as defined in Article 7 of the 1689 English Bill of Rights was incorporated almost verbatim into the US Constitution. It originated in the need to arm the men of the realm in order to raise a force for military or policing purposes, which came with the duty of each subject to possess a weapon other than a knife.[19] In England, bearing arms became a basic right *for all Protestants* in 1689, and this was understood as necessary for the right to self-defense, defined at that time as flowing from the natural rights of resistance and self-preservation.[20] Since that time, the right to armed self-defense has been seen as a means of preventing absolutism, part of the philosophical history of parliamentary monarchy, although some ambiguity remains as to its precise meaning and concrete application. Is it only to be exercised within citizens' militias, *or* is it an inalienable natural right for individuals to be able to preserve their lives and defend themselves against oppression (or, in practice, a privilege possessed only by a wealthy minority)? Throughout the nineteenth and twentieth centuries, England adopted a number of laws to regulate the bearing of arms by civilians, with the intention of stemming the proliferation of firearms and their anarchic use in the realm. These regulations failed to address either the social disorder caused by an armed population or the political question of self-defense. At the same time, though, the legitimacy of such regulations was never really questioned. In other words, in England, the regulatory framework for armed self-defense existed harmoniously alongside a Parliament that *represented* its subjects, and therefore limited the autonomous and individual manifestations of their privileges, such as their *becoming vigilantes*.

Any time the individual's access to weapons is defined and delimited, the citizens' right of jurisdiction is also being negotiated. Until the end of the nineteenth century, the judicial costs payable by plaintiffs were so high that in practice, only the richest members of society could afford to initiate legal proceedings.[21] Protests shook the country, and groups of citizens called for public meetings to discuss the high cost of justice and the inability of the legal system to protect people and property. These meetings gave rise to prosecution societies: members signed a charter committing to pool money as well as material and human resources to cover the costs of investigations, laying charges, legal counsel, and the arrest and detention of criminals.[22] The group's members also committed to help each other, by monitoring each other's properties, providing testimony, sharing information, and agreeing not to buy stolen goods or merchandise. These societies were essentially *judicial cooperatives*, more like mutual insurance for the defense of people and goods than self-help justice of the kind that developed in the United States. Prosecution societies saw themselves as supplementing the law and the justice system, not taking their place. Starting in the late eighteenth century, judicial cooperatives increasingly subcontracted out the dirty work of surveillance to squads of men recruited mostly from the poorest parts of society.[23]

Throughout the nineteenth century, self-styled groups of citizen vigilantes emerged throughout England, but as part of strictly regulated organizations: their money was deposited in banks, new members were voted in by existing ones, they hired guards, and judicial costs were covered, excluding for theft or events occurring outside the city or region. Because their charters were archived, we can estimate the number of prosecution societies (more than 500 in 1839) and get a sense of how they developed and the profits they generated through the criminalization of practices connected to the capitalist system and private property.[24] The state gave free rein to judicial cooperatives not out of weakness but as part of a historical process that sought to rationalize their usage. The history of the right to armed self-defense is inseparable from that of private judicial organizations as well as the genealogy of the liberal state. It is also a way of defining dominant modern subjectivity, emphasizing the figure of the model citizen with autonomous martial and judicial capabilities that allow them to defend their property as though it were their self. These judicial organizations built a very restrictive framework for their conception of armed self-defense. They based their legitimacy on the old duty to be armed in order to form citizens' militias in defense of the realm, and also on the individual right to self-preservation and self-jurisdiction extrapolated from that duty. This meant that when they formed structures for local law enforcement, they were supplementary to the sovereign power. This apparatus may have been not so much an extension of the sphere of self-defense to matters of social or national defense as an example of an extension of the entrepreneurial model of self-defense, or more specifically: "an extension of entrepreneurial initiative into the realm of criminal justice ..."[25] What we are seeing is an apparatus in the service of an ascendant merchant class, similar to medieval mercantile associations or the farmers' self-defense groups developing in France in the same period.[26] By forming organizations, individuals could exercise their right to armed self-defense collectively, thereby preventing their prerogative from being atomized, which would have made them lone vigilantes. Prosecution societies represented a consolidation of the privileges of the owning class, who did not seek to place themselves "above the law" but instead to create a "parajudicial apparatus" alongside it for self-defense.[27] These societies carried out their work efficiently and in harmony with the legislative authorities, not in opposition to them, and by so doing they consolidated a fundamental distinction among citizens, since only property owners could in fact fully exercise the natural right to self-defense.

On the other side of the Atlantic, a crisis of interpretation regarding the right to self-defense led to a fierce debate in American political culture. The two sides faced off from seemingly traditional ideological positions. Each side had a citational relationship with the legislation, experiments, and debates emerging from Europe's urban centers, but they also brought other issues to the fore. One side wanted to limit the ability of private individuals to use and carry weapons, believing that armed self-defense should occur within "well-organized militias." They were vehemently opposed to those who believed the bearing of arms was distinct from the history of militias and that it was an integral part of American citizenship that could not be limited or restricted. The two sides did agree, however, on the principal idea that all laws come from the people, and that the people—and therefore each citizen—is the original legislative body.

The long history of American militias during the colonial period shows that they were never clearly positioned as the primary source of the right to armed self-defense, but just as one of its expressions. The legitimacy of these militias came from the individuals who made them up, each of whom enjoyed an inalienable right to bear arms.[28] From the late 1600s through the 1800s, the right to self-defense underwent a stark mutation due to its transposition from England to colonial territory in the United States. It was unprecedented to express the right to self-defense as the right of citizens to (re)take up arms and to rely on their *sole* judgment for the *sole* defense of their persons and property, but this would become a key element of the young American nation and the constitutionality of its laws. Whether people acted together or formed groups made no difference; both were ways of exercising their individual right. The individual weapon is like an incarnation of Adam Smith's "Invisible Hand": it creates society.

Self-defense plays an active role in the American "imagined political community."[29] It is how the members of this community, American citizens, are interpellated as "eternal pioneers." They would come to be called frontiersmen, men portrayed as having built the country through their own strength and that of their arms, as defending themselves against every threat in order to push back the *frontier* (by building cities on supposedly savage, hostile territories, by exterminating the Indigenous nations they considered barbarous, by refusing the authority of the Old Continent as well as the positive laws imposed by the colonial government, and so on).[30] In practice, self-defense is a fundamental element of the colonial, racial, and social history of the United States of America, as well as the basis of its legitimating rhetoric.[31]

The right to bear arms was one of the ten amendments to the Constitution of the United States of America ratified on December 15, 1791, known as the Bill of Rights.[32] A first level of analysis generally frames the Bill of Rights as in opposition to local or federal rules on the bearing of arms, as these were seen as too restrictive. And yet, although the Second Amendment has historically been constrained by a large number of state and federal regulations, it has only been the subject of constitutional debate three times: in 1876, 1939, and 2008.[33]

The Supreme Court's 1876 decision in *United States v. Cruikshank* was of lasting importance. It followed the Colfax massacre, which took place on April 13, 1873, in the state of Louisiana. A Louisiana Republican militia, made up mostly of free Black men who were veterans of the Union Army, was defending the courthouse in the small town of Colfax. They were attacked and defeated by a white paramilitary force whose leaders would go on to form the White League, which had close ties to the Ku Klux Klan and was instrumentalized by the Democratic Party. Between 50 and 150 men were taken prisoner and massacred during the night. Only a few bodies were found, since most had been thrown into the river or burned. In 1876, the Supreme Court's decision confirmed that the right to bear arms (Second Amendment of the US Constitution) belonged to all citizens (per the Fourteenth Amendment, guaranteeing equal rights for all citizens before the law), including former slaves (Fifteenth Amendment). However, the decision also specified that the Supreme Court was not competent to bring criminal proceedings against members of the Ku Klux Klan who had violated the freedom of Black people to defend themselves, because the court's rulings were only enforceable against the federal government and not against the states, which were free to regulate individual liberty.[34] More than a hundred years later, the court's 2008 decision would confirm this position. In it, the Supreme Court ruled against the District of Columbia for forbidding citizens from keeping firearms in their home. This historic decision appears to be the last word in a debate that began more than 200 years earlier, and it came in spite of the social context of recent years, in which the possession and use of firearms has played a central role in American politics. It confirmed that the Second Amendment guarantees to all citizens the right to possess and carry weapons for their own defense.[35]

The individual and inalienable right to armed self-defense in the United States is important to our argument in that it is the condition of possibility for collective mobilizations in defense of the nation. The history of militias and self-help justice movements makes clear that they are not the origins of the principle of self-defense, but simply extensions of it. These movements can collectively be referred to as "vigilantism," as (with few exceptions) they all advocate for armed or paramilitary self-defense as well as for extralegal justice, accompanied by conservative and racist rhetoric.

Vigilantism, or the Birth of the Racial State

In the United States, the term "vigilante" is borrowed from Spanish, having descended from the Latin *vigilans*. Its recorded use goes back to 1824 in Missouri, where it referred to a "vigilant man," but it was mostly used in the second half of the nineteenth century in the context of "vigilance committees," while before that they were simply called "vigilants." Starting in the 1760s, groups of *vigilants* formed across the country, from the East to the Western frontier.

The first text about these vigilantes by one of their number was written in colonial Louisiana. It was intended to glorify vigilance committees, and it contains a theoretical argument for the legitimate use of armed defensive violence by self-proclaimed citizen vigilantes.[36] In 1861, Alexandre Barde wrote *Histoire des comités de vigilance aux Attakapas* (the history of vigilance committees in the Attakapas).[37] Barde was a settler who had arrived in Louisiana in 1842, where he worked as a journalist and sometimes as a teacher for white children on large plantations. His text is an interesting materialization of the racialization of vigilantism and stands as a record of colonial violence. It shows how this violence was romanticized, and he lays the groundwork for portraying the vigilantes, who are by definition white, as heroes.

Barde was affiliated with the Democratic Party and arrived in the Attakapas in 1859, at the beginning of the unrest in the lead-up to the Civil War. He got involved in the vigilance committees that were spreading across the region and became their historian. Vigilance committees were not born in Louisiana, but along the East Coast, and they moved gradually into the American West throughout the nineteenth century.[38] The membership of these groups, most of which were exclusively male, consisted of wealthy men, landowners, farmers, craftsmen, jurists, and men of letters, all of them committed to the defense of private property. They could involve as few as a dozen individuals or as many as 6,000, like the San Francisco Vigilance Committee at its peak in 1856.[39] Throughout the colonization of the Americas, groups of men formed themselves into militias and granted themselves exceptional rights of jurisdiction (judicial and policing authority). Vigilantism is one of history's largest manifestations of extralegal direct action, anti-abolitionism, and racist American terrorism and criminality. In contrast to the usual argument that vigilantism arose as a symptom of undeveloped political institutions that were weak and dysfunctional, our perspective is that the vigilantes are better understood as part of a process of rationalizing governmentality.

In his history of vigilance committees, Barde paints a picture of a golden age of French colonization, where good Christians, admirable fathers and hard workers all made the earth fertile and lived in peace.[40] This idyllic scene serves only to emphasize the fall: this first generation of white settlers were a family, and their justice occurred "within the family," in a spirit of clemency and indulgence. No one could be convicted since, according to Barde, they were brothers, cousins, friends, and neighbors who had all grown up together. However, he considers this kind of justice to be worse than any crime, since it does away with all the principles of justice, allowing a veritable "army of crime" to develop, complete with generals, officers, and soldiers, all striving toward a single goal: theft.[41]

Cows, horses, pigs, everything melted away in a few months, like snow; an Arab raiding party would not have been more able thieves or more ardent pillagers. These pasture pirates truly were enemies, and the weakness or complicity of jury members had permitted them to install themselves in a society that should have destroyed them itself.[42]

Beyond the familial nature of American colonial protojustice, the author identifies two reasons for this disastrous clemency. The first was a "nearly unlimited right of challenge," which meant that any lawyer could dismiss potential jury members until only the ignorant, complicit, or corrupt were left. The second was the need for a "unanimous verdict," which basically meant automatic acquittal due to the difficulty of getting all the jurors to agree. This is the context in which begins the history of vigilance committees in Louisiana:

> The day had come—a day that had been predicted a hundred times. Not a day of vengeance, because a court that used such a weapon would not be worthy of the name, but of expiation. It was a score to be settled with the dangerous classes: we have been keeping records of their past actions, and we would now go through them page by page. Their unpunished deeds would be weighed on a scale both terrible and impartial, like that of true justice, but this time we would be certain the scale was held by a sure and steady hand, and that the men behind it would be ready for any challenge they might meet.[43]

The vigilantes were going to "fight to purify our country."[44] Barde projected his own phantasms onto the popular imagination and described the vigilantes of the committees as beautiful, armed, and merciless, with a leader able "to make young girls fall wildly in love."[45]

Barde asks, how could "simple country folk" turn into heroic judges? Is it really legal for vigilance committees, even if made up of "honest citizens," to take on the work of the justice system? In Barde's telling, civil justice no longer existed, and the committees came into being on its ashes. The vigilantes were not judges; rather, vigilantism was simply an expedited modality of the judiciarization of conflict. It involved rejecting any notion of equity, including the adversary principle and the presumption of innocence. In defense of a minority, the trials' outcomes were decided in advance, and the accused were simply guilty parties waiting for their punishment. There were no judges in vigilantism then, properly speaking. There were no procedural codes or even clearly articulated lists of criminal offenses, whether felonies or misdemeanors. In the case of misdemeanors, the accused were found guilty and sentenced in advance. There were three levels of punishment: reparations to be made within a given time (generally between one and eight days), banishment and flogging if the deadline was not respected, and hanging for repeat offenders. For felonies, the committees saw only one remedy: the gallows.[46] Most of the vigilance committees existing during the late nineteenth century used flogging, banishment, and hanging in their push to drive out of the state every man considered undesirable, as threats to white colonial society. As the schisms that would lead to the Civil War deepened, vigilance organizations spread across the Southern states to enforce the racial order, part of the armed wing of white supremacist ideology: society must be cleansed.[47]

Above all else, vigilantism despised lawyers: "No lawyer will set foot here."[48] Vigilantism recognizes only one kind of defense, that of the members of a community, a people, or a society *against their enemies*—who are left utterly defenseless. The vigilance committees were thus a manifestation of a broader transformation of self-defense into legitimate defense—defending yourself against crime is legitimate a priori, and therefore so is any act of violence. The history of vigilantism is usually understood as a response to periods of chaos, where the old order is suspended, defeated, or overthrown, and the new order has not yet emerged.[49] On the contrary, vigilantism comes into being when a specific idea of justice (involving accused, judges, and lawyers) comes under fierce attack and is ultimately rendered inoperable. Looked at this way, the vigilantes are clearly not judges: they considered themselves the enemies of judges. They were not acting in place of judges—even once that place was vacant—or in their name. The vigilantes fought to make judges disappear by situating themselves as police, soldiers, court clerks, bailiffs, prison guards, and executioners simultaneously. Alexandre

Barde himself wrote positively of the fact that vigilantism is not a form of justice, but of war and hunting: a hunt for bandits, for the poor, for any troublesome people who "need to be wiped out."[50]

From this perspective, it becomes clear that the history of vigilantism represents a radical rupture with the classical idea of justice. Specifically, it breaks from theories of state formation involving the imposition of a centralized judicial structure whose legitimacy is based on the rule of law as enforced by a separate authority. The reason for this is that the vigilantes' version of history clashes with how the *hero* is usually understood in political philosophy. Classically, "heroic law" is only valid in *pre*-juridical periods, before a state succeeds in imposing itself, "where there are no human laws," as Vico described it in *The New Science*.[51] Hegel took up "the right of heroes" as well, arguing that pre-state violence is also the "foundational violence" of the constitutional state, taking the place of "the arbitrariness of force."[52] The hero puts an end to what social contract philosophy terms "the state of nature."[53] Then, once the state appears on the scene, vigilantes must leave or risk becoming anachronisms. However, the present relevance of vigilantism requires us to conceive of a different process: in this case, heroic law seems to have emerged in opposition to the state judicial system during its formation and was ultimately institutionalized in its place. It changes the traditional framing of the issue if heroic law arrives only after the fact, after the formation of the state (even if the state is still in an early stage of development), and goes on to contest it and even overthrow it in favor of a different judicial and juridical framework. Vigilantism is usually associated with the state of nature, and since it is the prime example of taking justice into your own hands, it represents the natural order reasserting itself against the state. Possibly, though, in this return to nature we are witnessing the establishment of an unprecedented and genuinely racial state, one whose laws are based on the rationalization of race. This is why vigilantes have never left the political scene in US history. They are neither an incarnation of an endless cycle of vendettas and personal vengeance repeating in the absence of public justice, nor symptoms of a revolutionary situation set to overturn the old order—vigilantes are the racial state's archetypal figures of the Great Man. The vigilantes actualize the morbid spirit of race—a spirit of "naive and ingenuous" men.[54] By making an institution of the historic character of a society of colonizers, the early vigilantes made white supremacy a concrete reality. In *The Philosophy of History*, Hegel reminds us that great men often meet bad ends, being killed, judged, or deported.[55] However, in the modern and contemporary history of the United States, those first vigilantes were replaced by a new generation, and vigilantism came to be celebrated and accepted. Vigilantism is a model of good citizenship—a good American citizen is a vigilant citizen. Vigilantes are the proud defenders of the American nation, they are heroes always ready for defense, and their culture contributes to the narrative of the white race while also making it a reality.

Barde's text is an early distillation of the basic elements that would make up the philosophy of vigilantes over the following decades and that continue to influence portrayals of vigilantes in popular culture today. In contrast with the allegorical representation of Justice, shown as a woman with her eyes blindfolded to represent the principle of impartiality, vigilantes hide their faces. They are portrayed as exceptional and personified, real and desirable, biased and pitiless. The allegorical figure of Justice stands over and between the parties in order to try the facts and judge blindly, without taking into account the parties' character. The vigilante, a masked enforcer, is immersed in the very society he means to defend by exposing criminals—he is the incarnation of a desire to punish, enacting a form of racial justice that seeks to execute those perceived as the natural enemies of private property, the family, and white society. While traditional justice is conducted publicly and openly, vigilantes act at night, whether in the name of God, in defense of honest people, or for the honor of women of their race. The vigilante's mask conceals his origins and his true identity, that of simply an average citizen who portrays himself as a worker, a peaceful farmer, a good Christian and father. It also emphasizes his gaze, as his eyes are the only features that reveal the rationality that guides his actions. The night makes his *vision* seem omnipotent, since despite the darkness, he is able to see through to the true nature of those who must be banished or punished. Unlike blind Justice, he is a character equipped with *super-vision,* and his actions are romanticized while the deadly violence is erased. He is a hero who can *unmask* and track down bandits, thieves, murderers, rapists, and criminals, a perfect allegory for a state that persecutes those who are not *innocent*, meaning not *white*.

White Justice

From Lynching to Legitimate Defense: "The Old Threadbare Lie"

Vigilante groups in the American West were associated with the practice of lynching from almost the moment they appeared. The word itself is a reference to the history of a vigilance group formed by Charles Lynch during the American Revolution (1765 to 1783). Legislators in Virginia had given Lynch and his men free rein to eradicate horse thieves and other bandits. They were authorized by law *to not respect the law*, and their acts were considered justifiable due to the immediacy of the threat. Before long, the "Lynch Law" was being applied all over the Southern states to persecute drifters, foreigners, white dissidents, and Black slaves and rebels.[1]

In the late nineteenth century, although lynching was still a part of vigilantism, a distinction emerged between spontaneous acts of lynching, carried out by crowds, and those committed by organized groups (most famously, the Ku Klux Klan). Even for those crimes committed by crowds, though, it is necessary to challenge the idea that these acts of violence can be dismissed as spontaneous and crazy, attributable to a crowd whipped up to furious, irrational vengeance. Numerous critical works have documented the individuals hiding behind the vague term "crowd," and they have shown that from 1880 until the end of World War II lynchings were simply a part of daily life, involving forms of social behavior considered *normal*, as the residents of a city or town gathering around a man who was to be tortured, mutilated, burned alive, or hung.

Schools closed for the occasion so that the children could watch the show. They were even allowed to play with the corpse. Families brought picnics, and after the execution, they would eat in the shade of the tree where the brutalized bodies still hung.[2] Lynching by crowds was not an exception to ordinary social life. At the turn of the twentieth century, in most cases of lynching, crowds had been unofficially given the responsibility to choose and carry out the punishment, encouraged by the negligence or active collaboration of judicial institutions that left the detained person without protection, being presumed guilty.[3]

Most cases of the lynching of African American men began with an accusation, a report, or a rumor (which, in the majority of cases, concerned the rape of a white woman), followed by arrest, detention, and trial. Frequently, vigilantes with ties to white racist organizations bypassed the normal legal process and gave the crowd the opportunity to punish the defenseless men. The crowd thus became the weapon by which vigilantes, who had also usually initiated the hunt, finished off their prey. Interpellated as a deadly force and confident in its right to punish, civil society became a mob that, as if by magic, was invested with the responsibility to commit a just crime, and also gained symbolic recognition for carrying out American justice.[4] Rather than distinguishing between two types of lynchings, we can adopt a sociohistorical perspective of the crowd and understand that these murders were not committed outside of time but rather were fully integrated in social life, in a context marked by the culture of vigilantism and the physical presence of active vigilance groups.[5] Lynchings were a "ritualistic affirmation of white unity."[6] If we hold on to the idea of lynchings perpetrated by a vague and faceless crowd whose murderous acts are unintelligible, we miss what was at play politically: these lynchings represent a shift from self-defense—an inalienable individual right—to defense of the race. It is no longer directed against individuals, whether white or (in most cases) Black, but rather against *all Black people*, everywhere.[7] Black people become an entity that is always in the crosshairs, always *killable*. In the late nineteenth and early twentieth centuries, the murderous white mob as a political subject incarnated the assertion *We are white America*. Although the vigilantes positioned themselves as knights faithfully defending the honor of *their* women, they left it to the crowd to put on the finishing touch, bringing justice in defense of *their* race.

Vigilantism and its accompanying political culture constitute a vantage point from which to consider the criminal acts made legal within a logic of parajudicial self-defense. They occurred within a history of racism where the rape of white women gradually became a charge capable of justifying the execution of thousands of innocent people. In her quintessential text *Southern Horrors*, based on a statement published in *The New York Age in* 1892, Ida B. Wells observes that during the Civil War, no measures were put in place in the Southern states to specifically defend white women who had been left alone on their plantations against the possibility of assaults by Black men.[8] And yet, there had never been more lynchings of Black men accused of rape than in the years after the war. Never before had a community experienced more torture and murder, carried out with impunity, under the pretext of defending the *honor* of white women. In this context, those cast as the victims and those cast as the aggressors play only a secondary role. What's essential here is the relationship between those who defend, those who are defended, and those who are left defenseless and made killable. Wells writes that in many cases, the women involved stated that the accused was innocent or even said they had been raped by a white man. Frequently, they had not been the victims of an attack of any kind.[9] They had sometimes been friends with Black men or had felt desire and carried on sexual or romantic relationships with men who were then incriminated, hung, shot, or burned alive—the women gave birth to children from these relationships. White women loved Black men in the South, and the men were tortured in the name of defending the women. Black women were raped by white men without any judge ever deigning to see it as a crime.

Wells's writings are not hopeful. The South will never be a land of justice, because the justice system's corruption means it works to acquit those she calls "the aggressors" (white men) and to unleash murderous crowds on "the victims" (Black men). She writes that the only times men threatened with lynching survived were when those men were armed and defended themselves:

> The only times an Afro-American who was assaulted got away has been when he had a gun and used it in self-defense ... When the white man who is always the aggressor knows he runs as great a risk of biting the dust every time as his Afro-American victim does, he will have greater respect for Afro-American life. The more the Afro-American yields and cringes and begs, the more he has to do so, the more he is insulted, outraged and lynched.[10]

This was Ida B. Wells's call for Black people to engage in armed self-defense.

During the whole of the Civil War and through the postwar years, in the period called the Reconstruction, protecting women—regardless of their class, and whether they were Black or white—was central to the political agenda of women's and feminist associations in the United States. Numerous feminist organizations, notably those in the Southern states, organized against laws denying civil rights to women and even making married women the property of their husbands (in Georgia, for example, a woman was not even considered the owner of her own clothes). These organizations called for "domestic protection" measures that would limit the legal, economic, and sexual power men had over "their" women.[11] If women needed to be protected from men (whether white or Black), this involved an assessment of the legal, social, and symbolic needs women had for protection. It also involved the promotion of a new norm of femininity that was less heteronomous, more combative, and less susceptible to sexual assault with impunity, less rape-able.

At the same time as African American abolitionists and activists were becoming more mobilized, the agenda of Southern white feminists changed as well. Their rhetoric did not yet systematically stigmatize Black men. For example, Rebecca L. Fulton, a segregationist activist, was one of the instigators of the campaign for the protection of femininity and young girls and notably supported a Woman's Christian Temperance Union (WCTU) petition about the age at which a young girl can legally consent to sexual relations. The goal was to raise it from ten years of age to eighteen. The WCTU was driven by a form of womanly Christian proselytism and mostly denounced the corruption of *white notables*.[12] Their rhetoric in the campaign to raise the age of sexual consent took aim almost exclusively at white men who sexually assaulted Black women and girls, who were thought to be more vulnerable due to their race and to their subordinate class position.[13] To Felton and numerous other white feminists, the rape of Black women by white men was more than just a moral failing and proof of a "disrespectful" attitude toward those women—it was also humiliating to white women and therefore a threat to the supremacy of the white race as a whole.[14] The campaign around the age of consent specifically, and the demands of the feminist movement for a *right of protection* more broadly, failed to achieve their goals in no small part because they were primarily directed at white men and denounced lynching as serving to mask the corruption of Southern institutions and notables.[15]

Felton had become the voice of Southern women, but she, like many other white feminists, also helped construct the myth of the Black rapist, which would be the primary factor in providing impunity for the murder and lynching of African American men from the late nineteenth to the mid-twentieth centuries. These feminists laid the rhetorical groundwork for a racist ideology, and the defenders of white supremacy rushed to develop it further as the economic and social consequences of emancipation materialized in a new generation of Black people who were born free. The stereotype of the "Black beast rapist" also emerged at this time.[16] Some white feminist activists endorsed the idea that Black men were a genuine threat to white women and used this to call for more protection. The stereotype not only produced a form of racial policing of the sexuality of *all women*; it also contributed to maintaining the sexual and racial division of labor in the post-slavery South by preventing the development of a Black elite. In the early twentieth century, educated African American men with access to the social and symbolic privileges of the white middle class were just as vulnerable to accusations of rape as Black workers, small merchants, and agricultural laborers—the Democratic white supremacists argued they were just using the education system to gain easier access to white women.[17]

Early in the lynching era, Ida B. Wells engaged with the rage that inevitably follows incidents of rape in order to understand the motivation of the murderous white mobs.[18] However, she quickly set this explanation aside. Just a few months before her statement in *The New York Age*, which would become *Southern Horrors*, she wrote an editorial in her Memphis newspaper, *Free Speech*, on May 21, 1892, based on three months of research, in reaction to the lynching of three of her Black friends. They owned a grocery store and had been accused of raping three white women, an accusation put forward by white business owners who felt the men were competing with them. In her response to this event, Wells concluded that rape was merely a pretext, concealing the deeper issue of maintaining the subordination of African Americans, preventing them from accessing citizenship, education, property, and wealth, and thereby blocking their upward mobility. The rage of the crowds was simply an act, and the claim that Black men were raping white women was an "old thread-bare lie . . ."[19]

"Women Must Be Defended"

Wells was a major figure in the anti-lynching movement, and she was one of the rare voices that refused to make rhetorical concessions: her political analysis of lynching viewed the slaughter of Black men and the rape of Black women as a single phenomenon. She was supported by some of the leading organizations in the Black feminist movement, such as the Woman's Era Club, but was criticized by others for supposedly being too aggressive in her activism.[20] This criticism was based on the idea that it was necessary to build a movement across racial lines, which meant making concessions to white women's organizations.[21] But Wells did not budge, arguing that making rape an issue for white women and lynching an issue for Black women would never lead to a coalition within the women's movement and could only maintain the racist and sexist system in all its horror.

We must ask the question, Who defends these murderous crowds? And what defense is possible against them? From 1900 on, the myth of the Black rapist was in full force and gave rise to what amounted to the codification of practices of torture—notably of emasculation—and the murder of victims. The murder of Jesse Washington in Waco, Texas, in 1916 stands out as one of the most egregious lynchings to have occurred.[22]

On May 8, 1916, Lucy Fryer was found dead in her home. Rumors of a rape spread quickly throughout Waco, and suspicion settled on Jesse Washington, a seventeen-year-old farm worker employed by the Fryers. A sham trial was held on May 15, in which the jury, the defense lawyer, and the judge were all convinced that Washington was guilty. He was sentenced to death and turned over to the members of the public present in the courtroom. There was an enormous crowd outside that included all of the city's notable citizens, and it had gathered around a stake to which Washington was tied and tortured for two hours. He was stabbed, emasculated, and his fingers and toes were cut off. Pieces of his body were sold as souvenirs, and photographs of the scene circulated as quaint postcards promoting local tourism.

The National Association for the Advancement of Colored People (NAACP) carried out an investigation a few weeks after the murder, interviewing white and Black residents of the town. W. E. B. Du Bois, cofounder of the NAACP, wrote an article about the experience, "Waco Horror," which he published in his newspaper, *Crisis*, in July 1916. Du Bois closed the text with a call for action against what he termed "the lynching industry."[23]

This ritualized horror spurred the movement against lynching to grow in intensity, as revealed by the increasing reach of petitions and campaigns by Black feminist organizations trying to stir up outrage and mobilize public opinion. In the 1930s, various Southern organizations joined the anti-lynching movement, as well as some religious groups and newspapers, which increasingly characterized lynching as a racist crime rather than as a legitimate response to the rape of white women. In November 1930, Jessie Daniel Ames, a white activist, launched the first anti-lynching organization in the white supremacist women's movement, the Association of Southern Women for the Prevention of Lynching (ASWPL). In practical terms, the organization was clearly based around racial segregation, and the word "women" in their name referred only to white women: they made up its membership and were its sole audience. For the first time, though, a white organization argued that Black men were not responsible for cases of lynching, and therefore that *they were not natural-born rapists*. In denouncing the slaughter, they joined the struggle against *both* racial violence and the sexual exploitation of women, which they understood had a racial dimension and was therefore plural (the sexual exploitation of white women and of Black women did not materialize in the same way). Ames clearly asserts that women (meaning white women) will "no longer remain silent in the face of this crime done in their name."[24] The ASWPL's press release presented the organization as the association of Southern women opposed to lynching in all its forms, regardless of the circumstances surrounding it.[25] The abolitionist press greeted this news with enthusiasm: "Southern women, whose chastity has been saved, according to widespread belief, for the past hundred years by lynchings, have initiated a movement to eradicate this protection by rope and faggot."[26]

Jessie Daniel Ames had been organizing for years against the "code of chivalry" that had existed in the southern United States since the nineteenth century. This code demanded that white women behave in a *ladylike* manner and incarnate the values that express this standard of femininity: chastity, piety, grace, and fragility. Becoming ladies—meaning, "real" white women—meant placing themselves under the protection of men. But their acceptance of these norms is also why they became heteronomous beings that *needed protection*. It was thus as ladies that white women accessed the status of women, along with the social and symbolic benefits that came with it, which were out of reach for African American women. However, white women remained responsible minors, and it was possible to distinguish those who were ladies, while exposing to violence those who were not and those who could never be, due to relations of domination. This was the case for women who spoke out against slavery or against segregation, who defended African American men, who had been raped by white men, or simply those who were subordinate to the dominant white class.[27]

To be vulnerable, fragile, and defenseless and to construct oneself in terms of becoming-whiteness—these are the specific conditions that had to be met to be *recognized* as a woman, and they immediately excluded all women of color, who were then literally left defenseless. The activity of the Woman's Era Club, one of the first and most influential Black feminist organizations, founded in Boston in 1894, was a direct challenge to the invisibilization of the violence done to Black women, who were never seen as victims and could be systematically exposed to rape with impunity:[28]

> We do not pretend to say there are no Black villains. Baseness is not confined to race. We read with horror of two different colored girls who recently have been horribly assaulted by white men in the South. We should regret any lynchings of the offenders by Black men, but we shall not have occasion. Should these offenders receive any punishment at all, it will be a miracle.[29]

In a sense, becoming a woman was the *medium* by which the white race materialized: by defending the honor of their women, men were able to naturalize a racially exclusive social group. The ASWPL's revolt against chivalry did not seek to challenge this racist apparatus but to make the defense of white women the sole responsibility of the women themselves, by extricating it from the genealogy of white patriarchy and from an idea of justice shaped by the culture of vigilantes. This meant the vigilantes were at last revealed to be *racist murderers*. The ASWPL's historic gesture deconstructed the sexist rhetoric surrounding racist violence that could justify the murder of African American men in the name of the sexual integrity of white women, or more specifically, in the name of a hegemonic norm of masculinity that had been growing whiter for centuries. If white women did not need defending, if they refused to be protected by their faithful knights, then all the violence was revealed for what it truly was: savagery.

However, the goal of bourgeois white women in the South was never to dismantle race but simply to produce a new norm of white femininity, which would then determine new modalities of racial production. In other words, although white Southern women of the dominant class initiated the creation of a new form of female political subjectivation (it is they who produced a racialized feminist *subject* on the political stage), they never stopped actively contributing to racial subjectivation: "we white folks." That they instrumentalized the rhetoric of defending women should in no way lead us to believe that white women were objectified. They remained impure subjects of white supremacist ideology, meaning they were at once the subject and object of policies in defense of the race. "Protection codes are thus key technologies in regulating privileged women as well as intensifying the vulnerability and degradation of those on the unprotected side of the divide between light and dark, wives and prostitutes, good girls and bad ones."[30]

Throughout the twenieth century, the defense of women remained a recurring theme in racist systems and apparatuses, taking different historical forms. The historicization of the premise "Women must be defended" has been the subject of important research in the fields of feminist theory and epistemology and of postcolonial and subaltern studies. Gayatri C. Spivak, in her text *Can the Subaltern Speak?*, introduced a phrase to define what she terms "imperialist subject-constitution": "White men are saving brown women from brown men."[31] The difference between the colonial context relative to the post-slavery context in the United States is that there is an extraterritorial dimension to the distinction between *our* women and *their* women. Discursively, this makes it possible to attribute violence against all women—but specifically against native women—exclusively to native men. Leila Ahmed describes the discursive theme of defending women in the context of colonial Egypt as a double-edged apparatus. It is used, on the one hand, to save native women from *their* men, thereby legitimizing any brutality committed against native people, regardless of sex, in the name of civilization, the superiority of the white race, and respect for women. On the other, it provides a means of impeding movements for the civil rights of white women in the home country. Only women considered sufficiently respectable are to be defended, meaning those who avoid excessive forms of emancipation that would, according to the bearers of imperial patriarchy, erase the difference between the sexes, which would be a sign of the degeneracy of the white race.[32]

In the early twenty-first century, calls to defend women are no less present, and feminist movements, although they struggle to be heard, respond by saying, "Not in our name!" This dynamic is the product of a political and historical conflict within feminism between the majority tendency that remains complacent—or complicit—with racist and/or nationalist political subjects, and a constellation that resists being subjugated to the demands of capitalism and to new imperialist ideologies. Additionally, the premise that "women must be defended" has mutated. It is still the case that only some women are to be protected while others are deprived of any protection, but this formulation now describes only a segment of contemporary power relations. A complex process of differentiation has constituted a third social group: that of women seen as solely responsible for their own protection, who are even produced as *subjects of defense* for a civilization, a race, or a nation. The history of women's presence in the military, and specifically in combat units, is part of the genealogy of this experimental minority. The paradigmatic example of this phenomenon is the Abu Ghraib prison and the photos taken in 2003 and 2004 depicting scenes of torture involving soldiers, both men and women, in the American armed forces. As agents of American defense policies, these women soldiers were granted powers for the self-defense of the nation, militarily trained and produced as "We, the United States," in order to brutally humiliate the Muslim enemy on behalf of American society. They are impure subjects, still objectified and interpellated as women. However, they are *liberated* women, part of a nation where equality of the sexes has become a civilizational principle, and they are feminists, in that they incarnate a dominant norm of white, capitalist, contemporary femininity that traces the new contours of race through its generalization.[33] The feminization of professions that have traditionally been reserved for men, such as the military, is supposed to be a marker of success for equality policies, but in this case, it conceals what is really underway. This new apparatus has a citational relationship with "the defense of women/the defense of the race," but it appears in a novel form: it is no longer a matter of defending *our* women, and going off to defend *their* women is somewhat out of date. Rather, now it is *our women* who are sent *to defend us* from *those men*—they are the ultimate weapon of civilizational domination. The artist Coco Fusco emphasizes that these women are not soldiers like any other: they are not sent to the front, and they are not just the effect of positive discrimination intended to help gender minorities. They were trained to produce and perform a form of femininity thought to be a particularly effective weapon against an enemy who, according to military leaders, embodies a form of masculinity that is eminently sexist, prudish, homophobic, barbarous, and even inhuman.[34] Scenes of humiliation, sodomy, obscene contact (physical contact, contact with underwear or with menstrual blood), rape, and torture have all the hallmarks of commercial pornography, making deliberate use of "young blond women," and they are intended to strike at the integrity and dignity of the prisoners while also, crucially, breaking their psychic defenses as well as the morale of the *Arab* population.[35] Sexual violence of this kind, deliberately carried out as a "technology of gender," is part of a codified military strategy to produce a new kind of vigilante: the woman vigilante.[36] Women soldiers engaged in torture are genuine subjects of national defense and are objectified as a new apparatus of emasculation, as a technology of domination serving hegemonic white, Christian, capitalist masculinity. Abu Ghraib was a carefully planned experiment, and it is an international symbol of the modern American culture of vigilantism.

The words "Women must be defended" characterized nearly 200 years of violence, in which faithful knights massacred men of color in the name of *their* women and the white race. Behind those words now, though, there is a new premise: "Our women defend us . . . and will sodomize *your* men in order to defend our civilization."

Self-Defense: Power to the People!

Doing Away with Nonviolence: "Arm Yourself or Harm Yourself"[1]

"A Winchester rifle should have a place of honor in every Black home."[2] These words, written by Ida B. Wells in 1892, capture the spirit of the latest wave of mobilizations. The issue of *legitimate* armed self-defense against the *illegitimate* violence of racism is central to the history of Black nationalism, along with the accompanying calls to arms.

From the late 1910s and throughout the 1920s, many articles were published in support of self-defense by intellectuals, artists, and journalists involved in the movement known as the Harlem Renaissance, all proclaiming the death of Uncle Tom. Marcus Garvey argued that there was a racist war going on in the country and around the world, and that African Americans should be united for the battle. In October 1919, he wrote:

> The Negro must now organize all over the world, 400,000,000 strong, to administer to our oppressors their Waterloo ... There have been many riots in the United States and England recently, and immediately following the war of democracy, there will be many more as coming from the white man. Therefore, the best thing the Negro of all countries can do is to prepare to match fire with hell fire.[3]

World War II was undeniably a turning point. The United States had been presenting itself internationally as a model democracy in the fight against the ravages of fascism in Europe, and this made racist violence on their own soil indefensible. Leading Black organizations recruited an increasing number of African American and Hispanic soldiers serving on the Japanese and European fronts, which led to mutinies. The NAACP's leaders saw that the postwar period would be decisive in the movement against lynching and for civil rights, and so they launched a campaign highlighting the contradictions of what they termed "Jim Crow democracy." In 1947, a petition filed by the NAACP with the United Nations triggered a massive response: "It is not Russia that threatens the United States so much as Mississippi."[4] The struggle against lynching gained an international profile, and the embarrassment reached all the way to the White House, where President Truman said, "We cannot escape the fact that our civil rights record has become an issue of world politics."[5] In 1954, Vice President Richard Nixon declared, "Every act of discrimination or prejudice in the United States hurts America just as much as an espionage agent who turns over a weapon to a foreign country."[6]

A few years later in the South, despite the recent legal civil rights victories in the struggle for desegregation, the emergence of a large number of Ku Klux Klan–inspired militias showed that the segregationist system was still firmly in place. White supremacist ideology was not only alive and well but enjoying a renaissance.[7] One particularly revealing event—known as the Kissing Case—marked the reemergence of the politics of self-defense. It occurred in Monroe, a city in North Carolina, in late October 1958. Sissy Sutton, an eight-year-old white girl, told her mother that she had kissed two young Black boys on the cheek, after having spent the afternoon playing with them a couple of days earlier, along with other children (the majority of whom were white and under the age of ten). Immediately, the girl's family rallied an armed mob that headed into the neighborhood where the young boys lived, with the goal of killing them and lynching their mothers. Their names were David "Fuzzy" Simpson and James Hanover Thompson, aged nine and seven. The two children were violently arrested by the police and accused of rape. They were thrown in prison, where they were mistreated and molested for days, without being allowed to see their families or the lawyers sent to defend them by African American organizations. Their mothers were persecuted as well: they were fired from their jobs and received death threats from the KKK, who burned several huge crosses in front of their house, fired shots at the facade and through the windows, and killed Thompson's dog. On November 4, the two young boys were taken to court, where the judge described the whole affair as a nasty consequence of *desegregation*, a direct result of racial mixing in the school system, which posed a threat to little white girls. Still without a defense lawyer present and without any arguments in their defense or cross-examination of the plaintiff, the judge found the two little boys guilty of sexual assault and gross indecency, sentencing them to imprisonment in a youth correctional facility (the Morris Training School for Negroes) until they turned twenty-one.

In Monroe, the local chapter of the NAACP had been on the verge of collapse, having dwindled to six members. Two years before the Kissing Case, in a last-ditch effort, Robert F. Williams, a militant communist, was elected chapter president. He presided over an explosion in active members, with 200 recruits joining in a single year, most of them from the working class rather than from the educated or middle classes, which were the NAACP's usual base. He also brought about a radical change in the chapter's philosophy and politics. Williams's family had been involved in the war against Southern racism and white supremacist militias for generations, and his service in the Marine Corps during World War II meant he had extensive weapons training.[8] Williams soon became an iconic (if controversial) figure in African American social movements, and he turned his NAACP chapter into a veritable "fighting unit," made up of military veterans committed to putting an end to racial injustice and the "invisible empire" (as the second iteration of the KKK described itself).[9]

When the NAACP's national directors refused to get involved in something they considered a "sex case," Robert F. Williams founded the Committee to Combat Racial Injustice and used it to elevate the Kissing Case to the level of international scandal.[10] His strategy was to give the case the largest possible reach, making use of committees in Europe that had formed as part of the anti-lynching struggle, in order to free the boys but also to put pressure on the NAACP, which seemed indifferent to their fate. The international press got involved quickly, and a photo taken by English journalist Joyce Eggington for the *London New Chronicle* transformed the Kissing Case into a symbol. She had snuck her camera into the prison where the young boys were being held by posing as a social worker, and she snapped a picture that would accompany a front page in the paper's December 15, 1958, issue. The picture, simply captioned "Why?," showed the conditions in which the children were being held, and it was picked up by other European newspapers. Following its publication, an international committee was formed to defend Thompson and Simpson, and its public campaign against racist violence in the United States resulted in millions of outraged letters being sent to Washington.

The Kissing Case was a turning point in the struggle against the segregationist system, because it involved two strategic shifts, both embodied in the person of Robert F. Williams. First, in the context of movements against colonialism, the systematic denunciation of American racism allowed segregation to be seen as a part of imperialism more broadly, and the violence directed against the Black minority as a form of internal colonialism. The Kissing Case represented the struggle against the brutality of white America. Second, the tone of the campaign around the Kissing Case was far from sympathetic, and it was a major contributor to the crisis over pacifist resistance that the leaders of the civil rights movement found themselves in. Although the rape and murder of Black children and adults continued in North Carolina and other nearby Southern states, preparations were underway for armed resistance. For Williams, armed self-defense was the only possible strategy for survival in the war against white supremacy and its armed wing, the KKK, and this made him a marginal voice within the large Black organizations. Williams's calls for armed self-defense led to him being considered an opponent of Martin Luther King Jr. and being banned from the NAACP in 1959, and also triggered FBI harassment.[11] The NAACP was frequently accused of having been infiltrated by communists, and it reacted by adopting an anticommunist line, supposedly to gain respectability. It turned against anti-imperialist activists and Williams in particular. Although he was ostracized, Williams received support from W. E. B. Du Bois and remained a major intellectual and political figure in Black movements. His political philosophy of communist self-defense would be fully fleshed out by the Black Power movement a few years later.[12]

The Kissing Case occurred in the wake of McCarthyism, and it was a symptom of anticommunist propaganda and politics, which were the basis of all the arguments used by the Southern press used to respond to the international outcry, and they also divided the African American civil rights movement by aggravating existing tensions. The question of violence as a national political strategy was a point of conflict with the leaders of the main Black organizations, who accused activists and intellectuals advocating for armed self-defense of having ties to communism. The integrationist politics of these organizations meant they had to constantly distance themselves from anti-imperialism and not show solidarity to revolutionary movements for liberation and decolonization internationally.

Because of the actions of Robert F. Williams and the Committee to Combat Racial Injustice, David Simpson and James Thomas were freed—conditionally—on February 13, 1959.[13] Williams published *Negroes with Guns* in 1962 while in exile in Cuba, and in this text he expanded on his ideas of armed self-defense. In striking detail, he described clashes in the race war that was underway in the Southern states, and he also laid out his position on the opposition between self-defense and the strategy of nonviolent direct action. In June 1961, during one of a series of rallies outside the Monroe public swimming pool over its exclusion of Black people, activists came under fire from armed white men. Williams and other NAACP activists repeatedly tried to file a police report, but each time, the Monroe police chief insisted he had not seen or heard anything.[14] The situation was the same after each act of violence targeting Black activists or communities. This story shows the strategy of systematic denial used by the white authorities. By adopting a hands-off approach and refusing to intervene, the police were themselves paradoxically engaged in a form of nonviolent direct action that allowed them to reframe acts of self-defense by Black activists and organizations as the initial aggression. Williams also listed the hateful cries he had heard: "Kill the niggers! Kill the niggers! Pour gasoline on the niggers! Burn the niggers!"[15] That day, confronted with the screams of the crowd, Williams and other militants had had no choice but to shelter in their car and draw their guns to avoid being lynched. Williams writes:

> What they didn't know was that we were armed. Under North Carolina law, it is legal to carry firearms in your automobile as long as these firearms are not concealed.
>
> I had two pistols and a rifle in the car. When this fellow started to draw back his baseball bat, I put an Army .45 up in the window or the car and pointed it right in his face and

didn't say a word. He looked at the pistol and he didn't say anything. He started backing away from the car.

Someone in the crowd fired a pistol and they again started to scream hysterically: "Kill the niggers! Kill the niggers! Pour gasoline on the niggers!" The mob started to throw stones on the top of my car, so I opened the door of the car and I put one foot on the ground and stood up in the door holding an Italian carbine.[16]

Williams's position is a classic one in philosophy of the right to self-defense. His view is effectively that as North Carolina was flouting the Fourteenth Amendment, it was clear the federal government had failed to uphold the Constitution.[17] Furthermore, state courts allowed the KKK and other racist militias (as well as the population that supported them) to carry out violent attacks with impunity, which therefore rendered those courts illegitimate and unable to deliver justice. In other words, the violence carried out by white people was legal but illegitimate, while that carried out by Black people in response was illegal but legitimate. He writes, "In a civilized society, the law is a deterrent against the strong who would take advantage of the weak, but the South is not a civilized society; the South is a social jungle."[18]

He advocated for self-defense to the extent that there was no justice for Black people in America. More specifically, the justice operating there was a white justice, one that exposed Black people to the highest risk of death. Those who murdered Black people went unpunished, so the justice system was their accomplice; the police were unable to protect Black people, but worse, they freely turned them over to their killers.[19] Self-defense is the last rampart in defense of one's life, and it was how Black people defended their very humanity.[20]

Although it shares certain themes typical of social contract theory, Williams's philosophy separated self-defense from the tradition of possessive individualism by breaking the link between the notion of self-defense and that of defense of one's self, understood as ownership of the individual's person and belongings. Defense of one's self in this case is not based on a subject of law that preexists the defensive act and is not carried out by an individual who has natural and legitimate rights of preservation and jurisdiction. Such subjects exist only inasmuch as they come to be, producing themselves in a polarized movement to have *their life be spared*.

To those who accused Williams of being an apologist for violence and playing into the hands of segregationists by provoking repression, he replied, "Self-defense is not a love of violence. It is a love for justice."[21] Williams is thus not creating an opposition between a strategy of self-defense and "the tactics of nonviolence."[22] In his opinion, self-defense becomes necessary when a strategy of nonviolence reaches a critical point at which continuing such tactics would be suicidal.[23] Williams categorically refused to make a commitment to nonviolence that would forbid activists from defending themselves against aggression and attack on the ground, rejecting the idea that this would be just *meeting violence with violence* or that it would lead to worse repression.

Here we touch on the heart of the debate on violence and nonviolence and whether the violence of the dominator *contaminates* the dominated. The use of violence is commonly rejected on two grounds: first, the concern that the dominated would become the dominator through mimesis; and second, for fear of a cycle of intensifying violence, as the dominators greatly increase their violence rather than ending it. To Williams, this is just an ideological debate and amounts to another way of disarming the oppressed, which explains his fierce opposition on principle to strategies of nonviolence. In his works, Williams uses a typical Marxist definition of violence as the midwife of history and, more specifically, as a fundamental principle of historicity and social change. Against what he terms white racist brutality, he believes that nonviolence and self-defense can be a useful combination, but that only violence is able to change "something as fundamental as racist oppression."[24] In his view, a strategy of defensive violence contributes to an insurrectionary dynamic that is the only way of transforming relations of power at their core. The strategy of nonviolence is useful for desegregating public transit, but it will never destroy the racist system itself, or the production of social and economic violence it enables.[25] Finally, Williams sees the use of violence as a way the civil rights movement could position itself in the heart of the conflict by declaring war against those who *defend their privileges* by attacking those who *defend their lives and their freedom*. This is why he situates himself as an internationalist and not as a Black nationalist. For him, it is not a matter of defending a nation, but of defending universal justice.[26] At precisely the same time as Williams was writing these lines in Cuba, Frantz Fanon—sensing the urgency of struggles for national liberation as well as his own imminent death—developed his philosophy of violent action, first in Algeria and then in his New York hospital bed.

The Black Panthers: Self-Defense as Revolutionary Politics

Robert Williams's writings were a major theoretical inspiration for the Black Panther Party for Self-Defense, and they were widely distributed and translated during the 1960s. As an influential figure in the US communist movement and a theorist of armed self-defense, Williams played a significant role in the civil rights movement's shift away from nonviolence.[27] The 1960s were marked by the highly visible use of violent direct action and, specifically, by the emergence of a semiology of bodies-in-struggle along with its associated mode of political subjectivation, and this spread far beyond Black social movements. A few years after the Kissing Case, the shooting of James Meredith during his March Against Fear across Mississippi in June 1966 (during which he had chosen to be unarmed and unprotected) marked a definitive break with the strategy of nonviolent resistance advocated by Reverend King. Following this attack, the leaders of various civil rights groups met to decide how to continue the march.[28] The march resumed with thousands of people participating, and while addressing the crowd, Stokely Carmichael, a member of the Student Nonviolent Coordinating Committee (SNCC), made his historic call for Black Power.[29] In this landmark march, beyond the particular disagreements between the groups, a struggle between two different political logics of violence came out into the open. Recent works on the history of the civil rights movement have clearly shown that it is an oversimplification to say there was an opposition, usually considered to have begun in 1966, between a nonviolent strategy (active) and a violent strategy (defensive). For instance, it is worth remembering that although Martin Luther King did not oppose the use of defensive violence (meaning self-defense in the strict sense), on this day in June 1966, he would not tolerate demonstrators being conspicuously armed, as he believed this would endanger other demonstrators by giving police the right to kill.[30]

The opposition to King crystallized around precisely this issue, notably in the form of the Nation of Islam. For Malcolm X, the philosophy of nonviolence promoted by King amounted to ordering Black people to disarm and not defend themselves against white people. Malcolm X argued that in practice, the injunction to remain nonviolent did not affect the relationships among Black people but those between races. King was not telling Black people to refrain from violence among themselves. In Malcolm X's view, though, that would be the only politically viable nonviolence principle, as it would contribute to unity and solidarity among Black people. It was not for nothing that white people considered Reverend King to be their only respectable interlocutor, and only his organization had received a significant level of support from them, including financially. In Malcolm X's words, by encouraging Black people not to defend themselves,

> King is the best weapon that the white man, who wants to brutalize Negroes, has ever gotten in this country, because he is setting up a situation where, when the white man wants to attack Negroes, they can't defend themselves, because King has put this foolish philosophy out—you're not supposed to fight or you're not supposed to defend yourself.[31]

In his view, nonviolence should be understood as, and limited to, an ethico-political question internal to organizing groups: it is a modality of political subjectivation that is only meaningful as a way of caring for an emerging *us*, and not as a *praxis of resistance and combat*.

King's ideas came to be in the minority relative to those developed by Robert Williams, Stokely Carmichael, Elijah Muhammad, and Malcolm X, whose death in 1965 and the trauma around it marked the emergence of a new generation of militants committed to defensive violence. The crisis within the movement also involved what was essentially a conflict between different ways of engaging with the *militant body* and a redefinition of the semiology of bodies in revolt.

Subjects following the nonviolent tradition are not passive, as their bodies are engaged in action and confrontation to defend themselves and their rights, which takes considerable strength. Their bodies incarnate a form of resistance whose conditions of possibility are total abnegation, unlimited endurance, and self-sacrifice (*without ever reacting*). By meeting these three conditions, nonviolent activists seek to make themselves the film on which the true image of crass violence and aggression can appear. They intend the effect of this appearance to be at once moral (this violence is unacceptable and illegitimate), political (this violence is illegal), and psychological (this violence is now intolerable even in the eyes of its perpetrators).[32] However, those within the movement who consider this strategy obsolete take issue precisely with the fact that nonviolent direct action involves bodies resisting by means of endless endurance. To a certain extent, nonviolent *and* violent defense of self are distinguished from each other not so much in terms of an opposition between passivity and activity or weakness and strength, but rather in terms of the temporality of active defense and its effects. In other words, they speak to two different ways of apprehending history. The first sees struggle as occurring gradually over time and accepts violence as a way of "working" history, as though to change its course by wearing away its banks, in a sense. Nonviolent action is a very laborious and painstaking process that wears down bodies as surely as it does history. In contrast to this teleological approach to defense, the second position takes a combative approach and reverses the logic: its political strategies of self-defense understand that history is only made through interruptions and shocks, when people "meet violence with violence."[33] Forget about changing history bit by bit—there needs to be a revolution. Metaphorically, it means striking, not grinding.

Self-defense is a martial practice, a philosophy of combat in which the moment—the revolutionary *kairos*—depends on landing an effective blow. In the Black Power movement, heavily inspired by Frantz Fanon, this problematic of explosive defense, of aggressive defense, took the shape of calls to respond blow for blow, *to show that one was able to respond*. And in these conditions, where you are staring down the barrel of a gun, the only response is a gunshot. Self-defense is then a counteroffensive, producing another semiology of the *militant* body, one based not on exemplary martyrdom but on inexorable and inescapable vengeance. It is not about the metaphysics of ends but the immediacy of a blow.

This explains the link between a politics of self-defense and one of representation and *affirmation of the self*. In the context of self-defense movements, defending while attacking is an affirmation of a right unjustly denied, and it is consequently an affirmation by the subjects who possess this right, or rather by those who seize a right they have been refused and give it to themselves. Explosive defense thus tends toward a declaration of war in all but name, meaning it tends to reestablish the modalities of combat *on equal terms*. Explosive defense is part of a martial philosophy in the sense that the terms and positions of relations of domination are no longer framed ontologically (dominator/dominated) or hierarchically (aggressor/victim). This classification has at least two effects: on the one hand, it restores the dignity and pride of oppressed minorities that are seen as having become belligerent; on the other, it permits the indefinite use of violence for however long the revolutionary struggle requires it.[34]

The emergence of the Black Panther Party for Self-Defense in November 1966 is emblematic of the repoliticization of armed self-defense within an internationalist framework, in contrast with the American segregationist and imperialist tradition. The party fully embraced the principle of armed self-defense, even including the term "self-defense" in its name in direct reference to the Deacons for Self-Defense. It also tried to widen the term's political meaning, situating it within the history of African American, anti-imperialist, and communist movements inclined toward self-defense as a condition for making a revolutionary political subject possible.

The Black Panthers adopted an intensely legalistic strategy of relying on the Second Amendment of the Constitution to win acceptance for African Americans' right to carry firearms, just like any other US citizens.[35] They adopted the practice of going out equipped with both weapons and a copy of the criminal code in order to follow police patrols and make their presence known if any arrests occurred, taking note of any procedural irregularities and informing the person being arrested or detained of their rights. As Bobby Seale, one of the Black Panther Party's founders, said in 1970, the only purpose of armed self-defense (which involves bearing arms) is to defend the lives of activists:

> There is a strict rule that no party member can use a weapon except in the case of an attack on his life—whether the attacker be a police officer or any other person. In the case of police harassment, the party will merely print the offending officer's picture in the newspaper so the officer can be identified as an enemy of the people ... no attempt on his life will be made.[36]

In California, the party's main enemy was the police, and so its choice of self-defense tactics and their staging were different from what was occurring in the Southern states, where the main purpose of self-defense was to protect the Black community from violence by fascist militias.[37]

As well, in the South, self-defense by racial minorities was criminalized, and local laws forbade racialized social groups from bearing arms. Following a strict dress code—all-black clothing with a black beret and a gun—the Black Panther Party for Self-Defense sought to recruit new members by incarnating a form of Black masculinity whose performance of power built pride, and by arguing for the necessity of constructing a Black community united against police brutality, white America, colonialism, and capitalism more broadly.[38]

The party's conception of self-defense mirrored the right to self-preservation, which is usually defined as a prepolitical act of resistance. In this case, though, it was a gendered and racialized performance that, although resembling intensely legalistic defensive zealousness, was in reality a powerful mechanism for political consciousness-raising.[39] Self-defense was not simply a means of struggle, nor even a pragmatic political choice compatible with other strategies, such as nonviolent direct action.[40] Self-defense was the very philosophy of their struggle. It had literally generalized and could be described as a revolutionary offensive, as *necessarily the only political line capable of overthrowing imperialism*. Seen from this angle, the Black Panthers had declared war—a civil war, a social war, a war of liberation—in which there was nothing to negotiate and nothing to defend, since the issue was never one of demanding those most basic of rights, ones that had always been denied and trampled.[41] Nothing to defend, other than an *us* that possesses nothing because, without the actions taken in its name, it is nothing—an *us* capable of anything.

In 1968, the Black Panthers abandoned the term "self-defense." As Christopher B. Strain writes:

> The Panthers began . . . as self-defense advocates; however, the group rapidly became a vanguard for social revolution, moving away from the *goal* of self-defense (that is, immediate self-protection) at the same time that they justified their actions using the *rhetoric* of self-defense.[42]

Several figures in the movement, such as Bobby Seale, felt that the attention paid to self-defense stemmed from a campaign of disinformation and destabilization intended to discredit the party's social and political activity. For instance, the allegation that the Black Panther Party for Self-Defense was just the Black Minutemen was clearly propaganda.[43] For his part, Huey Newton noted the counterproductive effects of militant rhetoric that takes self-defense in an excessively militaristic and macho direction, as this is too restrictive, dilutes the organization's finality, and does not fit with the movement's actions and ideology.[44] Alongside their martial training (shooting and safe weapons handling, martial arts), Black Panthers also had an obligation to think, read (especially Marx, Mao, and Fanon), and write.

> The pen
> is a weapon;
> ...
> it can deafen
> the ear with
> the roar of
> a people's voice
> clamoring for justice.
>
> It can kill
> lies emitted
> in ink from
> oppressor's presses
> making beasts
> of holy men
> justifying
> their slaughters.[45]

In addition, in line with its Ten-Point Program, published in 1966, the Black Panther Party's philosophy of self-defense manifested through its day-to-day actions in the struggle against social violence, which it termed the War on Poverty. These included organizing school breakfast programs in low-income areas; providing academic support for children and night classes for adults; creating schools and free clinics; and organizing vaccination drives, legal support clinics, social events, public transportation, grants for clothes and books, and so on. These baseline actions were minimized and rendered invisible by a systematic campaign of slander against the Panthers, and this was accompanied by unprecedented FBI repression to methodically decapitate the movement.[46] Moreover, and although it was created by the media and the state, the opposition between self-defense, on the one hand, and social self-determination and political mobilization on the other contributed to the idea of a sexual division of labor among party militants.[47]

SELF-DEFENSE: POWER TO THE PEOPLE!

Although it was just one political strategy among others, self-defense was also the subject of a narrative, the founding myth of the revolutionary subject. Long after it was crushed by the state, the Black Panther Party represented a political vision of defensive self-determination that served to *demystify the violence* of the oppressor. Elaine Brown, a leading party member, writes that the party saw itself as a revolutionary vanguard and that its primary goal before all else was to organize the *lumpenproletariat*, the poorest workers—underpaid, unemployed, or rendered unemployable—the overwhelming majority of whom were Black.[48] She describes the very bottom of the social ladder as made up of gangs and criminalized minorities, including racialized mothers providing for their families alone, prostitutes, drug users, dealers, petty criminals, slum dwellers, and homeless people. Any analysis, then, of capitalist modes of production must contain a critique of the systems of racism and sexism, which she describes as resting on three pillars: exploitation, based on the sexual and racial division of productive and reproductive labor, supported by the capitalist state; the systematic criminalization of racial minorities carried out by the carceral state; and imperialist militarization enacted by the colonial state. In telling the story of her journey as an activist, Brown shows how the party's use of macho semiology served as an initial tool of consciousness-raising, giving back the power to resist to those who had been beaten down—transforming the lumpen into a revolutionary army.[49] The first issue of *Black Panther*, the organization's newspaper, published on April 25, 1967, contained an argument in favor of armed self-defense using the term "gun power," describing how some of the Black population now had this power, whereas it had formerly been reserved for the police.[50] The "Brothers" in the Party were presented as "the cream of Black Manhood. They are there for the protection and defense of our Black community." It continued, "These Brothers have a political perspective. Most importantly, they are down here on THE GRASS ROOTS LEVEL where the great majority of our people are."[51] In other words, the Black Panthers wanted to situate their struggle within the material condition of the large majority of Black people: survival. This is why, as Brown writes, women activists were given the same consideration as men, since the gender and sexuality of Black people were another weapon to turn back against the oppressor: "Our gender was but another weapon, another tool of revolution."[52] However, this is precisely the problem—a division of weapons in which some are given firearms while others have only their sex involves forgetting the long and illustrious genealogy of African American women in struggle, which has always meant being armed. Even when understood as a weapon for self-defense, sexual identity is a double-edged sword, and the more space it takes up in the liberatory imagination, the more it can be turned back against activists of both sexes. The question is made more complex by the harsh critique of male chauvinism that also emerged from the Black Panthers: in order to be truly revolutionary, the struggle must support women's liberation with words and deeds.

A critique of macho tendencies in the Black Power movement eventually emerged within the party. As Elaine Brown wrote in her autobiography:

> They wanted so little from our revolution, they had lost sight of it. Too many of them seemed satisfied to appropriate for themselves the power the party was gaining, measured by the shiny illusion of cars, clothes and guns. They were even willing to cash in their revolutionary principles for a self-serving "Mafia." If a Mafia was what they wanted, I would not be part of it.[53]

Revolutionaries in the African American feminist movement were already rising to the challenge. They understood heterosexist machismo as one of the foundational pillars of the capitalist, imperialist system. Having power meant being a man, and being a man meant being white, and they thought it suicidal to make revolution wearing a white mask.[54] These debates about Black masculinity should be considered alongside the heated discussions occurring within the Black Panther Party around feminism, often considered a bourgeois struggle for white women, and around Marxism more generally. In 1967, during a meeting to organize support for Huey Newton, who had just been arrested, Stokely Carmichael gave a speech that shocked the most politically developed communist sections of the movement, including Angela Davis, who wrote, "Stokely, for example, spoke of socialism as 'the white man's thing.' Marx, he said, was a white man and therefore irrelevant to Black Liberation."[55] Conversely, Carmichael dismissed the idea that patriarchy, too, was a "white man's thing."

Some Black activists clearly embodied this "counterrevolutionary" turn, clinging to the reactionary myth that recognizing the superior power of Black masculinity could be a mode of political subjectivation.[56] Their starting premise is correct, in that not only are Black men excluded from the social and symbolic benefits of masculinity, but their very humanity is under attack—since the dawn of slavery, they have been humiliated, degraded, and emasculated by white men. And yet, the same activists take up this gendered and racialized framework as their own, and conclude that Black women—stigmatized as matriarchs, castrators, and Jezebels—had been passive collaborators and therefore needed to support the revolution by staying in their place as *women*. Like some sort of activist precontract, women would have to accept not being revolutionaries in order for there to be a revolutionary subject. In the ideological struggle over the resignification of power, overinvesting in chauvinistic masculinity (which has a citational relationship with *the white man*) and the obsession with forcing Black women into a norm of Victorian femininity (from which they have historically been excluded) is not the way to construct a Black political identity. Rather, it reinforces the ideological domination of white values.[57] Despite the critiques of white standards of beauty (notably the critique of smoothing and straightening hair), Black women were told to stay home and stay silent. They were forced to engage in a process of becoming white that also reified the normative potency of bourgeois masculinity, maintaining it as the signifier of power.[58] The backlash was immediate. As an organizational strategy, this amounted to condemning Black men and women to be mere mimics—grotesque, vulgar, monstrous, pathogenic—of the dominant norms of gender and sexuality, where they would be always off, outside, or too much. It reinforced the dominance of norms built on the stigmatization of figures cast as repellent, which allows those norms to constitute themselves as authentic referents, as *originals*.[59] Within the Black Panther Party, the critique of macho attitudes was official policy. In an interview with the *Guardian* in 1970, Bobby Seale said, "The fight against male chauvinism is a class struggle—that's hard for people to understand. To understand male chauvinism one has to understand that it is interlocked with racism." He continued, "In other words, the idea of saying 'keep a woman in her place,' is only a short step away from saying 'keep a nigger in his place.' "[60] His clairvoyance regarding issues of sexism and racism makes clear how intense the ideological class struggle over these issues was.

Rather than the typical analysis linking sexism and racism, interrogating this struggle allows us to redefine gender as an "ideological sign," meaning as a semiotic apparatus that produces—engenders—the norms of the dominant class as universal signifiers.[61] These signifiers encode the body so as to create socially perceptible and intelligible individuals who are therefore also acceptable and defendable, just as they encode social movements, making them audible and legitimate, or not. The summary murders of Black Panther militants through COINTELPRO cannot be understood separately from the

SELF-DEFENSE: POWER TO THE PEOPLE!

FBI's media disinformation campaign and production of phantasmic counterinformation. The FBI took full advantage of any accusation of assault, rape, or murder to revive the myth of Black men as violent, sexually predatory, and exceptionally virile, and of Black women as matriarchs, bad mothers on social assistance, and responsible for their *sons'* criminality.[62] The definition of racial violence (one ascribed exclusively to racialized minorities) is encoded ideologically in terms of gender (such violence is by definition uncivilized, masculine or macho, homophobic or unnatural), and this has made gender one of the most effective and enduring weapons for the ideological infiltration of the Black Power movement. The drive to reestablish a bourgeois patriarchy, with its own police, and to take up dominant gender norms (which are white by definition) as a regulating ideology represents one of the most effective and consistent modalities of an apparatus of domination for producing forms of ideological vulnerability within social movements. Self-defense is a dead end if it does not treat this semiotic class struggle as a priority.

Self-Defense and Safety

Safe!

In the late 1960s in the United States, mobilizations by racial *and* sexual minorities were at their apex, and the Black Panthers were the example to follow. In June 1969, the Stonewall rebellion marked a turning point in gay and trans liberation, echoing movements for women's liberation and antiracist and anti-imperialist movements. For all of them, the real killers were the state and its police. In 1965, LGBTQ activists began organizing against police harassment of sexual minorities. By the early 1970s, members of the Gay Liberation Front (GLF) were involved in numerous actions with or in support of the Black Panther Party, in a context where the connections between various anticapitalist, antiracist, and antipatriarchal struggles were increasingly central to the political analysis of many groups and coalitions.[1] "Our most immediate oppressors are the pigs . . . Every homosexual lives in fear of the pigs, except that we are beginning to fight back!"[2] Groups such as the Third World Gay Revolution (TWGR) and the Combahee River Collective continued holding this line even after it had become unpopular.[3] In early 1979, a dozen Black women were murdered, and the Combahee River Collective published a pamphlet in response: *Eleven Black Women: Why Did They Die?*[4] The collective refused to call for more protection by police or by patriarchs and instead reframed the question of safety in terms of "self-protection." This was based on a conception of sexism and racism as not simply two distinct relations of domination that can be stacked (as if adding one to the other resulted in a double discrimination) but as constituting a single apparatus for exposing people to the highest risk of death. The pamphlet is a veritable self-defense manifesto, listing bodily, personal, urban, and political resources and techniques for learning to defend oneself.

In 1969, a split occurred within the Gay Liberation Front, leading to the formation of the Gay Activists Alliance (GAA). The GAA intended to focus more of its political energy on the struggles of gay people, rather than on building links with other liberation movements and the political agendas of oppressed minorities. In one of the foundational texts of this period of the gay movement, *A Gay Manifesto* (written by Carl Wittman and signed and published in 1970 in San Francisco by the Red Butterfly, a branch of the GLF), the author critiques the idea that Black liberation or the struggle against imperialism should take precedence over gay liberation. In describing the physical violence experienced by sexual minorities, he addresses that carried out by "punks" before that inflicted by police. The author still supports a coalitional approach to struggle, but even as he writes that *all* men are socially constructed with male chauvinism, he states that solidarity with African American and Hispanic movements is made more difficult by the "supermasculinity" and "machismo" of men of color, which links them to ordinary acts of aggression.[5] Although he makes use of a Marxist analysis of oppression in the text (he recognizes that *we are all oppressed* by the same people "at the top"), the author is clear that the collective does not identify as Marxist but as "radical," and that all Marxist and socialist positions should incorporate gay liberation.

In 1973, the GAA formed a self-defense group in San Francisco, a squad of armed activists who called themselves the Purple Panther Division before quickly renaming themselves the Lavender Panthers. Under the leadership of the controversial Raymond Broshears, this group of gay and trans vigilantes announced their existence at a press conference on July 7 that clearly drew on the Black Panther Party's iconography: the panther logo (except purple) and the ostentatious bearing of arms (pistols and rifles). However, their stated goal differed from that of the Black Panthers. They did not intend to struggle against the criminal brutality of the police but rather to intervene quickly when violence against homosexuals was carried out in the public space by other minorities that did not fit the norm. They condemned the police's slow response and opportunistic mistreatment of victims, and their patrols were intended to defend themselves and others against punks, dealers, and gangs (who were explicitly Black, Hispanic, or Chinese American). The group stated they would "clean up" the area of homophobes. As Christina B. Hanhardt writes in her study of Broshears, for a short time in the early 1970s, he was a central figure in the gay liberation movement before disappearing from the activist scene. He gave the Lavender Panthers an unusual ideological profile, "[a] mix of libertarianism, anarchism, New Age and charismatic religious ideology, and sex radicalism."[6]

The rhetoric of "cleaning up" had already been used in 1966 by the San Francisco activist group Vanguard during their Clean Sweep action, and its critical significance was clear. The city bureaucrats and police were working for the economic interests of developers by cleaning up the city's marginal elements, and so Vanguard turned their own insult back on them in order to defend the ghetto. The action involved marching down Market Street pushing a broom while chanting, "All trash is before the broom."[7] The Lavender Panthers, however, used the language of "cleaning up" in an entirely different way from Vanguard and the clear picture given by their street theatrics. "Cleaning up" in this case meant keeping the streets safe from violence and protecting residents, which involved drawing a line between those considered neighbors and the *other* undesirables. Seven years after

Vanguard, although the local government and social services agencies had set up housing support programs, the process of cleaning up (spearheaded by the Lavender Panthers) still served the interests of developers and private landlords who wanted a well-policed gay community, as this created ideal conditions for investing and speculating in historic neighborhoods. Secure the streets and the lobbies and stairwells of buildings, too. Secure public transportation and businesses (notably by eradicating prostitution, pornography, and drugs). Such was the response to demands for the right to live in safety. "Be Safe!"—this buzzword let real estate speculators use racism and the struggle against homophobic violence as a Trojan horse.[8] In this way, San Francisco and New York (and in particular the Castro and East Village neighborhoods) could be seen as experimental sites in which that slogan and its associated politics of self-defense were in constant tension, causing many collectives to implode.

The Lavender Panthers disappeared in 1974. Two years later, another self-defense street patrol was started by a new organization founded in 1975, Bay Area Gay Liberation (BAGL). Some of the activists in this group saw their right to self-defense as the primary modality for resisting violence. Following the murder of a gay man in Tucson, Arizona, by students who were only sentenced to probation as punishment, activists formed the Richard Heakin Memorial Butterfly Brigade, also called the Butterfly Brigade. The group, composed almost exclusively of white men (one lesbian of color, Ali Marrero, participated), patrolled the streets of the neighborhood with whistles, notebooks, pens, and walkie-talkies, listing all the homophobic aggression they faced (such as insults from people in the street or from moving cars, harassment, and assault), notably by writing down license plate numbers. The whistles were a system for frightening, chasing away, and shaming hostile people as well as for protecting themselves in the event of a physical altercation.

They were also a sign of recognition within the community, a symbol of solidarity and commitment: "We were all taking care of each other," as Hank Wilson, one of the group's members, said.[9] Wilson was very clear about the group's relationship with the police: their strategy was to continue asking the police to act against homophobic aggression as a way of displaying how institutions did not recognize or take into account this violence.[10] The Butterfly Brigade's main goal was to build an alternative politics around safety. "We didn't want to give the community an illusion that someone was taking care of us. We wanted everyone in the community to feel like they were on patrol, all the time, looking out for everybody else."[11] For this reason, the Butterfly Brigade refused to have a uniform that would make its members stand out and look like a paramilitary group dedicated to everyone's safety. The idea was to develop a politics of solidarity, because each individual was only safe when everyone felt invested and committed to intervene anytime anyone was a victim of violence. Everyone needed to become an expert in self-defense. Yet, interpellating each individual—although, in practice, these were almost exclusively men—as a patrolman contributed to institutionalizing a safe dress code. It came to define who was a source of worry or suspicion and who deserved solidarity, resulting in a norm of white gay masculinity. An athletic build, short hair, mustache, jeans, T-shirt, leather jacket, and a whistle became the gay community's uniform in the Castro neighborhood.[12] The stigmatizing effect was immediate and transformed all other men into potential homophobes, making them seem like outsiders in the neighborhood.

Community self-defense settled into an easy relationship with early security measures (broken-windows policies, neighborhood watch), where "security" was held up as both a criterion for and a marker of a good quality of life.[13] Good gay lives, ones "worth living," are thus redefined within and by means of the regulation of obscenity, which simply amounts to repressing *unsafe* sexuality, those practices considered risky.[14] These practices traced the contours of which bodies were *worthy of being defended* and which were not—and were therefore responsible for the insecurity they experienced or caused. Some homophobic practices were indeed repressed, but this repression always simultaneously entailed criminalizing other forms of homosexuality and trans identity perceived as creating insecurity—whether moral, physical, sexual, political, social, or health—through noise pollution, unsanitary conditions, pornography, drugs, crime, vagrancy, and so on. Similarly, defining intolerant heterosexuality (homophobic, transphobic) in racist terms constituted it as a threat to quality of life in certain neighborhoods, and therefore to certain gay lives considered good and safe.[15] Drawing on an emotional essentialism of risk, the immediate effect of this apparatus was to make queers of color (African American, Indigenous, Hispanic) invisible, illegitimate, and unintelligible, which contributed to the prejudice that all homosexuals are white and all homophobes are Black. This process materialized as police surveillance, the repression of sexual and racial delinquency (the former considered obscene and the latter violent), the elimination of social programs, and the geographic displacement to other parts of the city of anyone abnormal and of poor, working-class, racialized minorities. Targeted and brutalized by the racist penal state, racialized minorities were primarily represented through the image of their *sons* who had been killed or imprisoned in defense of a safe and financially secure white middle class.[16] The members of this class were the only ones with the means to live in the refurbished buildings in "their" neighborhoods, and they demanded to be protected by the police at all times while doing so.

In a similar context on the East Coast of the United States, in New York, a self-defense group called Society to Make America Safe for Homosexuals (SMASH) was created in the same year as the Butterfly Brigade, and it was no less an example of collusion between self-defense and sexual and racial gentrification. SMASH developed a whole semiology of gay masculinity as powerful, vengeful, and ready to defend itself, constructed relative to a negative norm of racialized masculinity as young, criminal, and homophobic. There were also many other collectives existing at the same time as the two we have described that organized and mobilized to resist this logic and to demonstrate an alternative approach to the question of safety. All these groups faced continuous police brutality, as African American, socialist, and queer proles. It was with this in mind that, in the lead-up to the Revolutionary People's Constitutional Convention, organized by the Black Panthers, Huey Newton published his important text *The Women's Liberation and Gay Liberation Movements*, in which he called for a broad coalition across movements.[17] Newton evokes the fact that homosexuality elicits or provokes insecurity among heterosexual male African American activists. He is speaking to these men as one of them, writing in the first-person plural: "As we very well know, sometimes our first instinct is to want to hit a homosexual in the mouth, and want a woman to be quiet."[18] Between the lines of his conception of the dialectic of security/insecurity, Newton is denouncing a rhetoric of domination that constitutes *objective allies* as *subjective threats*. ("We are afraid we might be homosexual . . . We are afraid she might castrate us."[19]) Interpellated by white imperialist ideology as figures of sexist and homophobic violence, racialized men came to definitively embody insecurity. In order to understand this logic of security in its entirety, we must understand how it was reproduced within activist groups that took up its agenda and its vocabulary and that then saw other bodies as sources of insecurity. The bodies of women (straight or lesbian, white or Black), gays, and others were constituted as figures of insecurity for African American men, thereby ensuring that they could only become *subjects* within and by means of adherence to the dominant norm of masculinity. *To be recognized as a man means being recognized as white*, but also as heterosexual and petty bourgeois. As Newton wrote, "We must gain security in ourselves and therefore have respect and feelings for all oppressed people."[20]

Self-Defense and the Politics of Anger

Security can only be constituted as a norm of life when *insecurity* is being produced, against which the state appears to be (and presents itself as) the only response. During the 1970s, groups of Black lesbians, such as the Third World Women's Alliance, tirelessly challenged this logic and its effects on feminism's priorities. The police violence that they (and their children) disproportionately faced came along with the racist construction of Black women as being so capable of defending themselves that they did not need to be defended—or, worse, that they were a threat from which others had to be defended—especially when they were in a group.[21] Gente, a softball team founded in Oakland in 1974 that became a self-organized feminist self-defense group for Black lesbians, emphasized in an interview how lesbians of color were perceived as "invisible if we're alone, violent if we are together."[22] In March 1984, the bimonthly *ONYX: Black Lesbian Newsletter*, the leading African American lesbian periodical in the United States, published an issue whose cover showed a drawing of a group of Black women defending themselves from a white police officer on horseback who had just knocked one of them to the ground.[23]

Some activist groups made it their goal to obtain guarantees of security, but ultimately this meant not only excusing the state's violence but also predetermining modes of dissent and coalition building.[24] It created a certain type of militancy, a *protectionist* form of self-defense, whose emotional cartography contained dangerous pitfalls. Self-defense in that case consisted of taking up the injunction to "get to safety," engaging in protective actions based on how neighborhoods, streets, identities, individuals, and groups affected their collectives or causes—or in relation to *what did them violence* (such as an unfamiliar, threatening, or deviant person). Politics of security were thus coproduced by means of and within a system of affective marks: an emotional territoriality that not only divided up spaces, stigmatized bodies, and naturalized relations of aggression/victimization, security/insecurity, us/them, and fear/trust, but also mutated political subjectivation into sentimentality regarding danger and risk. It once again involved struggle taking an emotional turn. Coalition building requires a common denominator, but this in turn makes common denominators indefensible, and so it carries out a strategy of division on behalf of the apparatuses of power.

We should also take note of what these strategies did to the collectives themselves, to militant lives and bodies, and of the exhausting dead ends that sometimes led to self-destruction. The injunction to feel safe and secure among those like you is essentially a politics of controlling and limiting resistance movements, and even one of the most effective. Bunkered down in a strategy of separatism, whether it be thoroughly elaborated or not, activists seek to protect themselves by carving out spaces they can secure, in a mimetic response to official promises of security, repeating those promises and helping them spread. In their supposedly safe spaces, activists entrench themselves among those like themselves, who are, by definition, not dangerous. This safe togetherness is defined in opposition to an *unsafe* outside that evokes fear or hatred, and it is then unthinkable and unacceptable to believe that relations of power, conflictuality, and antagonisms also inevitably exist within such spaces, where they continue to operate uninterrupted. Staying inside an imposed framework of intelligibility in this way means, for those who understandably refuse to rely on the state's police or justice system, that the only defense against the unsafety lurking even within their own collectives is to further subdivide and delimit community spaces, to make them more secure still. This means cutting people out because the simple fact of their presence *might do violence* to someone else—excluding or excommunicating your peers because they fall short or have betrayed you by exercising power within the closed space. DIY judicial institutions constitute themselves as monstrous simulacra: while they refuse to rely on the dominant police and justice system, its de facto emanations are still invested with authority and allowed to colonize activist collectives. This day-to-day management of violence among activists—which plays out through subjective slights and wrongs—consumes a collective's time along with its members.[25] It cuts into the imaginary that makes it possible to create different modalities for working with violence. It is also emotionally and politically exhausting, undermining commitment and causing the process of political consciousness building to lose its focus.

The poet June Jordan provides a masterful description of the double consciousness involved in the *defense of self*. She was twice a victim of rape, and she describes how rape leaves you with a profound conviction of your own absolute powerlessness, as well as how political consciousness can act as a pivot point (or not) for restoring your power of action. Jordan writes that the first time she was raped, it was by a white man: after assaulting her for forty-five minutes, he dragged her into the shower and tried to force her to bend over to pick up a bar of soap so he could sodomize her: "He yelled, 'Pick it up!' He was ordering me to pick it up!"[26] In a fraction of a second, her fear evaporated—she would rather die than obey this white man. Race reanimated her paralyzed body. It was racism rather than sexism that served as the pivot point here, raising her power of action to a "do or die" level.[27] Jordan's rage expressed itself through self-defense and in reference to the existence of a community in struggle. She managed to strike him in the head and escape. Race activated her "self-protective rage"—a white man was raping a Black woman.[28] In that precise moment, this man became the incarnation of a predatory, murderous white masculinity that has always been the enemy of African American women. The second time, she was raped by a Black man, an activist with the NAACP. One night, she was out with friends and he invited them to come continue the evening at his place. Her other friends never showed up, so she found herself alone with this man. When he raped her, Jordan described being frozen in shock. What was happening was unthinkable, and it obstructed her power of action: he was Black and she was Black. She had not felt threatened:

> The issue of race was pivotal, except, this time, race paralyzed me to the deadly extent of self-effacement. Shocked that a "Brother" would violate me, his "Sister," I lost speed and resolute force of resistance and I never tapped into the rage necessary for resistance to the demons of domination.[29]

Race in this situation essentially neutralized her rage. She was stupefied by the unbearable injustice of having to be on guard, of having to defend herself, even with her companions in struggle. Along with the violent harm to her body, she felt guilty and outraged for having let her guard down and for getting assaulted in a place and by a person who were a priori safe and trustworthy. The rape lasted all night. The man let Jordan leave at dawn—her body was only pain, and her legs could hardly support her. Her body became, in her eyes, "the most defiled, filthiest thing in the world."[30] This disgust with herself almost drove her crazy. Jordan's experience of crass violence demonstrates how feminism had failed to build a community for *all women* that could be drawn on for self-protective rage.[31] The problem is thus not the fact that relations of violence continue to exist within such communities and that victims do violence to other victims. Rather, it is that a community that presents itself as united on the basis of a shared relationship of domination—of a common primary enemy—was unable to declare war on this enemy or to form a coalition in which Jordan could feel, if not safe, at least in a position to raise up her power without the risk of contributing to racism. Coherency is essential for movements that choose nationalist, separatist, or essentialist dynamics: the goal should not be safety in a phantasmic space of those like you, but rather building and creating territories in which to politicize and capitalize on rage in order to initiate and carry out struggle: "Show me the power and I will feel the pride!"[32] June Jordan is calling for the creation of other forms of community, formed not around reassuring subjects but around an enraged commitment to combat.

"Safety" is a *pharmakon*, a remedy, an injunction that brings relief. It is invoked when one is confronted with the politics of discriminatory management and the exponential production of risk and social insecurity that gradually makes life unlivable. It is a response to the *vital* necessity of moving through public and private space (without being attacked, harassed, or killed), collectively providing the material conditions for existence, having a roof over one's head, and creating other forms of life, exchange, countercultures, and practices of self. It is a response to the need for mutual aid and love. However, it is also a poisonous injunction, one that forces militant lives to withdraw, map out their fortifications, and purge their ranks. The more we protect ourselves against insecurity, the more we exhaust that power that community can otherwise signify for us—united in solidarity, a source of strength and anger—and the more we bring about a biopolitics on the scale of our struggles, a *bioactivism*.

From Vengeance to Empowerment

On a winter morning in the United States in 2008, someone called out to Suyin Looui in the streets while she was on her way to work, "Hot ching chong!" Furious and disgusted, she created a video game called *Hey Baby!*, in which women are the heroes. At the beginning of the game, you find yourself in the streets of a city that looks like New York or Montreal, armed with a gun. You are accosted by strangers: "Hey baby, nice legs!" "Do you have time?" "Wow, you're so beautiful!" "I like your bounce baby!" "I could blow your back out . . ."[33] At this point in the game, you have the choice to either answer with a nervous, timid "Thanks" and continue on your way (the harasser acts like he is going to leave you alone, but you run into him again a few seconds later), or you draw your gun and shoot him to death. The man lies dying in a pool of blood before being replaced by a tombstone on which the last words he spoke to you are written as an epitaph. You do not gain anything (there are an infinite number of harassers), but the chance to continue walking through the streets and getting accosted, which gives the game a Kafkaesque dimension.[34]

Like other contemporary feminist projects opposing street harassment, Suyin Looui's video game individually confronts us with the vengeful phantasm of carrying a weapon and with the ambiguous, sadistic satisfaction that comes from letting loose and blowing jerks apart.[35] However, it also confronts our power of action in the face of violence with the absence of *happy experiences* in contemporary society. Another reason why this game in which we are—*I am*—an ordinary hero is so enjoyable is that it shifts our sense of what is possible. The enjoyment challenges us to go back to the drawing board about what is possible to do to combat sexism—in the same way as does the ineffectiveness of public policy in eradicating it. And that is the game's premise: that a response to sexism is only conceivable by staging *face-to-face* encounters, where a single woman is confronted by a harasser. From this perspective, *Hey Baby!* runs counter to the imaginary used in the overwhelming majority of representations of violence against women, in which women are seen as a faceless group of defenseless victims.[36] The game represents an extreme counterposition, where the experience of sexism is first and foremost a *routine experience, gone through individually*. By arming women with Uzis and Kalashnikovs, as though that were a solution to sexist harassment in the public space, this game is a striking portrayal of self-defense that goes far beyond any legal definition of legitimate defense, the latter being classically based on the philosophical principles of immediacy and proportionality. Indisputably, the apparatus makes us uneasy: firstly because the solution it offers is disproportionate (a few words lead to men being executed by firearm), but then, more subtly, because it makes us smile and feeds our *imagined rage*.[37] The game's morbid premise is a phantasmagoric dramatization that provokes real satisfaction from those who share the ordinary experience of sexism (ordinary because it is routine, permanent, and licit). *Hey Baby!* frightens us as much as it cheers us up, and it gives us the opportunity to take a critical look at widely accepted representations of violence against women and at how these acts of violence are recognized. What would happen if all the violence rendered invisible were finally recognized for what it is and what it institutes, namely a continuous flow of solicitation and interpellation that requires our attention at every moment, like a player caught in the energy of a game. *Hey Baby!* stands out from mainstream feminist culture and discourse on the subject of sexist violence, its actuality is also a departure from the genealogy of feminist self-defense, and it serves as an illustration of a neoliberal turn in the feminist imagination. Although it hammers home its criticism on a number of points, the game's framing is nonetheless directly linked to a culture where self-defense is the focus of contemporary calls to guarantee security.

Inspired by the reference points of cultural products usually associated with young males (although adults and women may also consume these products), *Hey Baby!* is a first-person shooter, or FPS. It uses a perspective characteristic of war games, where the player views the action through the eyes of the virtual protagonist. Most FPS games give life to an ultra-violent capitalist, militarist imaginary, blurring the line between imperialist technoscience and science fiction. This imaginary is eminently gendered and racialized, which is clear from the target audience of these kinds of mass cultural products, as well as from the norms of gender, sexuality, color, and race that they contribute to reifying.[38] Although the enemies have well-defined identities (often they are the living dead, Nazis, extraterrestrials, communists, mafiosi, Russians, or even Afghan terrorists), the main character in an FPS game is a universal form without content, and it adopts a hegemonic viewpoint: that of a man with access to the resources reserved for dominant groups in the richest countries. However, in applying the FPS apparatus in *Hey Baby!*, Suyin Looui allows *us* to play the role of an urban feminist guerrilla in the first person. She has come up with a virtual space-time where we take pleasure in answering violence with violence. And yet *Hey Baby!* offers a clear personification of the ideal type of harasser: they are not white-collar men, men with white hair, or white men. Self-defense here is enacted through a form of virtual solipsism that also realizes the darkness of violence against women—dark and supposedly dangerous streets filled with dark-skinned strangers as aggressors. This contains two presuppositions that are as false as they are problematic: that sexist violence is the fault of young, racialized men from the lower classes, and that it occurs in the public space.

Regardless of our history, our identity, our experience, our shape, our physical and psychological abilities, or our wealth, skills, and social resources, we find ourselves exploring the virtual world through the scope of a gun that serves as superego: "I retaliate, therefore I am." This framing is a clear break with the rare games built around female characters, which are heavily plot-focused and require the player to identify, for better or worse, with characters who are overdetermined in terms of gender, sexuality, race, and class. They are third-person games, which makes it hard to see yourself as a hero whose traits embody dominant aesthetic norms (the best example is the iconic Lara Croft).[39] If FPS games constitute a space-time of principally masculine homosociality, *Hey Baby!* is not a parody but an attempt to resignify this space-time in *feminine* and *feminist* terms. A literal reading would situate this game within the dominant imaginary of armed self-defense, since it extends to women an extremely controversial *privilege* reserved almost exclusively for men—that of wielding virtual weapons. Taken this way, permanent, virtual exposure to extreme violence produces a form familiarity that entails degendering how violence is learned. Traditionally, socialization involving being desensitized to violence is a driver for constructing and embodying the identity and sexual identification that distinguish men from *Others*.

However, *Hey Baby!* can also be read as an empowerment narrative, one that seeks to produce a powerful subjectivity in order to counter the generally accepted victimizing representations that accompany political strategies based on seeking protection from the state. In this case, security is taken to mean returning to an unresolved theoretical tension at the heart of political and military philosophy: the proscription against doing justice oneself or seeking vengeance outside the political sphere. *Taking justice into your own hands* is generally thought of as amounting to a negation of the rule of law, which punishes without hate, and means getting caught in the distinctly negative motion of an endless cycle of reprisals, answering wrong with wrong. Yet, beyond the problematic of contractualism, there is also an economy of political emotions at work here. What relying on the justice system fails to address is the joy of vengeance, the fact that only by doing justice themselves can the subjects who *suffered* injustice, prejudice, or harm allow their rage and anger to keep them in a position that does not amount to *defenselessness*. Beyond simply restoring negative reciprocity—answering violence with violence—anger can be understood as a desire for vengeance and the pleasure taken from vengeance. Such anger belongs to subjects who, as opposed to victims, are not totally annihilated by the harm of the offense or the brutality of the injustice, and who have preserved the hope of restoring or repairing a state of equality.

In this case, a powerful subjectivity is reestablished through the overprotective mediation of weapons and through the immediate pleasure the game offers by giving us, at last, the chance to get revenge. It lets us feel jubilant and at peace, confidently facing the endless stream of harassers, in striking contrast with our daily experience that is usually told in the language of powerlessness. The *first-person* apparatus allows us to experience the pleasure of *getting out of it*. In the end, though, *Hey Baby!* departs from the characteristics that give FPSs their appeal, in that the game itself is simple, its plot is cripplingly weak by design, and the backgrounds are used over and over, indefinitely. It does not take long for easily slaughtering everyday sexists to get boring, which brings to the fore the repetitive character of sexist violence along with the futility and absurdity of such a disproportionate response. What good is an Uzi if harassers keep appearing forever? What is the use of slaughtering them if I will never be left alone? *Hey Baby!* thus offers a critical look at sexist violence: it is not unbearable because we are unable to do anything about it or to act on it, but because it is inescapable. The conclusion is then an aporetic one, as the pleasure found in being able to get revenge is replaced by the sad realization that revenge does absolutely nothing. It is precisely in that aporia that the exhaustion of the political resides—and not in the initial fact of framing the game in the solitude of an FPS, which causes the collective to disappear. This is because, when it comes to sexual violence, being one-on-one is eminently political.

However, the ultimate limit of agency in this imaginary experiment in feminist violence is the weapon itself. Beneath the appearance of a story about joyful vengeance, the game illustrates a distinctive principle of soft neoliberalism: autonomy, developing capacity, valorizing resources, restoring choice, and so forth. It can be summarized as follows: *power to*. In other words, when dealing with harassment, *you* have the power to defend *yourself*! *Hey Baby!* is a representation of feminist empowerment and joyous virtual solipsism, but it may not be the case that anger and rage are driving the action.[40] The gun is the main character, for it is the gun that restores the sexual and bodily integrity of the female victim. It defends *her*—it stands in for the husband, the state, and the law, as all of these have either failed or refused to protect *her*. It constitutes the metonymic figure of the protector, and it reifies the heteronomy of women relative to what take the form of a right to security. From this perspective, the game is essentially a critique of how women are excluded from guarantees of security, and it situates these guarantees as both the prize and the condition of possibility for full citizenship.[41] To a certain extent, like laws and husbands, the weapon appears as an object that materializes the third party or the authority to which defense is delegated and which is endowed with a violence that the subject is unable to express except through them. That the weapon makes you all-powerful only raises the question once again of your own power of action. Seen this way, the weapon is very much a classic apparatus for the delegation of the right to self-defense and self-preservation as it has been traditionally defined in classical political philosophy. More specifically, the weapon is an apparatus that brings about a tacit contract formalizing the submission of women through the very fact of their need to be defended. In other words, with a weapon, *I am defended*, and without one, *I am defenseless*.

Reprisals

Defenseless

For the past thirty years, almost every media campaign about violence against women—whether through graphics, on the radio, or on television—have all reenacted the exact same violent scene: *they reprised it*. By actualizing the vulnerability attributed to femininity rather than proposing alternative forms of femininity or tools to take reprisals in response to violence, these public campaigns have failed to prevent sexist violence.[1]

In France, the first national campaign about intimate partner violence was launched in 1989. If we consider only the period of 2006 to 2016, there were, first, the government's campaigns in 2006 and 2007. Accompanied by the words "I love you, a little, a lot, madly, not at all," we saw a young woman's badly beaten face and then her body in the morgue, covered by a blue sheet. There was a very similar TV ad in 2007, in which a woman who had been a victim of violence described what her husband had inflicted on her. It closed with the words "But fifteen days ago, it finally ended," over an image of a grave in a cemetery. And then there was the "Talk about it while you still can" ad, and its images of gagged women, promoting a crisis line that had been established. In 2009, a portfolio of the Office of the Secretary of State for Families and Social Services showed two children playing at being a couple in which the husband is violent.[2] In campaigns three years apart, in 2008 and 2010, the site stop-violences-femmes.gouv.fr was launched alongside a TV ad once again showing a woman's face covered in bruises. Campaigns run in France by organizations such as Amnesty International or UNICEF have been no different and also portrayed battered women and their abusers (such as, for instance, the "Violence is always in style" campaign). A poster released in 2014 featured a woman who is mixed-race or a descendant of immigrants from the French colonies (which is noteworthy because the subjects of previous campaigns had mostly been white women), whose face is split in two. One side of the photo is ripped into several pieces and glued back together, while the other side is intact. At the bottom, it reads: "Laws that stand up to violence." The slogan for the whole campaign was "The law protects you from violence against women."[3]

By mostly showing a woman—or more specifically, by systematically reifying female bodies portrayed as victimized bodies—these campaigns actualize vulnerability as an inevitability for all women. They show only swollen faces, injured bodies marked by blows (blood and bruises), crying, pleading, screaming, or, on the contrary, mute, broken down by close-ups, in pieces, frozen muscles, face in hands, prostrate. They display corpses, X-rays, graves, ambulances, sirens, devastated children who witness sexist violence or are themselves victims. The images in these campaigns exploit the full technical capacities afforded by current photographic and visual culture in order to make them seem as real as possible. These campaigns are supposed to prevent violence or raise awareness, and most of them claim to politicize the issue through their emotional interpellation of both public opinion at large and women victims in particular, encouraging them to react and speak up *before it is too late*.[4] They all promise to protect victims. More insidiously, these campaigns also address themselves to a third-party spectator, since they all state their intention to make visible to perpetrators of violence the moral implications of their acts. This mode of politicization of violence is based on three assumptions. The first is that making a problem visible makes it real. The second is that playing on emotions, specifically empathy, makes a phenomenon real *for everyone*.[5] And the third is that showing the consequences of an act or a practice can reach the perpetrators of those acts as moral subjects capable of becoming aware of the incivility, the immorality, or the danger (health, social, or human) of their actions.

Interpellation in this apparatus is by no means simple, incorporating a complex technology of the visible that articulates three perspectives, intersects three positions, "three emotions," "three intentions."[6] In *Camera Lucida*, Roland Barthes presents three analytical categories that are useful to us here: the Operator (the photographer, the one who presents for the seeing), the Spectator (the one who looks), and the Spectrum (the one who is presented and looked at). Looking, being looked at, presenting what is to be looked at. Barthes chose the term "Spectrum" to emphasize the role's dual nature: to be photographed, to be looked at, is at once to be put (or to put oneself) on display while also being frozen, captured in a present moment that has been forever mummified, which gives us the idea of spectral presence. The photographic apparatus has the unique quality of bringing a being into existence through the act of birthing an image that it displays and, at the same time, instantly mortifies. The process of objectification is experienced as "a micro-version of death ... I am truly becoming a specter."[7] This mortifying metamorphosis is capable of freezing even the most "alive" and spontaneous scenes for eternity, which is all the more fascinating when its object is a *staged scene* of violence, suffering, or death. In public campaigns concerning violence against women, the subjects of the photographs are perfect specters, as it were, performing as victims who were in fact killed by their attacker's blows. Why is it that representations of gendered power dynamics, even their most tragic manifestations, involve massively simplifying the mortifying (and infinitely reproducible) spectacle of the victimization of women?

In reading the photos used in these public campaigns, our first observation is that we did not choose to encounter these images: we encounter them by chance on our travels, as we take the subway or the bus or walk down the street, in certain government buildings, online, or on television.[8] It is a very real possibility that these pictures leave most of us indifferent, and this is all the more likely since our daily lives are overloaded with images, a constant flow of them that grows denser by the day.[9] Because they are constructed as advertising photos, their semiology is often basic, in that the meaning is simple, pure, and clear, and can be grasped without much thought. At this point, Barthes distinguishes two elements that together make a picture interesting: the *studium* and the *punctum*. *Studium* refers to shared tastes and to interest based on cultural and intellectual reference points shared by the Spectator and the image. This allows the image to be looked at—it is both intelligible and worthy of being looked at—with a kind of curiosity at once knowing, nonchalant, and distant. The punctum is, by contrast, the element that captures the Spectator's attention, the detail that pricks, wounding the Spectator, who then looks more closely and maybe even remembers the picture once the gaze is turned away.[10] Furthermore, the punctum is also what makes me accept that the characters and scenes in a photo exist beyond this entomological record: it is the striking detail that brings them to life, with their complexity and history, in the flesh and in three dimensions. This complexity is precisely why we should not hastily conflate the punctum with something shocking. In the pictures we are considering here, the punctum is nowhere to be found. The representation of violent acts, or rather their effects (blood, bruises, feigned suffering, tears, and cries . . .) is part of the studium, the usual assortment of conventional representations of gendered bodies (specifically, of a dominant norm of vulnerable femininity) and the universe of shared meaning coded through the semiology of gender. Using Barthes's term, such photographs can be called "unary," meaning they simply state what is already common sense.[11] They are slippery and banal, allowing the Spectator to pass by without looking at them, or to glance through them without being struck by their mortiferous brutality.[12] "We photograph things in order to drive them out of our minds," said Kafka to young Janouch.[13] What are we driving from our minds in this case? The obscene powerlessness of the victim bodies depicted in these photos? Or, on the contrary, what these bodies, these women, are and do *as well*?

These unary photographs depict prone, bloody, and beaten women as well as dead bodies, and they avoid all reflection. At the same time, they depict women who fit and incarnate all the aesthetic norms of dominant femininity: they are mostly young, white, and slim. Indeed, there is no element that brings us back to the complexity of the real, to the fleshiness of life. The picture reifies a norm of hegemonic femininity and associates it with a violent narrative. The photos of battered women take up all available space—regardless of where one's gaze lands, they colonize it. As Barthes writes, "The Photograph is violent, not because it shows violent things, but because on each occasion *it fills the sight by force*, and because in it, nothing can be refused or transformed."[14] It is this forced occupation that makes the violent dimension of these pictures a *mise en abyme*, a part reflecting a larger whole.

Furthermore, in doing away with the moment of surprise, with the unexpected and the never-before-seen, the Operator's perspective becomes omnipotent. Having chosen to represent only object-victims of violence, the photographer-subject imposes his point of view on the real while also taking pleasure in showing the spectacle of wounded, dominated, or even dead bodies he himself has staged. The tendency toward scopophilia raises once again the theme of the eroticism of domination.[15] It is clearly a form of sadistic voyeurism to forcibly place before someone's eyes a singular, simplistic perspective, and of eliciting in the Spectator, who can look without being seen, the same enjoyable power, the same *jouissance*, felt by the person freezing bodies whose flesh is marked by violence. The women being photographed (the Spectrum) are living subjects with complex experiences of life, but they are reduced to socii, to subjects of discussion, objectified by domestic violence statistics and dominant social norms. They are reduced to objects, inert and dead, to subjects frozen by the camera's lens, in an authoritarian testament to *what was* and imposing a grim fate on all women by essentially projecting onto them the menace of inevitable violence—*what has happened will happen*. We can gaze at their obscene suffering at our leisure, even out of the corner of our eye, and their bodies become objects of a "fetishist fascination."[16]

The eroticization of these defenseless women, these pure objects, takes up all the space in how gendered violence is represented, leaving none for other representations, images, or phantasms, and therefore for other narratives.[17] Such photos constrain and convert our gaze into a form of indifferent thinking; they exhaust and storm our imaginary by flooding it with pleasant powerlessness. *Who takes pleasure from seeing the suffering of others? Who takes pleasure from the spectacle of powerlessness?* It is quite unlikely that, in this case, those directed to incarnate powerlessness took any pleasure from the representation of themselves as *beaten*, their existences being such that they can identify with this brutal objectification of the self. It is much more likely that it brings up a slew of feelings and affects, like disgust, shame, rejection, empathy, refusal, a sense of injustice, hatred, denial. In such conditions, how can campaigns like these meet their stated goals to help or protect victims of violence? And therefore whom are they addressing?

Beyond the battered bodies themselves, the effects and consequences of the violent acts on the bodies in the photographs are clear on first glance. What haunts us in these photos are traces and signs of a power of action capable of stamping its mark on another's body—a capacity for extreme violence. These public campaigns are a tribute being paid to the aggressors. The fascinating part, then (the part that frightens, excites, or gives pleasure), is getting to see *what it is like to be powerful*, what it is like to be able to beat, strike, or injure while others are only capable of crying, screaming, or dying. The scopic drive thus indicates a degree of narcissism. In fact, the only *jouissance* here is for those looking upon their own power of action, those who, turning a corner in the subway tunnel, see themselves on a signboard, what they have done and what they can do. It is not the suffering of an object being placed before us, but the power of a subject. Campaigns like these are tragic because, fundamentally, they deal with the way men are supposedly overpowering. This power is presented as that of male bodies, though these are rarely shown, rarely staged, except through depictions of the efficacy, brutality, and licitness of their blows. The eroticization of suffering bodies constitutes a jouissance of the self, a grisly aestheticization of the acts of the perpetrators of violence. In other words, these campaigns both display and address the violent jouissance of perpetrators of violence.

The perpetrator is thus the fourth figure. He is a historic character standing outside the frame, but photography is like an ode to his striking power.

Phenomenology of Prey

The media had already begun denouncing *Dirty Weekend* in the weeks leading up to its release in 1991, calling the book inflammatory, immoral, ultraviolent, and pornographic, and its author mentally ill.[18] The British parliament debated banning its publication and distribution, which is the last time this occurred in the modern history of censorship in England.

Dirty Weekend obviously hit a sore spot. Most reviews of the book described it as glorifying violence without even bothering to justify it with a revenge motive. The violence, they claimed, is gratuitous, irrational, and limitless, whereas the book's heroine, Bella, is the very image of a victim become executioner. Associating her with obscene brutality—when carried out by a woman, brutality is always considered obscene—Bella is presented as a contemporary version of homicidal feminine madness, which thereby reduces her ethics to a pathology. However, if one were actually to read Zahavi's text, it is clear that these critiques completely overlook the central point of the novel. In this sense, they are symptomatic of a will *not to know*, a will that Zahavi's book jostled and undermined. In fact, Bella is a figuration of just how commonplace the experience of sexual violation is; her weekend of murder is a methodological fiction intended to examine this experience and make it felt, a way to use writing as a means to carry it up to the surface of the real, to impact and engage our consciences.

The novel also destabilizes a common ethical and political position in contemporary feminist currents that understands violence only as an expression of the power of action of the dominant and therefore not (or no longer) as a political possibility for feminism. From this angle, the novel is deeply shocking, because it highlights the *effects* of violence against women by describing what this violence does to Bella, as well as what she becomes capable of in turn. A "feminist serial killer" (as some journalists called her), Bella breaks with the feminist ethic of nonviolence (or rather, with an ethic too readily ascribed to the whole of feminism). She is the *dirty* heroine feminism needed in order to question its own relationship to violence: what we do *with* violence, *within* violence, what we make *out of* it. In the novel, there is no properly heroic conversion of a nice, fragile, vulnerable Bella into the blood-soaked vigilante standing up for women. What is at stake is something entirely different. The political content of the book lies elsewhere, in the heart of Bella's introspective, defeated, and desperate inner life, but also in the bodily experience of being out of patience. *Dirty Weekend* is a political story of muscles that, no longer exhausted and curled back on themselves, now reach out, grab a hammer, and smash in someone's skull. It is "political" in the most feminist sense of the term, in that the personal is political.

Bella lives alone in her tiny semi-basement apartment in a modest and perfectly typical building in Brighton, a coastal city in southern England. She is a young woman like millions of others, unremarkable and forgettable. She has no ambitions or pretensions in life, claiming not even the simplest and most stereotypical forms of happiness. "Losing seemed to suit her. It was something familiar, like an ache that's always there, but you know you'll miss it if it ever goes."[19] Bella is an antihero, an anonymous character, a woman who passes with hurried steps, a shadow in the crowd. That she is so ordinary is precisely what makes her a stand-in for every woman. As Zahavi writes, "Is she pathetic? Does her weakness repel you? Does the thought of her huge, demented, victim's eyes turn your stomach? Don't judge her. Don't judge her unless you've been there."[20] In other words, *we are all a little like Bella.* Who among us has not felt Bella's existential mediocrity, her anonymity, the familiar fear she carries within her, her abandoned dreams, her weariness with asking, her claustrophobia from living in a cramped space and from surviving in her body and in her gender, her humility before the hardships society reserves for her, when all she asks in return is to be left to her quiet life?[21] Almost every day, in ways both varied and repetitive, a myriad of insignificant acts of violence makes our lives miserable and tests our consent. Almost daily, we experience salacious stares, lewd harassment, degrading comments, unwanted acts, and nauseating brutality, all of which harm our bodies as surely as our lives.

These early pages describing Bella's life sketch an outline of what could be called a *phenomenology of prey*: a lived experience that we attempt to endure or normalize through a hermeneutics of denial, that we try to rationalize by making it more tolerable and livable. It is not long before Bella is targeted by an "ordinary" man (which is an important detail) who violates her in every way, after which she tries to maintain at all costs the fiction of a "Bella before the assault."[22] She tries to live as she usually does and to reassure herself by acting as if everything is fine. She seeks to protect herself by acting as if nothing happened, by de-realizing her own apprehension of reality. Across the street, a man watches her from his window night and day—but maybe she is just imagining that a man is watching her? Bella's existence is a constant effort to see *herself* as unimportant: her sensations, her emotions, her unease, her fear, her anxiety, her terror. The existential skepticism of victims stems from a generalized loss of trust, affecting everything that is experienced or perceived in the first person. When denial becomes impossible, she takes it on herself: she curls up inside her body, hides in her apartment, shrinks her living space, which, despite all her efforts, has been violated. Her daily life, in all its ordinariness, is that of prey, and she manages her life in order to safeguard its meaning and avoid acknowledging this fact, not least because being prey involves a form of attention being paid to her that she does not even give to herself. The assault does not, then, represent a rupture in Bella's uneventful life; it simply reveals the damage already caused by experiences of constant violence and the marks these have left in her body. Those experiences have constituted her body proper and her relationship to the world, framing the very way that the world appears *to her*, touches *her*. They have shaped the way her body inhabits, effects, and extends itself into the world. There is thus no way of returning to a *pre-assault* life. There is no way to go back, because there is no unharmed femininity to latch on to or recover, one that could be restored or un-violated.

Bella's story is also that of her neighbor, an average guy living in the building across the street, who one day decided to violate her. Why? Because Bella appeared so pathetic, so fragile, already such a victim. If we are each a little like Bella, it is because we, too, don't go out at certain times or down certain streets. We don't smile at strangers who speak to us, we just look down without responding and hurry home. We make sure to lock our doors and close our blinds, stay still and not answer the phone.[23] And, like Bella, we have spent tons of energy convincing ourselves that our perception of this situation does not deserve to make sense, that it is worthless and out of touch with reality. We spend energy concealing our feelings and intuitions, acting as if what's happening is fine. Or perhaps we know it is not acceptable to be spied on, harassed, and threatened, but we tell ourselves it happened because we were in a bad mood, or because we are impatient and paranoid, or we just had bad luck, since "this kind of thing" only seems to happen to us. Bella's experience is composed of an accumulation of small, common experiences alongside the minute details of each mundane tactic we all use each day to live normally. These tactics have their accompanying phenomenal work (perceptive, affective, cognitive, gnoseological, and hermeneutical) and, being based on denial and skepticism, they speak to the unworthiness of anything related to ourselves. In fact, this idea of normality orbits within criteria of acceptability (and also criteria of unacceptability, of repulsiveness) that are defined by the perspective of the man at the window: it is only by adopting his scale of acceptability and credibility that we consider it normal to be subjected to his *whims*, since, in his world, he considers it normal to act *as he pleases*.[24]

These experiences of the banality of power are commensurable, and they provide the vantage point from which to see

Bella as a tragic character in a feminist story, one meant to serve as an example. Bella's story only truly begins when she decides she has had enough. What occurs before this tipping point is not a novel, but simply a prologue describing *what it is like to be a woman*.[25]

Bella's neighbor—the man who watches her through the window, calls her on the phone, and wakes her up in the middle of the night—follows her one afternoon. He sits down beside her while she is taking a few minutes to enjoy the sunshine for the first time in weeks. He places his hand on hers, squeezing it to the point of breaking it. He forcibly kisses her and promises he will come to her house and "hurt her."[26] Bella waits. She waits her turn at the doorstep of her rapist's world. Telling him to stop did not help, nor did saying his actions were crazy or abnormal: he does not hear her and does not understand. She is in "empty space"—she loses her footing and cannot recover; she is disoriented and cannot make it make sense.[27] And yet, Bella decides to take action. Why this day in particular? Is she more exhausted than usual by her work to maintain a normal life? There is no way of knowing. It all happens like a movement, or rather a tension, within a single muscle, one she had not known existed, and this tension has fertilized "a hard little nugget of rage."[28] Bella no longer doubts. She no longer denies, waits, or politely protests while forcing a smile. She comes out from inside herself, she comes out of her house, and walks toward something:

> It was gone three, when she got to the North Laines. It's the part of town you go to if you want your head shrunk, or your palm read, or your destiny revealed. It's the mystic, altruistic part of town. It's where they take you by the hand, and lead you through your dreams.[29]

These wanderings lead her to an Iranian clairvoyant with an elliptical way of speaking, and she talks with him for some time.[30] She talks about herself, her life, her arrival in Brighton three years earlier, and what has been going on these past few months. She describes her exhaustion with being a woman, which reads like a fable of heterosexual disillusionment: the desire, the encounters, the sex, the free love, the paid love, the falling out of love, the disillusionment, the breakups, the abandonment because she has "let herself go."[31] It is the little things—no attention, no interest, not listening, not looking, no consideration, no care, no attachment—that have given Bella the profound conviction that she is "flotsam and jetsam ... The last in the race. Black clouds and no silver lining. Just another pebble on the beach. The last out of bed and the last in the queue. The last on anyone's list for anything."[32] This is a crucial part of the novel: Bella is talking with the clairvoyant but also to herself. She addresses him but is listening to herself. For the first time, she takes her own words, feelings, and judgments seriously. She makes herself real again. And beyond her neighbor's exceptional violence, all the ordinary violence becomes visible—violence where she knew the perpetrator, someone she might have been friendly with or considered close: teachers, loves, lovers, friends, bosses ... This reflective aside restores the density of her point of view, her perspective, her lived experience of the world. She makes the link between all these experiences, objectifies everything she has done, all the imperceptible ways she has resisted in order to get through this violence and survive. It is clear that if Bella is still around, it is only because she has long been an expert in self-defense, just of a form that is not recognized as such, without the label and with none of the prestige. Bella's daily self-defense techniques have been effective for the simple reason that they have prevented this violence from utterly destroying her. Avoidance, denial, deception, silence, arguments, explanations, smiles, looks, gestures, fleeing, dodging—these are unrecognized techniques for real combat. Bella becomes aware that although she has managed to defend herself, she is also exhausted from taking it on herself, and that in trimming down her world, she has cut to the quick of her being. She has made use of what was available, drawing on what she was taught and received as her heritage. These tactics, which at first glance seem like feminine cowardice, were the only ones able to effectively save her dignity, although at the cost of derealization. Regardless, she has survived this long, she has defended herself as best she could.

The question then becomes: What can she do now? What can she hope for? To defend herself. To defend herself still, but differently, moving from tactics to strategy. She will no longer hide in the world of the Other, dodging blows and gritting her teeth. It is not that Bella frees herself—she is not freer than before—she simply realizes that she is angry, which is enough to take action. The anger is hers. Bella is always polite, humane, and even almost kind to her victims. The difference now is she will no longer defend herself from violence by constantly doing herself violence—she is changing the rules for her own actions.[33] Rather than her actions involving taking it all on herself, she is going to focus on herself, care for herself, and act in the world. And to do this, she will, of course, have to *transgress* the existing rules.

Even brittle little Bella can raise a hammer.[34] On Friday night, it is she who visits her perpetrator's home in the middle of the night and slips into his bedroom. It is she, this time, who explains the new rules, as he does not know the game has changed. It is she, again, who strikes him several times, smashing his head and leaving him dying in a pool of blood. This is a point of no return, and from now on, Bella will take care of herself by treating her reality as important, which makes her no less Bella. She has never wanted to inconvenience or bother anyone, but in fact she has been taught how to kill men all her life, and they have done so much to bring her to this point. They have taught her violence well, and it does not take much will or much strength to engage in violence. It does not take much technical skill or training, which is precisely why it is easy to violate a woman. She has seen it done, she has seen how it is done, she has endured what it does. Over the following weekend, the men she encounters will go through it. Yet these murders are never senseless: without knowing that Bella has changed the rules of the game, all the men she meets over those two days insult, harass, hit, or rape her, threaten her with death, or violate another woman, just as they usually do.[35]

Really, it is Bella herself who has reached a certain level of maturity, one at which violence suffered must become violence done. Like a distorted version of Jean-Jacques Rousseau's Émile, Helen Zahavi's Bella is a very good student. She has never practiced martial arts or received any special training, she never learned to use a hammer, a knife, or a pistol, and yet, under the surface, her experiences of violence have served as lessons in feminist self-defense.[36] Without her even realizing it, they have given her the resources needed to reason, judge, act, and strike—that is, to approach the world. Bella tries out her body and learns by doing. She begins to trust her feelings—her hate, rage, fear, and joy—as well as her deductions. No, you can't mock a man with a limp erection, you can't accept a ride home, you can't go down a dark alley, you can't stand within reach of a hand that might slap you, you can't let them too close to your neck—unless, that is, you are armed and determined to strike hard.[37] She begins to give significance to her own choices: is it too much to ask to live without being violated? Bella's two days represent the temporality of a feminist self-defense course, complete with accelerated practice, shared experiences, awareness gained, and recommendations.[38] It is not that Bella *has learned to fight*; it is that she *has unlearned not to fight*. Adopting a feminist strategy of self-defense means never having to distill reality in order to extract what is effective from a move (immobilize, hurt, kill), but instead leaping into the thick of violence's social reality to train bodies already traversed by violence. It means engaging muscles already familiar with violence but that have fundamentally never been taught or socialized to train themselves for violence, *for action.*

Although there is change, there is no real metamorphosis in *Dirty Weekend*—Bella stays the same throughout. She becomes neither a hysterical woman driven by cruelty nor a magnificent murdering heroine. Helen Zahavi wants her character to keep her feminine ordinariness, which is at once unique and commonplace. The author repeatedly specifies that Bella just wanted to be left alone, but despite her steely patience, this was not possible. It took two days of astonishing violence for her point of view to be considered, for it to matter to *others.*

The Epistemology of Concern for Others and Negative Care

In turning to violence, Bella undergoes a mutation, but the experience this produces is not unfamiliar: Bella the killer has the same experience as Bella the victim. The viewpoint has changed, but her lived experience is continuous throughout. Bella has not then undergone a metamorphosis, but rather an *anamorphosis*. She remains the same, even as the way she sees herself and others see her changes. What is it like now to be, not just a woman, but Bella? What is it like to defend yourself? What is it like to be Bella seen from this new angle? We can think of it as if it were an anamorphosis in a painting, which, when seen from a different angle or from closer up, reveals an object, an animal, or a face. We can borrow from Dürer's description of this art of deceiving the eye: he calls anamorphosis "the art of the secret perspective." Ultraviolent Bella is still Bella; it is just another view of her, a hidden, forbidden, and taboo vision of which Bella herself is not aware. *Dirty Weekend* has the excellent quality of not making any moral judgments or ontological distinctions between defenseless Bella and Bella the killer.

Conversely, for the novel's male characters (those responsible for harassment and assault) the change in perspective brings about the utter collapse of *their world*. In other words, these changes in perspective are not brought about through choice or goodwill but rather through relations of force, through laying waste: viewpoints are the materialization of positions within relations of force, and only violence is able to shift the balance.[39] In *Dirty Weekend*, Bella's vengeance is not about the punitive murders she carries out, and she in no way resembles the classic figure of the vigilante. She does not even fully turn herself into a *hunter*—something else is at work here. Her murders are brutal because they transgress the schema of intelligibility within and through which some worlds are experienced; they illuminate blind spots, dead angles, and secret sensations. The murders thus create the cognitive conditions of possibility for *empathy*. Forcing the other to see the world from a different perspective, to make the other feel, not quite what one feels, but astonishment at perceiving, feeling, and living something different:

> She gave the small one a second or two. A second or two, to let him look up. She let him look up and lock eyes with her. They looked at each other, the small one, the still one. The knowing look that passed between them. The look of surprise at the way things turn out. Hunter become quarry. Quarry become hunter. Executioner condemned. Condemned—executioner. The knowingness of the looks that passed between them.[40]

From now on, the prey do the hunting.[41] This is a tale of the revenge of the powerless, the defenseless, and the fragile. It is not a novel of resentment but a fictional illustration of the historicity of relations of power (prey do not always remain prey), based on a phenomenology of violence. A particularity of Zahavi's novel is that by focusing on a single character, it describes a process of building political consciousness without the involvement of a collective, which repoliticizes individual experiences. Apart from the Iranian clairvoyant she meets by chance and who represents Bella's inner life, no one else is involved in the change of viewpoint occurring within Bella herself. Bella liberates herself alone. Helen Zahavi explores a familiar *topos* of feminist theory: the politicization of lived experiences of domination and the construction of a revolutionary political subject. For Bella, political subjectivation entails a singular, intimate, and phenomenal process: Bella is not part of a collective movement or even of a *political subject* (there is no "We women . . ."), and she creates chaos at the heart of a dominant scheme. To put it differently, she brutalizes oppressors/aggressors so that they see and feel and experience in their flesh what it means to *get acquainted* with another viewpoint, to be an outsider, ignored, erased, and, by definition, obscene. It must be recognized that for victims of violence, building political consciousness is not always the result of a collective effort, since it is likely that for most of them, no collectivity is possible—the collective doesn't walk you to your door or follow you to the bedroom. This means there are some kinds of domination that properly de-realize people's lived experience, existences, and bodies, that properly exclude individuals from the very possibility of constructing a world in common with others, or that only intermittently allow the creation of worlds in common. Bella is alone; she is alone in her home and experiencing harassment with no one to talk to or ask for help. She is not engaged in self-defense by choice, but out of pure necessity.

Through Bella, Zahavi speaks to the others—to the men, the *hunters*. She wants them to enter into Bella's world. Her project is thus akin to a brutal pedagogy: *what is it like to be a woman?* This is not a game. It doesn't end with the conventional apologies and profuse regrets. It is a political revolution, and what's more, it is an ideological revolution: think like prey, live like Bella, suffocate as she does, feel, move about, sweat, shiver, and disappear the way she does:

> Let them quake when we walk behind them. Let them quicken their steps, and hunch their shoulders, and hurry home in the dusk. Scurry home, dogs. Avert your eyes as we pass. Let fear creep up and whisper in your ear . . .
> Swill-fed pigs. Sniveling toads. Syphilitic scum. Nothing you were and nothing you shall be. The dust in my eye. The shit on my shoes . . .[42]

At first, the hunters fail to understand, because such an encounter is literally incomprehensible.[43] They turn a blind eye and a deaf ear and they sit tight in their positions: *they do not disarm*.[44] The following formulation holds true for every hegemonic position, not just for the issue of gender:

> Indeed, there is no polite way of asking, and that has been clear for quite some time. And since we cannot ask for it, we need to strike first.[45]
>
> . . .
>
> You can't expect them to tread softly, like a Bella. You can't expect them to hesitate when every building, every patch of grass, every dim-lit street, every station, every subway, every blind alley belongs to them and they can enter if they wish. You can't expect them to feel like a Bella, who felt like a trespasser in her own home.[46]

Zahavi's novel can serve as a basis for theorizing what we call "dirty care"—a negative form of care. Building on the phenomenology of prey, it is possible to trace a different genealogy of the ethics generally ascribed to women, those in marginalized positions, and minority groups. It is the ethics around the tendency to consider others, to pay attention to them and take care of them, to take responsibility for them—to care, in short. This has been theorized in a current of feminist philosophy not as, of course, something women are predisposed to by nature, but as the historical product of the way groups in a minority position are disproportionately assigned to reproductive tasks. It is as much a product of the sexual and racial division of domestic labor as it is of its liberalization (which resulted in the emergence of the caring professions). Historicizing this division of labor has made it possible to demonstrate the relationship to the world it implies, its ethical implications, and the moral attitudes it produces, and to define them as the acts of attention to others that establish a morality of care.[47]

Our goal is to supplement these analyses from a different genealogy. Our hypothesis is as follows: concern for others arises within and by means of violence, and it generates an ethical position quite different from affective proximity, love, and compassionate attention, or abnegation in the most demanding forms of care (although such care can give rise to negative emotions for those who provide it, these will always be a combination of desire and repulsion).[48] Enduring violence generates a negative cognitive and emotional attitude that determines the individuals who experience it as always on the lookout, paying close attention to the world and to others. They live in a state of "radical anxiety," and it is exhausting to have to deny, minimize, defuse, endure, reduce, and avoid violence, to have to seek shelter, protect yourself, defend yourself.[49] This means developing a series of rationalizations in order to understand others and to make your own actions seem reasonable and normal, for instance movements, attitudes, and actions deployed to avoid irritating others or to not encourage or trigger their violence. It also means living with the affects and emotions (which, although nearly imperceptible, are constant) and getting used to their violence, desensitizing yourself and accepting it.

"Concern for others" here has nothing to do with *doing* something to help, care for, comfort, reassure or protect them; rather, we are concerned for others in order to anticipate what they want, will, or can *do to us*—which might devalue, exhaust, insult, isolate, injure, worry, deny, frighten, or de-realize us.

This kind of attention paid to others does not a priori presume any kind of attachment, closeness, or commitment—it is very much occurring under duress.[50] Such attention could just as well be described as a long labor of denial, avoidance, and defusing; it is also a way of maintaining distance (maintaining safety), of fleeing, or even of preparing for conflict, for combat. This understanding of attention is the defining characteristic of dirty care, and it allows us to identify two more major elements. Firstly, the kind of attention required of the dominated consists of always projecting yourself onto the intentions of others, melting into their representations as a way of defending yourself. This is a product of the dominated's knowledge—their incredibly in-depth knowledge—of the dominant groups. However, their meticulous objectification of the other and the necessity of making others the object of their attention, knowledge, and care is far from a sign of the subject of knowledge's epistemic privilege. Rather, it grants the object disproportionate power. The object becomes the center of the world, and the subject apprehends it from *nowhere*. The subject of knowledge orbits around this focal point. In this case, the subject of knowledge does not occupy a hegemonic position, a position looking down from on high, or a position of authority within the knowledge process—subjects are in a position of heteronomy before their object-king. This can only occur because the object confuses itself with objective reality, and its point of view sets the tone for what is real.[51] The object dominates: its perspective totally subsumes that of the subject, its worldview wins out and its framework of intelligibility reigns supreme. Furthermore, the subjects' work in paying attention to their object is exhausting: the level of attention must be high to gain the knowledge needed for self-defense. This intense focus occurs continuously and without interruption, or almost. The need to be on the alert nearly every instant leads to exhaustion and prevents subjects of knowledge from paying any attention to themselves. Their own representations, impressions, desires, intentions, and emotions take the back seat, where they are treated as if they were doubtful, fantastic, false, trivial, insignificant. When the labor power put into this process of knowledge runs out, restoring it is a slow and painstaking process, requiring a level of self-denial that intensifies the derealization of one's own viewpoint and of the lived world. The usual framing of the ethics of care is missing this dark side, an ethics of powerlessness visible through all the effort spent to defend oneself, despite it all. In this negative sense, dirty care is the care we give to ourselves, or rather to our power of action, by becoming experts on others in order to save our own skin. Put differently, the ceaseless effort to know others as well as possible in an attempt to defend ourselves from what they might do to us is a technology of power that manifests through the production of ignorance—and not ignorance of ourselves but of our power of action, which *we* come to see as alien and alienated. Authentically modest witnesses, submissive, drained, and docile, the dominated are assigned a cognitive relation and alienating gnoseological labor.[52] They develop knowledge about the dominant, which constitutes an archive of the ways the dominant are phenomenally and ideologically all-powerful.

Secondly, what about the "object-king"? In all the literature concerning what might be called the collection of "epistemic injustices," there are numerous works dealing with dominant knowledge and epistemic privilege.[53] In this field, the elaboration and study of the concept of *agnotology* have shown that positions of hegemonic power bring about the active production of ignorance.[54] This production is complex and involves the negation of outside viewpoints, the universalization of a situated viewpoint that is considered reality itself (the real *in itself*), and incorrect or biased processes of perception (or blindness). It involves myths, dispossession of knowledge, and denial, as well as socially centered criteria for scientific admissibility, authority, and credibility. And it also involves a double standard in archival practices and principles of veridiction (that determine what is *worthy* of being preserved and memorized, what is objective, neutral, and scientific, what constitutes an event or a fact). As a consequence, the production of ignorance entails active amnesia, revisionism, scientific doxa, and ideological production, in the proper sense. Early feminist epistemologists laid out the concept of ignorance, and it constitutes a central theme in Black literature (which Charles W. Mills, in reference to Ralph Ellison's novel, called "epistemological novels") and in critical whiteness studies.[55] This concept makes clear the asymmetry between the cognitive and gnoseological exploitation of the dominated and the countless social and symbolic benefits it accrues for the dominant. In being ignorant, the dominant adopt a cognitive posture that stops them from truly seeing others, being concerned for them, taking them into account, and knowing or considering them. This allows the dominant to find more time for themselves: to get to know themselves, like themselves, listen to and cultivate themselves. By making themselves the sole object of attention and care, they give themselves more importance, weight, and space, thereby reproducing the material conditions that allow their domination to endure.

And yet, there is attention of a sort paid to the dominated. As the novel *Dirty Weekend* shows, the harassers, aggressors, and rapists depicted seem to be obsessed with hunting Bella, or any other rape-able body. Interpellated as hunters, the existence of a form of knowledge exclusive to hunting implies the dominant have a skill that should not be ignored: to know their prey *in a certain way*, for instance knowing their habits, territories, hiding places, and their defensive strengths and reserves . . .[56]

In his essay "Michel Tournier and World Without Others," Gilles Deleuze cites Tournier's book *Friday, or, The Other Island*:

> He discovered that for all of us the presence of other people is a powerful element of distraction, not only because they constantly break into our activities, but because the mere possibility of their doing so illumines a world of matters situated at the edge of our consciousness but capable at any moment of becoming its center.[57]

For the hunter, however, the world is without Others: there is no one beside me or behind me to inject another perspective into my own, no alterity to sustain the density of the real, defined as that which I do not perceive but which is perceived or perceptible only through the Other. If the Other is nothing more than prey that I chase, hunt, and capture, whether with my gaze or through the sights of a gun, and if reaching toward or touching the other means killing them, then the real has done away with the very category of possible. The Other is no longer a presence that brings me back to the "relativity of Others" (the non-known or non-perceived) and thus to everything that may exist outside of my own perception.[58] For the hunter, Bella's frightened face is not "the expression of a frightening possible world, or of something frightening in the world—something I do not yet see."[59] It is merely a sign that the hunt is drawing to a close. Bella, for her part, takes aim at no one. She has no one to follow, hunt, or capture. Still, though, Bella is on alert: the Other has also disappeared as a perspective and as a presence that reassures her of the existence of the real they both inhabit. The Other is an imminent threat, always a few steps behind her, ready to ravage her. For

Bella, this is a world in which anything can happen, a world that is always conspiring behind her back. It indicates a reality that threatens her and imposes itself on her, even if, at the expense of the actuality of her own perception, she does not see it herself, which puts her life in danger.

When prey start to hunt, they do not become hunters themselves. They are defending themselves out of necessity. Yet, as this world of predation generalizes, everyone is transformed into prey. This is the eradication of any kind of alterity, or rather, it means *enclosing the possible within an order defined by threat and danger*, and it is also the eradication of political conflictuality. *Dirty Weekend* is a tale of self-defense, and it allows us to grasp that the apparatus of power that distinguishes between those who hunt and those who are hunted is not seeking to impose a hunt of all against all. Rather, it seeks to reduce everyone to prey, diluting and invisibilizing relations of domination in a world made unlivable for everyone, but in which only some are killable and continue to be pursued.

On the evening of February 26, 2012, in Sanford, Florida, in a majority white neighborhood, Trayvon Martin, a seventeen-year-old African American teenager who had the hood pulled up on his sweater, had just left a store with a bag of candy in his pocket. He was on the phone with his girlfriend. George Zimmerman, a volunteer with the local neighborhood watch program, was nearby in his car and called the police.[60] He stated that a suspicious person who seemed to be high on drugs was walking through the neighborhood checking out houses. He was told to do nothing and to wait for police to arrive. From the testimonies of several neighbors, it seems that an altercation occurred between Zimmerman and Martin, with Zimmerman being much bigger and ten years older than the young high school student. When the police arrived, Zimmerman was bleeding from the nose and Trayvon had been shot in the chest, seemingly at point-blank range. After weeks of withholding information, the police finally provided the family and the media with the recording of the 911 call, which revealed there was a first shot fired (which seemingly missed or was fired as a warning), and then Trayvon can be heard pleading and crying, and then there was a second gunshot. Shortly after police arrived, witnesses came forward to say Zimmerman had fired a first shot for no reason while he was holding down the teenage boy, who was unable to flee or move and was pleading with his killer.

In the state of Florida, the laws governing legitimate defense are particularly loose and grant "immunity to people who act to protect themselves if they have *a reasonable fear* they will be killed or seriously injured."[61] State law thus gives wide latitude to any person to carry and use a weapon with impunity. The risk of killing others can be made legitimate by a *feeling* (one needs to reasonably feel threatened). Basing legitimate defense on *reasonable fear* is not, by definition, a sufficient criterion for determining where *legitimate defense* ends and *paranoid murder* begins. Zimmerman was questioned by police and released. Although the Sanford police could find no proof that Zimmerman reasonably felt threatened and acted in self-defense, he was not charged. Only after the demonstrations began that denounced this heinous, racist crime was an investigation of the crime as second-degree murder launched, leading to Zimmerman's arrest (he was immediately released on bail) two months after the event. The trial opened a year and a half later, in June 2013, and—despite a lack of proof to legitimate using the right to self-defense and despite the devastating witness statements and recordings—Zimmerman was acquitted. In the year before Trayvon Martin's murder, George Zimmerman had called the police forty-six times, regarding alarms going off, nuisance behavior, neighbor disputes, road rage, and, most commonly, the presence of a "suspicious person."[62]

George Zimmerman was a vigilante for the racial state. Trayvon Martin was defenseless against the threat of becoming, as a young African American man, killable prey in the name of legitimate defense. The political and legislative framework surrounding this murderer's acquittal is a sign of a technology of power that literally whitewashed Zimmerman on the basis of his own fear as prey. Fear as a projection thus leads to a world where the possible is mixed in with insecurity, and this fear now determines every good citizen as a potential murderer. This weapon allows an unprecedented emotional subjugation of bodies, and also a muscular government of individuals under tension, of *lives lived on the defensive.*

Acknowledgments

Author's Acknowledgments

A portion of the research that led to this book was supported by a grant from the Schomburg Center for Research in Black Culture, in New York, as well as by a grant from the Mellon Foundation that allowed me to teach and conduct research as part of the Critical Theory Department at the University of California, Berkeley. This book also owes its existence to the conversations, correspondence, and debates I've been fortunate enough to have over the years with colleagues, students, and friends, which formed a community for testing ideas. And finally, it was deeply inspired by the practices, ideas, and commitments I've shared within activist collectives and struggles. Conflictuality clearly also served as an incubator for the book's substance, despite the difficulties this entailed, but I would never have managed to bring it to a conclusion without the support of those listed here, to whom I express my sincere gratitude. Thanks to Oristelle Bonis and Carine Lorenzoni, Gael Potin, Kira Ribeiro, Nedjma Bouakra, Francesca Arena, Sarah Bracke, Nathalie Trussart, Elodie Kergoat, and Amanda Bay. Special thanks to Souen Fontaine, whose company, affection, and friendship I value so deeply.

I would like to thank Isabelle Clair, who was the first to read over this text and who, since 2013, has been at once my favorite partner for discussing ideas, a companion both in research and the struggle for feminist research, and a dear friend. Thanks as well to Judith Butler: the confidence, attention, and goodwill they showed toward me quite simply made this book possible. Finally, thanks to Grégoire Chamayou for his unfailing friendship that has grown no less intellectually and emotionally close with time.

Mwen, chabine, manda liv là sa a fanmi an-mwen Dorlin: a nous, Kimbe raid pas molli ...

Translator's Acknowledgments

This translation would not have been possible without the assistance of Cédrine Michel, who, although formally a consultant on this project, played a role much closer to that of co-translator. Cédrine and I would also like to thank Tammy Kovich for her assistance with research, and Jessie Kindig of Verso Books for her editorial support throughout.

Notes

Prologue: What a Body Can Do

1 Joseph Elzéar Morénas, *Précis historique de la traite des Noirs et de l'esclavage colonial* (Firmin Didot, 1828), 251–2. [Unless otherwise noted, translations of French sources are our own. —Trans.]
2 Michel Foucault, *Discipline and Punish*, trans. Alan Sheridan (Vintage Books, 1977).
3 Judith Butler, *Frames of War: When Is Life Grievable?* (Verso, 2009), 1.
4 See the introduction by Grégoire Chamayou in *Kubark: Le Manuel secret de manipulation mentale et de torture psychologique de la CIA*, trans. Émilien et Jean-Baptiste Bernard (Éditions Zones, 2012).
5 When he defines *life*, Georges Canguilhem notes that "life is not indifferent to the conditions in which it is possible," which defines *polarity* in its true sense: *life is polarity* and *life is a polarized activity*. See Georges Canguilhem, *The Normal and the Pathological*, trans. Carolyn Fawcett (Reidel, 1978), 70.
6 The video is 9 minutes 20 seconds long. It is available on YouTube.
7 These L.A. riots are not to be confused with the Watts Rebellion, which occurred in 1965. See Mike Davis, *Dead Cities* (Verso, 2006).
8 A second trial took place in Federal Court in February 1993, over the violation of Rodney King's civil rights, in which two police officers implicated in the beating were sentenced to thirty-two months of prison time (the other two were acquitted again). During the trial, the judges granted that the police officers had acted within the legal scope of their duties during the first few minutes of the arrest, arguing that the first wave of beatings was justified by King's recalcitrant attitude. It was only on account of the "useless" beatings that followed that the two were convicted.
9 See Seth Mydans, *New York Times*, March 10, 1993.
10 I am using this expression deliberately, since George Holliday is white; in reality, it would be necessary to enter into detailed

analysis of the mobilization of national and international "opinion" around the Rodney King case. What interests me here is the performative dimension of racial identity produced, among other things, by the courtroom and the temporality of the trial.

11 Judith Butler, "Endangered/Endangering: Schematic Racism and White Paranoia," in *Reading Rodney King/Reading Urban Uprising*, ed. Robert Gooding-Williams (Routledge, 1993), 15.
12 Butler, "Endangered/Endangering," 16.
13 For example, in a study published in the *Journal of Health and Social Behavior* in 2005, the authors attempt to demonstrate on the basis of clinical research that African Americans feel more anger than whites, and have fewer resources to manage their emotions in "socially acceptable" ways. Such publications are part of a broader and continuously renewed production of racist knowledge, particularly in psychopathology, psychology, and psychosociology. J. Beth Mabry and K. Jill Kiekolt, "Anger in Black and White: Race, Alienation, and Anger," *Journal of Health and Social Behavior* 46, no. 1 (2005): 85–101.
14 Butler, "Endangered/Endangering," 20.
15 Ibid., 16.
16 The ontological status of evidence in the judicial system is a narrative construction. This becomes only truer wherever visual evidence is being considered as the record of a fact. They do not allow us to immediately grasp a truth but rather the manifestation of what is perceived as visible, sayable, and therefore a legitimate form of evidence. The judicial field offers a particularly rich terrain of investigation into gnoseological constructions of perception (schematizations) through sociohistorical definitions. This hermeneutics is less about constructing evidence piece by piece than it is about deciding what counts as legally "objective" evidence. This process also drapes itself in the claim of being guided solely by the "naked truth" of facts. See Kimberlé Crenshaw and Gary Peller, "Reel Time/Real Justice," in Gooding-Williams, *Reading Rodney King/Reading Urban Uprising*, 56–70.
17 Ibid., 61. The authors describe a narrative technique of "disaggregation."
18 Butler, "Endangered/Endangering," 20.
19 "Total control" and "dangerous intent" were the terms used by the police officers during their hearings at the first trial. "Attributing violence to the object of violence is part of the very mechanism that recapitulates violence, and that makes the jury's 'seeing' into a complicity with that police violence." Ibid., 20.

The Production of Disarmed Bodies

1. The distinction between a weapon and an improvised weapon is that the former was designed to harm or kill, while the latter is an object used in this way, although this is not the primary function. In the case of France, the legal distinction is laid out in article 132–75 of *Le Code pénal* (the Criminal code).
2. Synod of Mans, 1045. "And no one but armed chevaliers and their servants will be permitted to bear arms, with swords reserved for chevaliers and with simple cudgels for their servants, who like others must enjoy security." Romain Wenz, "'À armes notables et invasibles': Qu'est-ce qu'être armé dans le royaume de France à la fin du Moyen Âge," *Revue historique* 671 (2014): 549. See also Pascal Brioist, Hervé Drévillon, and Pierre Serna, *Croiser le fer: Violence et culture de l'épée dans la France moderne* (Éditions Champ Vallon, 2008).
3. Romain Wenz observes that the legal concept of "bearing arms" originates in the Code of Justinian, which regulated the production and trade of weapons and was taken up in a slightly modified form at the end of the Middle Ages. At this time, groups of armed individuals were the principal targets, following royal proclamations in the thirteenth century intended to limit violence between subjects by reinstating the *quarantaine-le-roi* (King's Quarantine, a forty-day period of reflection instituted by Philippe Auguste, also known as Philip Augustus, in the event of private wars or conflicts, which Louis IX reinstated in 1245) as part of the banning of wars between nobles. Gradually, it meant that to "go armed" became a specified and documented fact. See Wenz, "À armes notables et invasibles," 551.
4. Established and formalized in 1260, this ban was also written into a 1311 ordinance and should be considered in relation to the laws banning wars, duels, and tournaments.
5. Infractions were punishable by fines: sixty pounds for nobles, sixty sous for others. Wenz describes these amounts as being linked to both ability to pay and the risk presented to the king himself, whose authority is significantly more threatened by expeditions of armed nobles than by a gathering of commoners. See Wenz, "À armes notables et invasibles," 553.
6. Ibid., 554.
7. André Corvisier and John Charles Roger Childs, *A Dictionary of Military History and the Art of War* (Blackwell, 1994), s.v. "weapons."
8. Ibid.

9 "Apart from officers, nobles, and those under our orders," subjects were forbidden by an edict published on November 25, 1487, to carry "bows, crossbows, halberds, spears, voulges, daggers, or other offensive weapons." Wenz, "À armes notables et invisables," 557. For more on the subject of elite armed forces formed to engage in war and protect the king's person, as formalized under Louis XIII, see Rémi Masson, *Défendre le roi: La maison militaire au XVIIe siècle* (Éditions Champ Vallon, 2017).

10 Wenz, "À armes notables et invisables," 562. Weapons were considered "invisible" if they were carried in anticipation of a confrontation: "The expression literally means 'attacking weapons' and must be understood as a judicial construct joining two previously distinct crimes: *portatio armorum* and *invasio cum armis*." It would soon by replaced by the term "prohibited weapons." Ibid., 564.

11 Ibid., 564.

12 For the duelists, what is at stake is the restoration of their honor by means of a ritual that lets them continue producing virility: such a face-off could only occur between peers (a community of equals, which is simply the community of *virs*). The goal was not to deconstruct a relationship of domination but rather to reaffirm the community of men of honor—the loser still "saved" his honor by showing he had the courage to show up to the site of a duel. See François Guillet, *La Mort en face: Histoire du duel de la Révolution à nos jours* (Aubier, 2008). Robert Nye, *Masculinity and the Male Code of Honor in Modern France* (Oxford University Press, 1993).

13 Noble women could take advantage of a similar privilege, even though weapons and martial training for women remained unorthodox, if not exceptional, as the figures of the Princess of Montpensier and of the women who participated in the League and then in the Fronde show. See Éliane Viennot, "Les femmes dans les 'troubles' du XVIe siècle," *Clio* 5 (1997); Nicolas Le Roux, "Justice, Justice, Justice, au nom de Jésus-Christ: Les princesses de la Ligue, le devoir de vengeance et l'honneur de la maison de Guise," in *Femmes et pouvoir et pouvoir des femmes dans l'Occident médiéval et moderne*, ed. A. Nayt-Dubois and E. Santinelli-Foltz (Presses universitaires de Valenciennes, 2009), 439–58; Sophie Vergnes, "La duchesse de Longueville et ses frères pendant la Fronde: de la solidarité fraternelle à l'émancipation féminine," *XVIIe siècle* 2, no. 251 (2011): 309–32.

14 In *The Book of the Courtier* (1528) by Balthazar Castiglione, the perfect courtier is described as a master of all sidearms, trained for combat.

NOTES TO PAGES 4 TO 7

15 An edict of Henri XV forbade pages, lackeys, students, and clerks to carry a sword, since these categories did not have any "civil responsibilities." Brioist, Drévillon, and Serna, *Croiser le fer*, 45. The first light firearms appeared in the first quarter of the fourteenth century, with the arquebus invented in 1425. The musket appeared a hundred years later, in 1525, and its mechanism steadily improved over the decades following.

16 Robert Muchembled and Jean Birrell. *A History of Violence: From the End of the Middle Ages to the Present* (Polity Press, 2012), 301. See also Norbert Elias, *The Civilizing Process*, vol. 1, *The History of Manners* (Blackwell Publishing, 1969).

17 The first fencing school in Europe opened in Bologna in 1413.

18 See Achille Marozzo, *Opera nova chiamata duello, o vero fiore dell'armi*, 1536.

19 The foil is one of the first of what could be called training weapons: a sword fitted with a button that allows blows to be landed without causing injury. See Pierre Lacaze, *En garde: du duel à l'escrime* (Gallimard, 1991).

20 Egerton Castle, *Schools and Masters of Fencing: From the Middle Ages to the Eighteenth Century* (George Bell and Sons, 1885), 46.

21 Norbert Elias and Eric Dunning, *Quest for Excitement: Sport and Leisure in the Civilizing Process* (Blackwell Publishing, 1994). Benoît Gaudin notes as well that high kicks (aimed at the plexus, shoulders, or head) were introduced into French kickboxing as the bourgeois class entered the training halls and gradually appropriated these techniques. Citing Georges Vigarello, he points out that "high movements and the aerial element have long been exclusive to the nobility," although such movements are not very effective as defensive techniques. See Benoît Gaudin, "La codification des pratiques martiales: Une approche socio-historique," *Actes de la recherche en sciences sociales* 179 (2009): 26; and Georges Vigarello, *Une Histoire culturelle des sports, techniques d'hier et d'aujourd'hui* (Robert Laffont, 1988).

22 Louis Sala-Molins, *Le Code noir ou le calvaire de Canaan* (PUF, 1987), 20.

23 From the *Ordenanzas* of Santo Domingo, 1768. Reproduced in Manuel Lucena Salmoral, *Les Codes noirs hispaniques* (Paris, UNESCO, 2004). Regarding the criminalization of weapons, see p. 260. Regarding the length of machetes, see p. 269.

24 Ibid., 115. This shows two different modalities of the process of racialization: in the Spanish part of Hispaniola, the colonial administration granted mixed-race persons a relative privilege by creating an intermediary class distinct from "Negros" using legislation about access to weapons, which also assured the

administration of their loyalty. By contrast, in the French part of the island, although slave laws connected race to the condition of slavery until the end of the 1750s, several decrees were issued to draw a clear, discriminatory color line through the "free" population: they forbade, for instance, freed slaves and free people of color to "carry a machete (1758) or a sword (1761)." In the same period, such people were banned from "buying or selling of gunpowder or munitions without the authorization of the governor"; they were barred from certain professions, posts, and ranks (priesthood, nobility, medicine, surgery, and officership in the military) and were also forbidden to have a white name (they were forced to take on an African last name) or to be called Sir or Madam. See Dominique Rogers, "Raciser la société: Un projet administratif pour une société domingoise complexe (1760–1791)," *Journal de la Société des Américanistes* 2, no. 95 (2009): 235–60.

25 Norma R. Yetman, ed., *Voices from Slavery: 100 Authentic Slave Narratives* (Holt, Rinehart and Winston, 1970), 149.

26 This right was coupled with a strict ban on native people carrying weapons. See Édouard Sautayra, *Législation de l'Algérie* (Maisonneuve & Cie, 1883), 26. From the order issued by the governor-general on December 11, 1872, cited in Olivier Le Cour Grandmaison, *Coloniser, exterminer: Sur la guerre de l'État colonial* (Fayard, 2005), 260.

27 From the first article of the order issued on December 11, 1872, cited in Olivier Le Cour Grandmaison, *De l'Indigénat: Anatomie d'un "monstre" juridique: le droit colonial en Algérie et dans l'Empire français* (Zones éditions, 2010). Section IV, "Code(s) de l'indigénat: 'code(s) matraque(s).'"

28 Similarly, in August 1777, a "Black police" was established in France by a royal decree: "We have been informed that the number of Blacks here [in France] has grown to such a degree, due to the ease of travel between France and the Americas, that each day we are depriving the colonies of a portion of the men necessary for agriculture. At the same time, their presence in our kingdom's cities, especially in the capital, is causing tremendous disorder. Furthermore, once they return to the colonies, they bring with them an independent and restless attitude that makes them more trouble than they are worth." All Black people were thereby banned from coming to France, and settlers were permitted to bring only one slave back as a personal servant, who must be billeted at their port of arrival. Free people of color had to obtain a "certificate of presence" by declaring themselves to the admiral upon arrival. "Déclaration pour la police des noirs," Versailles,

August 9, 1777. The full text of the declaration is available in French at staraco.univ-nantes.fr. The same system of passes was established in Algeria in 1897. Olivier Le Cour Grandmaison notes that in 1871, a system of *livrets ouvriers* (workers' passports) was established in metropolitan France, and this would become a major tool used to control the working class. It was abolished in 1890. See Grandmaison, *Coloniser, exterminer*, 255. See also Robert Castel, *From Manual Workers to Wage Laborers: Transformation of the Social Question* (Routledge, 2017); and John Torpey, *The Invention of the Passport: Surveillance, Citizenship and the State* (Cambridge University Press, 2009).

29 Sala-Molins, *Le Code noir*, 122.

30 The Black Code forbade slaves to vend in markets, notably due to fears of poisoning. See Caroline Oudin-Bastide, *L'Effroi et la terreur: Esclavage, poison et sorcellerie aux Antilles* (La Découverte, 2013).

31 The Count of Elva to the Marquis of Fénélon, August 5, 1763, Archives nationales d'outre mer, Collection 84 66, fol. 334. Cited in Jean-Pierre Sainton et al., *Histoire et civilization de la Caraïbe*, vol. 2 (Éditions Karthala, 2012), 326–7.

32 "Recently in Martinique, thirteen Black people were put to death, including some who were only fifteen years old; the decision indicated that they tried to escape." Joseph Elzéar Morénas, *Précis historique de la traite des Noirs et de l'esclavage colonial* (Éditions Firmin Didot, 1828), 89. Also relevant is this case from November 30, 1828: "One person named Élisée and ten of his fellows were sentenced to death for having, in attempting to escape, sought to rob their masters of their value." Elisée's mother, Agnès, was forced to attend the execution before being imprisoned for not turning her son over to the authorities and for having fed him while he was in hiding. Remember that throughout the slavery era, the conditions were such that settlers had no incentive to preserve the value represented by their slaves: while the price of slaves was around £1,700 to £2,000 at the end of the eighteenth century, the courts paid £2,000 per "head of Negro executed" to their owner as compensation. On slave resistance and its repression, see Elsa Dorlin, "Les Espaces-temps des résistances esclaves: Des suicidés de Saint-Jean aux marrons de Nanny Town," *Tumultes* 27 (2006): 11–16.

33 Morénas, *Précis historique*, 89.

34 Ibid. As well, as part of the systematic negation of "the right of self-preservation," the institution of slavery forbade slaves *to care for* themselves. They were forbidden to defend their bodies from disease through the criminalization of health care practices: the

use of plants and self-medication, preparing remedies, caring for the sick (see the February 1, 1743, ordnance). With thanks to Hourya Benthouhami-Molino for drawing my attention to this text, see Samir Boumediene, *La Colonisation du savoir: Une histoire des plantes médicinales du Nouveau Monde 1492–1750* (Des Mondes à faire, 2016). See as well Londa Schiebinger, *Plants and Empire: Colonial Bioprospecting in the Atlantic World* (Harvard University Press, 2017).

35 This derogatory form of justice was strengthened through the establishment of a provost tribunal (a temporary criminal court with no right of appeal) under the Restoration in 1815, in order to judge so-called political crimes in Martinique. It sentenced hundreds of slaves and free people of color to decapitation on suspicion of poisoning between 1822 and 1827. Joseph Elézar Morénas notes that this allowed slaves to be arrested, sentenced, and punished on the same morning. Many slave owners made use of this process to get rid of elderly slaves, whom they would accuse of poisonings in order to receive financial compensation. See Morénas, *Précis historique*, 322.

36 Sala-Molins, *Le Code noir*, 176.

37 Ibid., 319.

38 Ibid., 322.

39 Hourya Bentouhami, in her as yet unpublished research, uses the heuristic concept of "the double" in her discussion of the broader ontological status of subjugated, racialized, and dominated subjectivities. I'm grateful to her for her kindness in allowing me to read over her manuscript. [See Hourya Bentouhami, "Notes pour un féminisme marron: Du corps-doublure au corps propre," *Comment s'en sortir?* 5 (2017): 108–25. —Trans.]

40 "The *Indigénat* system, framed as a set of legal exceptions, shouldn't be understood as existing outside of the judicial norm in metropolitan France and should be seen in the context that created it: the French state and the nation ... This is one of the major contributions made by some recent work on the colonial state that tried to shed light on the tensions and contradictions that came along with the expansion of metropolitan states as they became imperial ... These new perspectives, first developed on the other side of the Atlantic, emphasize ... continuity, and consider the colonies not as special cases, but as one extreme of a spectrum." Isabelle Merle, "De la 'légalisation' de la violence en contexte colonial: Le régime de l'indigénat en question," *Politix* 17, no. 66 (2004): 140.

41 Regarding the head tax, it was imposed in the colonies at the end of the nineteenth century and referred to a personal tax each

colonized person had to pay to the French state as a financial contribution to France's colonial project (described as the "development" of the colony and its resources, and "access to infrastructure," "peace," and "colonial protection"). See also Catherine Coquery-Vidrovitch, *L'Afrique occidentale au temps des Français: Colonisateurs et colonisés* (La Découverte, 1992), 108. The list of offenses is cited in Merle, "Légalisation de la violence," 105. In her treatment of Algeria, Isabelle Merle distinguishes between, on the one hand, the exorbitant "high-policing" power held by the administrative authorities (the governor) to deal with actions they considered serious or threatening to public safety, without the need to define these acts in advance, and on the other hand, "practices of 'community-based repression' and 'low policing,' which was the responsibility of the administration's lower-ranking agents," based on an unending list of crimes and infractions (ibid., 147). An 1881 decree extended the *Indigénat* to Cochinchina (southern Vietnam), New Caledonia, and the territories of French West Africa. These special infractions were the subject of criticisms—including by the inspectors sent to assess the colonial administration, notably the mission led by Fillon and Revel (New Caledonia, 1907), which was a crucial source for Merle's research. See as well the critiques emerging from anticolonial works, such as *L'Indigénat: Code de l'esclavage* (Petite bibliothèque de l'Internationale syndicale rouge, 1928).

42 Olivier Le Cour Grandmaison describes a category he calls the *sacer*: "For the French, regardless of their status, their person and their property were considered sacred, in its sense of 'untouchable,' since *sacer* refers to a person who will make unclean anyone who touches them. Any physical or symbolic threat made against them would be immediately punished using derogatory measures that allowed for specific and particularly harsh punishments." Grandmaison, *Coloniser, exterminer*, 261. To further demonstrate his point, he also cites a text by Sautayra (*Législation de l'Algérie*, 269) that lays out the "disrespectful (actions) and offensive words directed toward representatives or agents of the state, even while not exercising their functions ... Rackets, raucous scenes, arguments and other disorderly acts, especially in the marketplace, that are not sufficiently serious to constitute crimes ... Public speaking with the goal of weakening respect for authority" (ibid., 253). Sautayra, *Législation de l'Algérie*, 269.

43 "Confronted with a world configured, the colonized subject is always presumed guilty. The colonized does not accept his guilt, but rather considers it a kind of curse, a sword of Damocles."

Franz Fanon, *The Wretched of the Earth*, trans. Richard Philcox (Grove Press, 2005), 16.
44   Fanon, *The Wretched of the Earth*, 15. See as well "The work of the colonist is to make even dreams of liberty impossible for the colonized. The work of the colonized is to imagine every possible method for annihilating the colonist." Ibid., 50.
45   Ibid., 19.
46   Ibid., 16.
47   See Elsa Dorlin, "To Be Beside of Oneself: Fanon and the Phenomenology of Our Own Violence," *South as a State of Mind* 3 (2016): 40–7.
48   Fanon, *The Wretched of the Earth*, 16.
49   Ibid., 17.
50   Ibid., "Magical superstructure" (18); "Ecstasy of dance" (19).
51   "Slaves belonging to different masters are also forbidden to gather by day or by night, for weddings or any other reason, whether on their master's property or elsewhere, and especially not on the roads or in remote locations." Sala-Molins, *Le Code noir*, 122.
52   Although music was outlawed by the Black Code in the seventeenth century, rules regarding gatherings, dancing, and music depended on the discretion of residents and so varied by territory. In Guadeloupe, for instance, Article 16 was seldom enforced. See Luciani Lanoir L'Étang, "Des rassemblements d'esclaves aux confréries noires," *Bulletin de la Société d'histoire de la Guadeloupe* 152 (2009): 3–14.
53   Jean-Baptiste Labat, *Nouveaux voyages aux Isles françoises de l'Amérique*, vol. 4 (Cavalier, 1722): 153–4. [Jean-Baptiste Labat's travel memoirs have been published in English only in an abridged form that does not include this section. See Jean-Baptiste Labat, *The Memoirs of Père Labat: 1693–1705*, trans. John Eaden (Routledge, 1970). —Trans.] See also Médéric Louis Élie Moreau de Saint-Méry, *Danse* (self-published, 1796): "When one has not seen this dance, one would hardly believe how lively and animated it is, and how much grace it derives from the strictness with which the musical rhythm is followed. The dancers replace one another without respite, and the negroes are so intoxicated with pleasure, that it is necessary to force them to conclude dances of this sort, called Kalendas." Quoted in Lilian Moore, "Moreau de Saint-Méry and 'Danse,'" *Dance Index* 5 (1946): 238.
54   This was the case in Louisiana, Guyana, and Haiti (where it was also known as the *chica* in the Saint-Domingue era), as well as in Martinique and Guadeloupe. See André Thibault, ed., *Le français dans les Antilles: Études linguistiques* (L'Harmattan, 2011), 38. Similarly, in Madagascar, Mayotte, and Réunion, there was the

moringue (or *moraingy*), a martial dance built around acrobatic movements, kicks, and wrestling techniques. Although it disappeared in the 1950s, its practice was revived in the 1990s. See Jean-René Dreinaza, *Techniques et apprentissage du moring réunionnais* (Comité Réunionnais de Moring, 2000). Guillaume Samson, Benjamin Lagarde, and Carpanin Marimoutou, *L'Univers du maloya: Histoire, ethnographie, littérature* (Océan éditions/DREOI, 2008).

55 For details on bamboulas, see Jacqueline Rosemain, *La musique dans la société antillaise 1635-1902 en Martinique et Guadeloupe* (L'Harmattan, 1986); and Jacqueline Rosemain, *La danse aux Antilles: Des rhytmes sacrés au zouk* (L'Harmattan, 1990). Bamboulas were sometimes even encouraged by white people to promote "the drunkenness and debauchery of negroes," with the goal of growing their "herd." Lanoir L'Étang, "Des rassemblements d'esclaves aux confréries noires," 6.

56 For the Indigenous connection, calendas notably incorporated Native American sacred objects, such as amulets found on the ground by slaves during their work. See Odette Mennesson-Rigaud, "Le rôle du vaudou dans l'indépendance d'Haïti," *Présence Africaine* 18-19 (1958): 43-67.

57 This list of practices is drawn from Thomas J. Desh-Obi, *Fighting for Honor: The African Martial Art Traditions in the Atlantic World* (University of South California Press, 2008), 132. In regard to the danmyé ladja, there is the film *Ag'ya*, a study of *biguine* and danmyé ladja by the African American dancer, choreographer, and anthropologist Katherine Dunham (1909-2006), who made it during a trip to Haiti, Jamaica, and Martinique in 1936. She developed a choreography called *Ag'ya* in 1938 that was danced for the first time in Chicago. It was last viewed by the author in July 2016 on YouTube, under the title *Ag'ya Danmye Ladja Compilation* and posted by the account Capoeira Science. For more on the moringue, see André-Jean Benoît, *Sport colonial: Une histoire des exercices physiques dans les colonies de peuplement de l'océan Indien, la Réunion, Maurice, des origins à la fin de la Seconde Guerre mondiale* (L'Harmattan, 2000). In his work, Thomas A. Green includes the following in his list of unarmed combat techniques among people of African origins: *mani* (Cuba), *chat'Ou* (Guadeloupe), *ladjiya* (Martinique), *pingé* (Haiti), *congo* (Central America), capoeira (Brazil), *broma* (Venezuela), and *susa* (Suriname). Thomas A. Green. "Surviving the Middle Passage: Traditional African Martial Arts in the Americas," in *Martial Arts in the Modern World*, ed. Thomas A. Green and Joseph R. Svinth (Praeger, 2003), 129. In the United States, the *juba*, a martial

dance and musical form among slaves, frightened and fascinated white people with its rapid leg movements. See Saidiya V. Hartman, *Scenes of Subjection* (Oxford University Press, 1993).

58 Although capoeira is well studied, this is much less true of the Caribbean martial arts, with the exception of the moringue and the danmyé. Concerning the latter, we have the excellent work done by Pierre Drus under the direction of Gerry L'Étang: Pierre Drus, *Aux sources du danmyé: Le wolo et la ladja* (Université des Antilles Guyane, 2011). There is also his contribution to the organization AM4, available at am4.fr.

59 Richard Burton provides an analysis of the tension between oppositional cultures and political resistance, drawing on various cultural spheres (such as Haitian Voodoo and Jamaican Rastafarianism), arguing that cultural forms are a substitute for resistance, as resistance is impossible. Cultural opposition manages to threaten power structures while also offering a means of self-defense and permanent resistance. See Richard D. E. Burton, *Afro-Creole: Power, Opposition and Play in the Caribbean* (Cornell University Press, 1997), 263–5. See also Christine Chivallon, "Créolisation universelle ou singulière?" *L'Homme* 3, no. 207–8 (2013): 37–74.

60 For "perfect legacy" (*legs idéal*), see Thierry Nicolas, "Politique patrimoniale et 'patrimonialisation' aux Antilles françaises," *Techniques and Cultures* 42 (2003): 131–40. Capoeira is the classic example, probably the most well-documented practice of its kind at this time. See Maya Talmon-Chvaicer, *The Hidden History of Capoeira: A Collision of Cultures in the Brazilian Battle Dance* (University of Texas Press, 2008). See also Benoît Gaudin, "Capoeira et nationalisme," *Cahiers du Brésil contemporain* (EHESS, 2009). Benoît Gaudin, "Les maîtres de capoeira et le marché de l'enseignement," *Actes de la recherche en sciences sociales* 179 (2009): 52–61.

61 See Julian Harris Gerstin, "Traditional Music in a New Social Movement: The Renewal of Bèlè in Martinique (French West Indies)," doctoral thesis, University of California, 1996.

62 In the Caribbean and Brazil, there are techniques resembling *n'golo*, a traditional West African martial art, and Senegalese wrestling, *làmb,* although it remains difficult to establish the link. See Yvonne Daniel, *Caribbean and Atlantic Diaspora Dance: Igniting Citizenship* (University of Illinois Press, 2011), 162. Talmon-Chvaicer, *The Hidden History of Capoeira*, 19.

63 Chivallon, "Créolisation universelle ou singulière?," 54.

64 Pierre Dru provides a precise analysis of this point in his work on the danmyé published on lesperipheriques.org. The same idea is

present in capoeira as *malandragem*, which refers to all the "tricks" developed by practitioners to survive under wretched conditions. During combat itself, the malandragem refers to "the way misdirection, shrewdness, and trickery allow for victory using the art of the feint, by means of deception, rather than by strength." Adriana Albert Dias, *Mandinga, Manha and Malicia: Una historia sobre os capoeiras na capital da Bahia 1910–1925* (EDUFBA, 2006), 18. Cited in Monica Aceti, "Des imaginaires en controverse dans la pratique de la capoeira: Loisir, 'métier' et patrimoine culturel immatériel," *STAPS* 1, no. 87 (2010): 109–24. [Aceti provided a French translation of Dias, on which the present English translation was based. —Trans.]

65 In particular, the martial dance *ladja* involves magic that allows fighters to build their strength—*achté un pwen*.

66 Médéric Louis-Élie Moreau de Saint-Méry, *La Description topographique, physique, civile, politique et historique de la partie française de Saint-Domingue*, vol. 1 (1797–1798). Reproduced in *Société Française d'Histoire d'outre-mer* (2004): 64.

67 The Haitian Revolution made Voodoo a key ingredient in the narrative around slave liberation, with one example being the Bois Caïman ceremony on August 14, 1791, where the main actors in the future insurrection apparently made a "blood pact" that has since become part of the Haitian national myth. However, the importance of Voodoo in the Haitian Revolution is still a subject of debate. In 1958, Odette Rigaud wrote, "Here we find one of the most peculiar phenomena in the history of Haiti, despite the importance of the social experiment carried out by Markandal, Biassou, Dessalines and Toussaint-Louverture and of occult knowledge, the negroes were not brought to independence by any man, but rather by an occult flame from which the greatest and purest of Haitian heroes was born: the religious fervor inspired by African Voodoo in the negroes of Saint-Domingue. This was, in practical terms, the most effective of all the weapons used during what are called the wars of Independence." Odette Menesson-Rigaud, "À propos du vaudou," *Bulletin du bureau d'Ethnologie* 3, no. 16 (1958). Cited in Menesson-Rigaud, "Le rôle du vaudou dans l'indépendance d'Haïti," 56. Her position was criticized by the historian Gabriel Debien, who maintained there was insufficient proof to conclude the existence of a Voodoo culture common to all slaves touched by creolization. Gabriel Debien, "Les travaux d'histoire sur Saint-Domingue, chronique bibliographique (1957 et 1958)," *Revue française d'histoire d'outre-mer* 47, no. 167 (1960): 257. For more on Voodoo in

Saint-Domingue, see Pierre Pluchon, *Vaudou, sorciers, empoisonneurs: De Saint-Domingue à Haïti* (Karthala, 1987); David Geggus, "Marronage, Voodoo, and the Saint Domingue Slave Revolt of 1791," *Proceedings of the Meeting of the French Colonial Historical Society*, vol. 15 (1992): 22–35; and Laurent Dubois, *Avengers of the New World: The Story of the Haitian Revolution* (Harvard University Press, 2005).

68 For an example of this attitude as it concerns the martial practices of other colonized peoples, see Olivier P. Nguema Akwe's section on *mesing*, a martial art that combines wrestling and sorcery, practiced by the Fang warriors (modern-day Gabon) against the French army. In the early twentieth century, Colonel Wobert spoke of "defensive sorcery." Olivier P. Nguema Akwe, *Sorcellerie et arts martiaux en Afrique* (L'Harmattan, 2011), 70. Another example is the Boxer Rebellion in China at the end of the 1890s, which emerged from a long tradition of secret societies. The movement was organized in mixed groups with the goal of expelling the Manchus and westerners from China, and it used a self-defense system based on boxing and magic. In 1910, Jean-Jacques Matignon, a French army doctor, described this "sacred boxing": "Their movements are accompanied by incantations, chanted wailing, and strange movements acting on energy. They are truly as if possessed, as though under the ecstatic effect of some euphoric drug. They invoke the support of Chen Wu, the god of magic, and Kuan Ti, the patron of armed groups. Many of them are only teenagers, or even children, boys and girls, some of whom must be only twelve years old. Those are the worst of them. If these would-be boxers had kept to their dance and kickboxing training, their actions would have only been of interest to a future history of sports. The bothersome part is they also represent the awakening of a new Chinese patriotism." Jean-Jacques Matignon, *Dix ans au pays du dragon* (Maloine, 1910), 12.

69 Settlers are still trying to pierce the mystery of these practices and rituals in order to capture them, seeing them as a source of knowledge they could benefit from, notably in the realms of botany and medicine. See Schiebinger, *Plants and Empire*.

70 Thomas Madiou, *Histoire d'Haïti* (Imprimerie J. H. Courtois, 1847), 99–100.

71 This was also the reason given by the authorities for banning danmyé in Martinique, where, starting in 1947, numerous municipal decrees were issued to criminalize the practice. See the documentary film by Narinderpal Singh Chandock, *Le Danmyé, l'art martial créole* (ISP Production, 2014).

72 James C. Scott, *Domination and the Arts of Resistance: Hidden Transcripts* (Yale University Press, 1990), 37.
73 See Franz Fanon's discussion of the concept of recognition in his book *Black Skin, White Masks* (Pluto Press, 2008), 163.
74 In the conclusion of *La Force noire*, Mangin acknowledges that the Senegalese are a crucial intermediary between the colonizers and the colonized: "Retired infantrymen will provide just the kind of leadership native societies need. We saved those peoples from oppressive domination, breaking the old leadership that constrained them most cruelly, and we have replaced those leaders with a distant, paternal administration. An intermediary is needed between these few administrators and the natives ... Former soldiers will serve as the frame and the cornerstone in the construction of a new edifice, and to hold all the parts together, there is patriotism, 'social cement,' in the fine words of Gustave Lebon." Charles Mangin, *La Force noire* (Hachette, 1910), 346–7.
75 Charles Mangin was a general in the French army who lived from 1866 to 1925.
76 *La Force noire* is part of a larger corpus of works on the fringes of literature, made up of instruction manuals written for officers and noncommissioned officers serving in the colonial army.
77 Mangin, *La Force noire*, 274.
78 Dino Costantini, *Una malattia europea: Il 'nuovo discorso coloniale' francese e i suoi critici* (Edizioni PLUS, 2006), 181. For more on the "civilizing mission," see Costantini's chapter on Henri Massis, who advocated for an ultraconservative form of Catholicism and defended Mussolini's conquest of Ethiopia. [The author refers to a French translation by Juliette Ferdinand published by La Découverte in 2008, under the title "Mission civilisatrice." —Trans.] For Massis's writings, see Henri Massis, *Défense de l'Occident* (Plon, 1927), and Massis, "Manifeste pour la défense de l'Occident," *Le Temps*, October 4, 1935.
79 Like other military men, Mangin praised animist peoples and scorned Muslims, advocating for the proportion of Muslim soldiers in the colonial forces to be reduced from a third to a fifth by increasing the proportion of non-Muslim Black people. See Mangin, *La Force noire*, 274. For Mangin's views on the "primitive patriarchy," see p. 243.
80 Ibid., 236.
81 Ibid.
82 Ibid., 285.
83 Ibid., 248.

84 Mangin's stated goal was to build a colonial armed force of ideally 500,000 men (although he admits that a realistic goal attainable without conflict in the short term would be between 100,000 and 200,000). This army would be made up of volunteers (recruited between the ages of sixteen and thirty-five who would then become professional soldiers eligible for retirement after twelve or fifteen years of service. A 1906 law in fact already allowed for native soldiers to retire from the military after fifteen years of service. Mangin understood that demographic information could only be approximate, because colonized men did not know their age; in fact, there was no system of public records, and setting one up was out of the question (ibid., 279–80).

85 Ibid., 312–13.

86 Ibid., 272.

87 In Algeria, the French state could enroll imperial subjects in the army without granting them civil rights, while in Senegal, civil rights were granted in some areas. In 1916, in defense of the nation, the Empire delved ever deeper into its human resources. The French high command organized massive campaigns to mobilize the colonies, but revolts broke out in many places across the Empire. "It was one of those rare moments," writes Éric Deroo, "in which equality was put on the table as a possibility for the Empire's subjects (citizenship for decorated military men and the wounded, promotions, lower taxation, pensions, reserved jobs, etc.). In reality, almost none of these promises were kept after the war." Éric Deroo, "Dying: The Call of the Empire (1913–1918)," *Colonial Culture in France Since the Revolution*, ed. Pascal Blanchard et al. (Indiana University Press, 2014), 136–7.

88 Mangin, *La Force noire*, 273.

89 Ibid., 350. This point raises, of course, the issue of recruitment, which Mangin argues should always be either voluntary or mixed, meaning "voluntary and constrained." The constraint can be delegated to "native leaders" and other local authorities, who would be responsible for providing the Empire with a quota of men—for instance, one-tenth of those fit to bear arms. Puppet leaders kept in power by the colonial authorities would thus have a convenient way of getting rid of any opposition or restive elements. All the while, Mangin wants to convince us that the recruits are fighting in order to acquire "the right to a gun." He gives the example of a recruitment camp where the large number of applicants led a French officer to propose a trial in which he greased a pole and recruited only those who could reach the top. See Mangin, *La Force noire*, 289. The historian Gilles Manceron

remarks, however, that the low wages paid, along with the harmful consequences of military service to agricultural and civilian labor, made it difficult to encourage voluntary service. The French authorities quickly set up a system of direct and indirect constraint. On the eve of the first global conflict, in 1910, Adolphe Messimy, at that time minister of the colonies and later minister of war in 1914, declared in *Le Matin*: "Africa has cost us piles of gold, thousands of soldiers, and rivers of blood. The men and blood will be paid back with interest." This statement was echoed by the publication of Mangin's book, which was ultimately unsuccessful, and the Black army he had hoped for, vigorous, warlike, and grateful, would remain a colonial fantasy: "In a 1915 letter addressed to the Governor General of French West Africa, the Governor General of the Ivory Coast, Gabriel Louis Angoulvant, described a 'manhunt.' The population resisted conscription in various ways: by putting forward unsuitable men while the youth fled the village, self-mutilation, mass desertion, and attacks on camps in order to free the recruits." Gilles Manceron, *Marianne et les colonies* (La Découverte, 2003), 210.

90 "Foreign armies" also referred to foreign volunteers, professional fighters who stepped forward while conscription was struggling to get underway. They made up the bulk of the foreign regiment under Napoleon and later became the Foreign Legion, which was created in France in 1831. See Walter Bruyère-Ostells, *Histoire des mercenaires de 1789 à nos jours* (Tallandier, 2011). Regarding mercenaries, see Niccolò Machiavelli, *The Prince* (Hackett Publishing Co., 2008), 220–1: "I submit, then, that the armies with which a prince defends his state are his own troops, mercenaries, auxiliaries, or a force combined of these elements. Mercenary and auxiliary armies are useless and dangerous. If a prince bases his government on a foundation of mercenaries, he will never have any stability or security. Mercenaries are disorganized, ambitious, undisciplined, and disloyal; bold among friends, among enemies cowardly; unfearing of God, unfaithful to man. Your defeat is staved off only as long as an attack on you is staved off: in peacetime they plunder you; in wartime, your enemies do."

91 In his description of the situation in Italy, controlled by the church or by a few principalities whose citizens knew nothing of arms, Machiavelli had this to say about mercenary armies: "Moreover, the mercenaries devoted all their professional skill to eliminating hardship and anxiety for themselves and their own troops; they did not kill one another in battle, but rather took each other prisoner without demanding ransom. They did not attack cities by

night; the mercenaries within the walls made no sorties on the enemy in their tents, constructed neither palisades nor ditches around their camps, and did no fighting in winter." *The Prince*, 231–2.
92 The world is our country: *Orbs patria nostra*.
93 Mangin, *La Force noire*, 323. Mangin backs up these words with an example: the Germans had had no issue with using foreign troops, brought from peoples and regions that had been freshly conquered, in combat against the French. A few years later, during the First World War: "The image of the native infantryman was used to convince the French nation of the abilities of native peoples in war, and also to stigmatize the Germans, who were portrayed as even more barbarous and savage than the natives. The famous postcard depicting an African infantryman guarding German prisoners behind barbed wire captures the spirit, with a phrase he addresses to a passing father and son: 'Ti viens voir li sauvages!' (an approximate English translation would yield: 'You's come here an' get a look at da savages!')." Deroo, "Dying," 137.
94 Accordingly, the conquest of Tonkin between 1884 and 1885 was carried out almost entirely (with the exception of officers of all grades) using infantry from French Indochina, a total of almost 16,000 men. In 1894, the conquest of Madagascar was done with Senegalese troops, and the same for Dahomey. See Manceron, *Marianne et les colonies*, 155.

Defense of Self, Defense of Nation

1 See Article 51 of the Charter of the United Nations from 1945: "Nothing in the present Charter shall impair the inherent right of individual or collective self-defense if an armed attack occurs against a Member of the United Nations, until the Security Council has taken the measures necessary to maintain international peace and security."
2 Hugo Grotius, *De jure belli ac pacis, libri tres* (1625). Translated by Richard Tuck as *The Rights of War and Peace: Book 1* (Liberty Fund Inc, 2005), 134.
3 Catherine Larrère, "Grotius et la distinction entre guerre privée et guerre publique," *Penser la guerre au XVIIe siècle*, ed. Ninon Grandé (Presses universitaires de Vincennes, 2012), 84. Larrère's analysis of Grotius follows that of Richard Tuck. See Richard Tuck, *The Rights of War and Peace: Political Thought and the*

International Order from Grotius to Kant (Oxford University Press, 1999).

4 According to Catherine Larrère, Grotius shifts the idea of war in this way to deemphasize the idea that war is rooted in justice ("just war") in favor of the idea that it is rooted in legality: "legitimate war," which could only occur between two legal entities, meaning states. Larrère, "Grotius," 92.

5 In line with the bill Dubois-Crancé brought to the Constituent Assembly in 1789, this one was brought forward by Jean-Baptiste Jourdan and largely drafted by Delbrel. See Philippe Catros, "'Tout français est soldat et se doit à la défense de la patrie': Retour sur la naissance de la conscription militaire," *Annales historiques de la Révolution française* 348 (April 2007): 7–23.

6 Ibid., 27.

7 Ibid., 8. The quotation is from the first article of the law of September 5, 1798 (Fructidor 19, year 6).

8 Annie Crépin, *Défendre la France: Les Français, la guerre et le service militaire de la guerre de Sept Ans à Verdun* (Presses universitaires de Rennes, 2005), 37.

9 Up until 1905, certain exemptions and privileges were in place that allowed military service for breadwinners, academics, seminarians, and so on to be reduced to one or two years instead of three. An unresolved tension remained, though: training professionals from within this citizen army (nearly 600,000 men in active service) created a military class, a conservative elite made up of the sons of the bourgeoisie, that used schools and private meetings to ensure its material and ideological reproduction. Furthermore, all soldiers were stripped of their civil rights (since they could no longer vote or run for office, in accordance with laws passed on November 30, 1875, and December 9, 1895) during the period of their conscription or, in the case of officers, for the duration of their service. The army saw itself as a school for civic-mindedness, noble and disinterested (serving the rights of Nature and France, rather than a certain class or party), but it had become a society within society, a school for violence. See Madeleine Rebérioux, "L'Armée nouvelle," *Introduction à Jean Jaurès* (1969).

10 Dubois-Crancé, in an unsuccessful bill submitted to the Constituent Assembly in December 1789, states, "I say that it is now a right for every Frenchman to serve his country, that it's an honor to be a soldier when in the service of the most beautiful constitution in the world." See also the Mably citizens' militias. In regard to the "right of defense" properly speaking, although

rarely invoked at that time, it does appear in two opposing traditions: an aristocratic one, where the right of defense serves to distinguish between classes of citizens, and a Jacobin one, where military service was an assertion of liberty. See Philippe Catros, "Tout français est soldat," 17.

11 In regard to the participation of freed slaves, Laurent Dubois quotes Léger Félicité Sonthonax, commissioner of the Republic in Saint-Dominque, who declared that even if France were to abandon the colony "without arms or ammunition, the last neighborhood still flying the Republic's flag would be defended by an army of Black people. They are the veritable *sans-culottes* of the colonies, they are the people, and only they are able to defend the country." See Laurent Dubois, "'Citoyens et amis!' Esclavage, citoyenneté et République dans les Antilles françaises à l'époque révolutionnaire," *Annales, Histoire, Sciences sociales* 2 (2003): 28.

12 Furthermore, as Éric Deroo explains, troops from the French Empire were not "the only groups sacrificed on the front lines" during the war from 1914 to 1918. In-battle losses by overseas battalions made up of forced or volunteer recruits (600,000 subjects were enlisted and 430,000 served on the various fronts) were about equal to those by battalions made up of French *poilus*, as infantrymen were called, who averaged 22 percent to 24 percent of the overall body count. However, the battalions made up of subjects of the French Empire were further decimated by the climate and unhealthy conditions in northeastern France, not just by the enemy's bombs and bullets. On all of these topics, see Deroo, "Dying," 135.

13 Paola Tabet, *La Grande arnaque: Sexualité des femmes et échange économico-sexuel* (L'Harmattan, 2004).

14 The division of martial labor should be understood in terms similar to the sexual division of reproductive labor, a strategy whose success involved increasing the number and diversity of techniques and strategies used to constrain the bodies of women of different social classes.

15 On this point, I could refer to another text by Paola Tabet that at first glance would seem relevant to the sexual division and the use of tools and weapons. Paola Tabet, "Les mains, les outils, les armes," *L'Homme* 19, no. 3–4 (1979): 5–61. Reprinted in *La Construction sociale de l'inégalité des sexes: Des outils et des corps* (L'Harmattan, 1998). However, Clotilde Lebas critiques Tabet, arguing that she underdetermines "tactics" involving the use of tools as improvised weapons. See Clotilde Lebas, "La violence des femmes: Entre démesure et rupture," ed. Coline

Gardiand and Geneviève Pruvost (La Découverte, 2012), 252: "Paola Tabet's description falls short on how the gendered distribution of tools and weapons contributes to the domination of the male class over the female. She only considers the material distribution of these tools. Of course, this unequal sharing of weapons and tools produces, imposes, and delimits sexual territories, but ordinary objects can be used, manipulated, and given new purpose in tactics that can shake the whole system of territories built on the binary categorization of bodies."

16 Dominique Godineau, *The Women of Paris and Their French Revolution*, trans. Katherine Streip (University of California Press, 1998), xviii.

17 Zalkind Hourwitz was a revolutionary who perfectly described the line dividing white, Catholic men who owned property and were free from those excluded by the Enlightenment: "All that is required in order to be a citizen or even a legislator in this land of freedom and equality is ownership of a white foreskin." Zalkind Hourwitz, in *Courrier de Paris*, January 24, 1791. Cited in *Apologie des juifs: 1789*, ed. E. Varikas and M. Löwy (Syllepse, 2002), 20.

18 Most of them would later become members of the Society of Revolutionary and Republican Women.

19 Godineau, *The Women of Paris*, 108. Godineau goes on to cite the passage in the petition in which the women citizens assert that the right to arm themselves is a natural right "possessed by every individual for the defense of life and liberty." This is reminiscent of Robespierre's April 27, 1791, declaration that "every citizen has the right to be armed in defense of the nation."

20 *Adresse individuelle à l'Assemblée nationale, par des citoyennes de la capitale, Le 6 mars 1792*, cited in Claude Guillon, *Notre patience est à bout: 1792–1793, les écrits des enragé-e-s* (Éditions Imho, 2009), 114–15. Guillon emphasizes in his commentary that the petitioning women addressed the men as "Sirs" rather than as "citizens" because these men were unjustly appropriating natural rights for themselves. This led the president of the National Assembly to begin his reply with a sharp, "Miladies" (ibid., 112).

21 Quoted from a rule in the Cordeliers District from July 25, 1789. Cited in ibid., 111.

22 Ibid., 122.

23 For "monstrous gender mutations," see Elsa Dorlin, *La Matrice de la race: Généalogie sexuelle et coloniale de la nation française* (La Découverte, 2006).

24 See Sylvie Steinberg, *La Confusion des sexes: Le travestissement de la Renaissance à la Révolution* (Fayard, 2001).

25 Plato made such a depiction in the *Timaeus* during his reflections on the wandering womb. See Dorlin, *La Matrice*.
26 The Society of Revolutionary Republican Women, May 13, 1793, outside their Museum section. Cited in Claude Guillon, *Notre patience est à bout*, 121. See also May 12, 1793, at the Jacobins Club (ibid., 118).
27 The reference to Amazon battalions was widely taken up by the Society of Revolutionary Republican Women. For instance, outside their Museum section on May 13, 1793: "Let companies of Amazons emerge from the neighborhoods and markets of this immense city! This is where the real women citizens are found, those who have kept the purity of their values in this den of corruption and are the only ones who have felt the price of freedom and equality." Ibid., 120.
28 Frank Hamel, *A Woman of the Revolution: Théroigne de Méricourt* (Brentano's, 1911), 285. The original French text is available on Gallica, the online portal of the National Library of France. [The speech is translated in its entirety in Frank Hamel's book on de Méricourt, available on archive.org. —Trans.]
29 Ibid., 287.
30 Jean Jaurès, *L'Armée nouvelle* (Jules Rouff et Cie, 1911). [No complete English translation of this text exists in English. Abbreviated editions are available on marxists.org and on archive.org. —Trans.] Jean Jaurès, *Democracy and Military Service*, trans. G. G. Coulton (Simpkin Marshall Hamilton Kent & Co., 1916).
31 See August Blanqui's 1880 pamphlet, "L'Armée esclave et opprimée," translated as "The Army Enslaved and Oppressed" by Mitch Abidor on marxists.org. See as well August Bebel's 1898 text "Assassinations and Socialism," translated by Boris Reinstein and also available on marxists.org.
32 Jean Jaurès, *L'Armée nouvelle*, 149. [This passage is missing from the abbreviated translation, but the related discussion is available. —Trans.] Jean Jaurès, *Democracy and Military Service*, 35.
33 Ibid.
34 Ibid., 152.
35 Ibid., 154–63. [See 36–8 in the abbreviated translation. —Trans.]
36 Ibid., 163. "And such are the conclusions that he arrives at, this man whom most of our high-ranking officers consider the genius behind the renewed French strategy, this man whose thinking has marked every part of the instruction at the *École supérieure de guerre*, our preeminent school for officers. The nation no longer takes to the field, but merely lines up to watch their glorious

champions fight, only able to support them with their empty cheers. And that is what Captain Gilbert proposes, after summoning all able-bodied Frenchmen to attend the tragedy." Ibid.

37 Jaurès considers the Swiss military exemplary in this regard, since the Swiss reservists have a role no less active than that of the elite troops. They are an active reserve able to mobilize at any time.

38 For "armed nation," see ibid., 177. For "implacable in defense," see Madeleine Rebérioux, "L'Armée nouvelle."

39 Rosa Luxemburg, "L'Armée nouvelle de Jean Jaurès," trans. Daniel Guérin. German text first published in the *Leipziger Volkszeitung* on June 9, 1911. [Translation from the French edition available on marxists.org, which is without page numbering. —Trans.]

40 Ibid.

41 Ibid.

42 Ibid. Luxemburg critiques Jaurès for encouraging socialists to trust in the law and for the suicidal "constitutional insurrection" strategy that he lays out at the end of *L'Armée nouvelle*. Luxemburg writes that "giving in to the illusion that legalistic phrases will in any way triumph over the interests and power of capitalism is the most harmful position the proletariat could adopt." Ibid.

43 Georges Yvetot (1868–1942) was an anarchist in the tradition of Proudhon. He was secretary-general of the CGT in 1902. Georges Yvetot, *Nouveau manuel du soldat: La patrie, l'armée, la guerre* (Fédération des Bourses du Travail, 1905).

44 Ibid., 7.

45 "Militarism was born when the few took for themselves what had belonged to all and decided to keep it by force." Ibid. "We are all proletarians, meaning we are the ones who today bear all the weight and sadness of society." Ibid., 9. Proletarians have nothing to defend—this could well be Yvetot's definition of the term, in line with that of *The Communist Manifesto*. For "the religion of violence," see p. 8.

46 Ibid., 9. Yvetot also denounces the years of training that occur before service even begins, in the form of young children playing games and hearing stories that amount to role-playing at war and that acclimatize them to violence.

47 Ibid., 10.

48 Here, he is referencing Anatole France ("The army is a school of crime"), but in this section he also cites a slew of authors: Seneca, Erasmus, Montaigne, Ronsard, Bossuet, La Bruyère, Fénelon, Rousseau, Voltaire, Girardin, Maupassant ...

49 Ibid., 14.

50 Ibid., 16.
51 Ibid., 32. It should be noted that the tension between creating self-defense groups in view of an insurrection and forming dedicated militias to defend the working class during struggles—notably against repression by law enforcement and attacks by fascist groups—crystallized in the 1930s as a dichotomy between mass self-defense and self-defense groups. This ultimately led to the formation of fixed teams of marshals, which made self-defense less relevant as a mass strategy for the working class, and which had been advocated for by the International. On one side of the issue, the anti-militarist politics of the French communist movement led to skepticism toward specialized self-defense formations, which were seen as a paramilitary "masquerade": against the Blackshirts, the only "uniform needed for defense is the factory worker's blue coveralls, the construction worker's vest, the worn cardigan and coarse corduroy of agricultural workers and poor farmers, the jacket of salaried workers and government employees, the rail workers' blue overalls." See Jean Lagarde, "La lutte de masse antifasciste: Corrigeons les erreurs et renforçons l'activité de notre travail d'autodéfense," *L'Humanité*, March 28, 1934. This position was in line with the International, which clearly stated that self-defense should be understood as an organizing principle of the worker's movement overall, which included among other things encouraging workers to fraternize with soldiers assigned to carry out repression. On the other side of the issue, the Communist Party of France (CPF) forbade the arming of workers, but the debate shifted with the rise of fascist groups and the need to "protect" the party. On the socialist SFIO party's left fringe, there was an action-ready combat formation made up of revolutionary militants and led by Marceau Pivert. But the CPF, to avoid being outflanked by far-left workers' militias organized by Trotskyists or on Pivert's model, favored a "republican" form of mass self-defense (symbolized by the use of a badge in the French national colors) and created teams of marshals. Although the marshals' stated purpose was to defend union members from fascists, in practice they were also used to avoid clashes and to control both demonstrations and the demonstrators themselves in order to prevent any "excesses" that could trigger police repression. Paul Vaillant-Couturier, "Qu'est-ce que l'armement du prolétariat?," *L'Humanité*, January 28, 1935; Georges Vidal, "Violence et politique dans la France des années 1930: Le cas de l'autodéfense communiste," *Revue historique* 640 (2006): 901–22; Philippe Burin, "Poings levés et bras tendus: La contagion des symboles au temps du Front populaire," *Vingtième siècle*

11 (1986): 5–20. (My thanks to Vanessa Codaccioni for her bibliographical assistance on this point.) Transforming self-defense into marshaling also involved turning an insurrectional defensive strategy into the self-discipline of social movements. It brought with it an inevitable stigmatization of actions termed violent carried out by their own members, for provoking repression or adding to its intensity.

52 Edward William Barton-Wright (1860–1951) was born in India and studied in Germany and France.

53 Sadakazu Uyenishi is the author of a famous jujitsu manual first published in 1905, called *Text-book of Ju-Jitsu* (Alcuin Classics, 2011). The cinematic images from the book were reanimated in a video available on the Bartitsu Society YouTube channel. Yukio Tani was also recruited as a wrestler for the music hall shows organized by William Bankier that helped to popularize jujitsu. In France, Émile André published a book summarizing cane and stick fighting techniques, and it is available online on the website of the FFAMHE. Émile André, *100 façons de se défendre dans la rue avec armes* (Flammarion, 1905).

54 Graham Noble, "An Introduction to E. W. Barton-Wright (1860–1951) and the Eclectic Art of Bartitsu," *Journal of Asian Martial Arts* 8, no. 2 (1999): 50–61. Bartitsu was popularized in 1903 by Arthur Conan Doyle when Sherlock Holmes used "baritsu" to fight Professor Moriarty in "The Adventure of the Empty House."

55 Edith Margaret Williams (1872–1971) was born in Bath. She married William Garrud in 1893 and settled in London, where her husband worked as a physical education trainer in several universities in the city. He met Edward William Barton-Wright in 1899.

56 Titled *Jiu-Jitsu Downs the Footpads,* directed by Alf Collins and featuring Edith Garrud in 1907, it was one of the first martial arts films. Sadly, it appears to have been lost.

57 The WSPU was founded in 1903 by Emmeline Pankhurst (1858–1928), to get women the right to vote and full equality. Three of Pankhurst's daughters, Christabel, Sylvia, and Adela, were also prominent militants. The latter two quit the WSPU during an internal schism over the radical character of its methods. In 1905, following the failure of the first major suffrage campaign, the WSPU adopted the motto "Deeds, not words" and proceeded to upend the feminist movement's repertoire of actions by engaging in direct action and civil disobedience (occupying offices, chaining themselves to the gates of Parliament, property damage, vandalism, attacks on public and private buildings, hunger strikes . . .). This earned them the disapproval of most feminist

organizations involved in the campaign for the right to vote, along with that of the press and political parties. They were targeted by brutal police repression, and several activists were injured, arrested, and imprisoned, then force-fed in prison during hunger strikes in which they were demanding to be treated as political prisoners. In 1909, Emmeline Pankhurst met Gandhi while he was in London; a few months later, Gandhi stated that the WSPU's cause was just, but that its actions were against the principle of nonviolence on which civil disobedience should be based (*Satyagraha*, "holding firm to truth" in Sanskrit). During the war, the WSPU campaigned for women to be enlisted in the war effort. This position cemented the division between Emmeline and Christabel Pankhurst on the one side and Adela and Sylvia Pankhurst on the other. Sylvia was a militant communist involved in the International (though she was excluded in 1921 over her opposition to Lenin), and she advocated for an antimilitarist feminism, critical of bourgeois parliamentary democracy. She therefore rejected the WSPU's strategy of prioritizing the right to vote at the expense of the rights of women workers. The WSPU dissolved in 1917. In 1918, a law was passed granting the right to vote to all women over the age of thirty; the age was lowered to twenty-one ten years later. See Emmeline Pankhurst, *My Own Story* (Virago, 1979), first published by Eveleigh Nash in 1914; Paula Bartley, *Emmeline Pankhurst* (Routledge, 2002); Katherine Connelly, "Sylvia Pankhurst, the First World War and the Struggle for Democracy," *Revue française de civilisation britannique* 20, no. 1 (2015).

58 The club's opening was announced in the *Votes for Women* journal in December 1909. Activists from the Women's Freedom League also trained there. See Elizabeth Crawford, *The Women's Suffrage Movement: A Reference Guide 1866–1928* (UCL Press, 2001), 240; Tony Wolf, *Edith Garrud: The Suffragette Who Knew Jujutsu* (Kathryne Wolf, 2009).

59 In 1913, the government was confronted with the opposition parties' outrage over the barbaric practice of force-feeding imprisoned activists on hunger strike. It thus passed the Cat and Mouse Act, an amendment that would allow prisoners to be released to regain their strength before incarcerating them again. The Bodyguard Society intervened in this process to prevent the police from recapturing activists who had been temporarily freed.

60 "But the evil of pinning faith to indirect action is far greater than any such minor results. The main evil is that it destroys initiative, quenches the individual rebellious spirit, teaches people to rely on someone else to do for them what they should do for themselves;

finally renders organic the anomalous idea that by massing supineness together until a majority is acquired, then through the peculiar magic of that majority, this supineness is to be transformed into energy. That is, people who have lost the habit of striking for themselves as individuals, who have submitted to every injustice while waiting for a majority to grow, are going to become metamorphosed into *human high-explosives* by a mere process of packing!" Voltairine de Cleyre, "Direct Action," in *Exquisite Rebel: The Essays of Voltairine de Cleyre—Feminist, Anarchist, Genius*, ed. Sharon Presley and Crispin Sartwell (State University of New York Press, 2005), 284. In her opposition between political action (political representation and electoralism) and direct action, Voltairine de Cleyre gives the following definition of the latter: "Every person who ever thought he had a right to assert, and went boldly and asserted it, himself or jointly with others that shared his convictions, was a direct actionist." Ibid., 273. To de Cleyre, direct action can be either peaceful or violent, but in the former case, it has nothing in common with the way political action trains you to accept injustice. Direct action is thus always violent, in that it expresses how "it is impossible that life continue to submit." Ibid., 280.

61 H. Irving Hancock, *Physical Training for Women by Japanese Methods* (Putnam's, 1904).

62 H. Irving Hancock, *Le Ju-jitsu et la femme: Entraînement physique au féminin*, trans. C. Pesseaud (Berger-Levrault, 1906), 1. Quotations are drawn from Fernand Lagrange's introduction to the French edition.

63 On this issue, see the works of Anaïs Bohuon, to whom I express my thanks for pointing me toward her work.

64 Charles Pherdac, *Défendez-vous mesdames: Manuel de défense féminine* (Rueff, 1912).

65 Cited in Michel Brousse, *Les Racines du judo français de la fin du XIXe siècle aux années 1950: Histoire d'une culture sportive* (Bordeaux University Press, 2001). Michel Brousse points out that the few French women who practiced jujitsu and judo at that time were allowed to participate in competitions, and some earned their black belt. Mixed fights and female championships were held (notably in 1955 in Morocco) before being banned in 1957, when the French Judo Federation excluded women from competitions and from receiving a black belt. The federation's doctors argued that women's practice should be restricted to technical execution, quickness, and flexibility, using only movements suitable for their "sex" and that preserved their "grace." See Brousse, 281–2.

66 See Willy, "Jiu-Jitzu féminin," *L'Auto* 1878, December 6, 1905; and Michel Corday, "Le sport et la femme," *L'Auto* 2199, October 23, 1906.

67 See "Jiu-Jutsu: Comment une femme peut se défendre," *La Femme d'aujourd'hui*, July 1905. Jean-Joseph Renaud, "La défense féminine," *V.G.A.* 533, December 5, 1908. The former is an illustrated article, while the latter, published three years later, is a long report in full color showing jujitsu holds. The holds were performed by Mademoiselle Didier, an actress at the Odéon, and the sports journalist Rouzier-Dorcières, a famous fencing duelist who took the side of jujitsu in the early twentieth-century debate over the relative merits of wrestling techniques from the Greco-Roman tradition and Japanese martial arts.

68 William Ewart Fairbairn, *Self-Defense for Women and Girls* (Faber and Faber, 1942). William Ewart Fairbairn, *Hands Off! Self-Defense for Women* (Appleton-Century Company, 1942). Released later in the same year, the latter text is really just a reworked version of the former.

69 William Ewart Fairbairn (1885–1960): After the war, he became a teacher for the Shanghai police special forces.

70 For the effect of the war on the feminist movement, see Françoise Thébaud, *Les Femmes au temps de la guerre de 14* (Stock, 1986); Laurence Klejman, "Les Congrès féministes internationaux," *Mil neuf cent: Revue d'histoire intellectuelle* 7 (1989): 71–86; Christine Bard, *Les filles de Marianne: Histoire des féminismes 1914–1940* (Fayard, 1995). On the influence of the English suffragist movement in the United States during the same period, see Sandra Adickes, "Sisters, Not Demons: The Influence of British Suffragists on the American Suffrage Movement," *Women's History Review* 11, no. 4 (2002): 675–90. Edith Garrud stopped teaching in 1925 and closed down her dojo.

71 See Maureen Honey, *Creating Rosie the Riveter: Class, Gender, and Propaganda During World War II* (University of Massachusetts Press, 1984).

72 These two posters were rediscovered in the 1980s and were conflated to create a contemporary feminist icon, although these images are emblematic of American patriotism during the war years and of its regressive impact on the rights of women. The war was hardly over when the large majority of women were made to return to textile factories or to the home, forced to forget both their skills as workers and in self-defense. The 1950s involved even more forgetting in order to produce a patriarchal and racist ideal of *way of life* under the docile and mollifying gaze of the new housewife.

Testaments of Self-Defense

1. From a set of documents retrieved from the Ringelblum Archives in Warsaw, Poland. Document number 426. Ring II/333/ Mf/ ZIH-802; USHMM-57. Translated into French by Ian Zdanowicz. My thanks to Ian Zdanowicz for pointing these documents out to me and translating them. Thanks as well to Tommy Kedar, who brought several important sources to my attention.
2. Hanna Krall, *Shielding the Flame: An Intimate Conversation with Dr. Marek Edelman, the Last Surviving Leader of the Warsaw Ghetto Uprising*, trans. Joanna Stasinska and Lawrence Weschler (Henry Holt and Co., 1986), 7.
3. I am referring here to Hannah Arendt's idea of worldlessness. See Hannah Arendt, *The Human Condition* (University of Chicago Press, 1958).
4. The Armia Krajowa (the largest organization resisting the Nazis in Poland) provided "90 pistols with ammunition, 600 grenades, 15 kg of plastic explosive, and a few automatic rifles. The Polish Workers Party sent 10 rifles and 30 pistols ... We can safely say that the support given by the Polish Resistance was minimal. The Jewish fighters were to remain tragically isolated." Henri Minczeles, *Histoire générale du Bund: Un mouvement révolutionnaire juif* (Denoël, 1995), 339. On the arms and equipment collected by self-defense groups, see Emmanuel Ringelblum, *Ktovim fun geto*, vol. 1 (1961), 332–3. Cited in Yisrael Gutman, *The Jews of Warsaw, 1939–1943: Ghetto, Underground, Revolt*, trans. Ina Friedman (Indiana University Press, 1982), 349–50.
5. Cited in Minczeles, *Histoire générale du Bund*, 339.
6. Gutman, *The Jews of Warsaw*, 315–16.
7. See *Journal* by Hirsch Berlinski, a fighter from the ZOB (Jewish Combat Organization). Cited in Rachel L. Einwohner, "Availability, Proximity, and Identity in the Warsaw Ghetto Uprising: Adding a Sociological Lens to Studies of Jewish Resistance," *Sociology Confronts the Holocaust*, ed. Judith M. Gearson and Diane L. Wolf (Duke University Press, 2007), 286.
8. See Hirsch Berlinski, *Zikhronot* (Yalkut Moreshet, 1964), 14–16. Cited in Gutman, *The Jews of Warsaw*, 287. Another armed organization was also formed, the Jewish Military Union (Zydowski Zwiazek Wojskowy—ZZW).
9. Ibid., 305.
10. [On related themes, see Wladyslaw Szlengel, "Counterattack," trans. John Carpenter and Bogdana Carpenter, *Chicago Review* 52, no. 2/4 (August 2006): 287–91.—Trans.]
11. Krall, *Sheltering the Flame*, 6.

NOTES TO PAGE 56

12 Ibid., 10.
13 "He had a girlfriend. Pretty, blond, warm. Her name was Mira. On May 7 he came with her to our place in Franciszkanska Street. On May 8 he shot her first and then himself. Jurek Wilner had apparently declared: 'Let's all die together.' Lutek Roblat shot his mother and sister, then everybody started shooting. By the time we managed to get back there, there were only a few people left alive; eighty people had committed suicide. 'This is how it should have been,' we were told later. 'The nation has died, its soldiers have died. A symbolic death.' You, too, probably like such symbols? 'There was a young woman with them, Ruth. She shot herself seven times before she finally made it. She was such a pretty, tall girl with a peachy complexion, but she wasted six bullets.'" Ibid., 5.
14 In January 1943, at a time when there were only 500 members of the ZOB remaining, there was another raid. Only 80 fighters survived. Marek Edelman wrote: "For the sake of exactitude I'll tell you that 'our barrels' from which the fire blossomed—at that time there were only ten of them in the Ghetto ... Aniclewicz's group, which was taken to the Umschlagplatz and did not have arms, started hitting the Germans with bare fists. The group of Pelc, the eighteen-year-old printer, when taken to the square, refused to board the train, and Van Oeppen, the commander of the Treblinka camp, shot all of them, sixty men, on the spot." Ibid., 61–2.
15 Emmanuel Ringelblum, "'Little Stalingrad' Defends Itself," *To Live with Honor and Die with Honor! Selected Documents from the Warsaw Ghetto Underground Archives 'O.S.' ('Oneg Shabbath')*, ed. Joseph Kermish (Menachem Press, 1986), 595.
16 Armed self-defense was an ethical gamble, sharing little with the aesthetic of heroism. However, in a clandestine Polish newspaper from April 30, 1943, there is an argument that self-defense and dying with weapons in hand would transform the Jews into a *people*: "From a helpless people, a flock slaughtered by the German murderers, the Jews have risen to the level of a fighting people. And even if they do not fight for their existence—which is out of the question, considering the absolute superiority of the enemy—they have nonetheless demonstrated their right to national existence." "The Greatest Crime in the World," *Mysl Panstwowa* [Government thinking], April 30, 1943, Yad Vashem Archive, 0-25/25. Cited in Gutman, *The Jews of Warsaw*, 404. Thanato-ethics thus provided substance to a national mythology, which in subsequent narrative construction would be drained of its original meaning in favor of nationalist rhetoric based in dialecticizing the victim/hero relationship.

17 Front Odrodzenia Polski, "Around the Burning Ghetto," *Prawda Mlodych* [The truth of the young], April–May 1943, 279–80. Cited in Gutman, *The Jews of Warsaw*, 406. We see here the idea that for the FOP, although the Jews and Poles have a common enemy in the Germans, their war is not the same.

18 See the classic text by Jesse Glenn Gray in which he discusses this fascination with scenes of battle at length, in reference to Kant's concept of the sublime. He provides a good example of the excessive aestheticization of combat and how it contributes to the ongoing construction of contemporary normative heroic virility. Jesse Glenn Gray, *The Warriors: Reflections on Men in Battle* (Harper Colophon Books, 1970).

19 Krall, *Shielding the Flame*, 36–7.

20 Minczeles, *Histoire générale du Bund*, 339. The Bund was founded October 7–9, 1897, near the city of Vilna. Over the Rosh Hashanah holiday, a dozen syndicalist delegates, eleven men and three women, most of them workers and intellectuals from local organizations and clandestine newspapers, met and created the General Jewish Labour Bund (Algemeyner yidisher arbeter-bund in lite, Poyln un Rusland). Their goal was to create a Russian social-democratic party and rally Jewish workers to it. It rapidly became "the only socialist organizational structure with a solid existence east of Poland ... The founding of the Bund signaled a new era in the organization of the Jewish proletariat. During the first two or three years of its existence, the Bund called 312 strikes in 14 factories, affecting 44 economic sectors. In 157 of these stoppages, 27,890 workers participated ... New relationships were formed between those involved in the socialist project. Transfiguration is not too strong a word, because social-democratic militants distinguished themselves from their fellows through their commitment to purity and to their ideals. This manifested itself in countless details in daily life: physical hygiene, clean clothes, and the refusal of vulgar talk, obscenities, and cursing. This new kind of behavior was also integrated into their relationships with workers, which play an incalculable role in the development of the Jewish workers' movement. Women ... became equals as comrades." Nathan Weinstock, *Le Pain de misère: Histoire du mouvement juif ouvrier en Europe*, coll. [Re]découverte, vol. 1 (La Découverte, 2002), 116. The Bund reached a peak of 33,000 members in 1906 before being targeted by severe repression.

21 Szmul (Artur) Zygielbojm, "The Last Letter from Szmul Zygielbojm, the Bund Representative with the Polish National Council in Exile," *Yad Vashem Archives*, O-55 (2016): "To our

appeals for help, the outside world sent its answer. Through the underground radio, we received the news that brave and loyal Artur Ziegelboim, our representative with the Polish government-in-exile, had given us the only aid within his power. During the night of May 12 he committed suicide in London as a gesture of protest against the callousness and indifference of the world ... The meaning of Artur's suicide was bitterly clear to all of us. He was tendering us the balance sheet of all his efforts on our behalf. Through an edition of *The Bulletin* issued on the Aryan side, we let the underground know that another fighter, who had suffered and fought with his ghetto comrades until his last breath, had fallen in far-off London." Bernard Goldstein, *Five Years in the Warsaw Ghetto: The Stars Bear Witness*, trans. Leonard Shatzkin (Viking Press, 1949), chap. 6.

22 "The important thing was just that we were shooting. We had to show it. Not to the Germans. They knew better than us how to shoot. We had to show it to this other, the non-German world." Krall, *Shielding the Flame*, 3.

23 Weinstock, *Le Pain de misère*.

24 [We rely here on Shlomo Lambroza's translation of these phrases. See his "Jewish Self-Defense During the Russian Pogrom of 1903–1906," in *Hostages of Modernization: Studies on Modern Antisemitism 1870–1933/39*, vol. 2, ed. Herbert Arthur Strauss (Walter de Gruyter, 1933). —Trans.]

25 Minczeles, *Histoire générale du Bund*, 95. See also Henry J. Tobias, *The Jewish Bund in Russia, from Its Origins to 1905* (Stanford University Press, 1972); I. L. Peretz, "Impressions of a Journey Through the Tomaszow Region," in *The I. L. Peretz Reader*, ed. Ruth R. Wisse (Yale University Press, 2002).

26 Stephen P. Frank, *Crime, Cultural Conflict, and Justice in Rural Russia 1856–1914* (University of California Press, 1999), 157–8.

27 Also at play is the distinction between "violence" and "defensive violence," and in this case, the line is not clearly drawn between self-defense and terrorism. In 1901, during its fourth congress, the Bund adopted a resolution banning terrorist acts.

28 The differences between these two tendencies should not overshadow their commonalities. In 1909, during the Poale Zion party's congress in Vienna, a motion was passed to establish connections with other Jewish workers' parties. The support of the party's leader, Bev Borokhov, was crucial to this, though he drew the ire of Poale Zionists in Palestine, who accused him of abandoning the Palestinian aspect of the party's program when he declared, "We are not a party for Palestine, but for the Jewish proletariat." The Russian section of the party thus left

the Zionist Organization. See Weinstock, *Le Pain de misère*, 238.

29 The assault lasted several days, spilling over into other neighborhoods and surrounding towns until martial law was declared on April 21. See Monty Noam Penkower, "The Kishinev Pogrom of 1903: A Turning Point in Jewish History," *Modern Judaism* 24, no. 3 (2004): 188.

30 Local Jewish religious authorities informed the local police of the campaign calling for a massacre, but nothing was done to prevent it. (Ibid., 189.)

31 Ibid., 187.

32 Ibid., 188.

33 In regard to the reaction of intellectuals, Leo Tolstoy had remained silent during the massacres of 1881–83 but spoke out against the "horrible events in Kishinev." Maxim Gorky published a collection of essays, *Sbornik*, and turned the proceeds over to the victims. Ibid., 190. In regard to the international press, see the April 28, 1903, edition of the *New York Times*.

34 Hayyim Nahman Bialik, "The City of Slaughter," in *Complete Poetic Works of Hayyim Nahman Bialik*, ed. Israel Efros (Histadruth Ivrith of America, 1948), 129. See also *The Literature of Destruction: Jewish Responses to Catastrophe*, ed. David Roskies (Jewish Publication Society, 1989); and Michael Stanislawski, *Zionism and the Fin de siècle* (University of California Press, 2001), 183.

35 Penkower, "The Kishinev Pogrom," 193. See also Lambroza, "Jewish Responses."

36 Minczeles, *Histoire générale du Bund*, 98.

37 From the "Self-Defense" entry in the Jewish Virtual Library, jewishvirtuallibrary.org.

38 In the fall of 1903 in Gomel, a pogrom was prevented by self-defense groups jointly organized by the Bund and Poale Zion, in which 200 combatants drove back the mob and also the army and police, who had been complicit. In Zhytomyr in May 1905, self-defense groups from the Bund were able to limit the horror, although 29 people were killed and 150 wounded. In the fall of 1905 in Ekaterinoslav [modern Dnipro], during the revolution, self-defense groups from the Bund, Poale Zion, and Jewish student organizations drove back the mob and managed to defend not only the Jewish neighborhoods, but also non-Jewish working-class areas at risk of being pillaged and burned. They pursued pogromists who succeeded in robbing Jewish shops or homes. See Theodore H. Friedgut, "Jews, Violence, and the Russian Revolutionary Movement," *Studies in Contemporary Jewry* 18 (2002): 52–3.

39 Born in Ukraine in 1880 and died in the United States in 1940. See Ze'ev Vladimir Jabotinsky, *Story of My Life*, ed. Brian Horowitz and Leonid Katsis (Wayne State University Press, 2015).

40 Ilan Pappe, *Across the Wall: Narratives of Israeli-Palestinian History* (I. B. Tauris, 2010), 115.

41 In 1921, Jabotinsky was elected a member of the Zionist Organization, though he was critical of its compromises with the British. He was expelled over his secret agreement with the anti-Semitic and anti-Bolshevik leader of the Ukrainian government-in-exile, Symon Petliura. See Marius Schattner, *Histoire de la droite israélienne: de Jabotinski à Shamir* (Éditions Complexe, 1999), 69.

42 Two years earlier, Jabotinsky had founded Betar (Brit Yosef Trumpeldor, "the Joseph Trumpeldor Movement"), which would go on to become the youth wing of the Hatzohar.

43 Ze'ev Vladimir Jabotinsky, "The Iron Wall," *Jewish Herald*, November 26, 1937. Available from the Jabotinsky Institute on Israel's website, under reference number F-1923/204/EN.

44 Schattner, *Histoire de la droite israélienne*, 176. Wingate went on to be a leader of the Chindits, the United Kingdom's special forces during World War II, and was active in the Burmese Campaign, where he conducted offensive operations far from the front line and ultimately lost his life. Many Israeli politicians participated in the Special Night Squads, including Moshe Dayan (head of the Israel Defense Forces from 1955 to 1958, minister of defense in 1967) and Ygal Allon (one of the first leaders of the Palmach in 1941, minister repeatedly between 1961 and 1977). Moshe Dayan, *Moshe Dayan: Story of My Life* (William Morrow and Company, 1976), 44–7.

45 This "ethical" principle of restraint was also political, because it was the condition Britain placed on the Haganah in return for arming them during the 1936–39 uprising, which was officially illegal.

46 In the same ideological vein, the Stern Gang also emerged from far-right Zionist currents and carried out attacks against the British authorities, going so far as to make overtures to Nazi Germany. The Stern Gang, named for its founder, Avraham Stern, called itself Lehi, an acronym for *lehomi herouth leIsrael*; Stern founded it in 1940 after a split with the Irgun occasioned by the outbreak of the Second World War and the cease-fire agreement with Britain signed in 1939.

47 See Einat Bar-On Cohen, "Globalization of the War on Violence: Israeli Close Combat, Krav Maga and Sudden Alterations in

Intensity," *Social Anthropology/Anthropologie sociale* 18, no. 3 (2010): 267–88.
48. One of the core ideas of self-defense is to break down the notion of safe distance: to be at a distance is to be vulnerable (in range of a kick or a punch, for instance), while being close to the attacker's body means finding opportunities to strike their vulnerable points (the throat, vital organs, or joints).
49. Physiological and emotional work would become an essential characteristic of krav maga: learning to react quickly, to keep your muscles ready, to turn fear into a trigger for attack rather than letting it be an obstacle to defense. It involves using not only your muscles but also your emotions, affects, and hormones for maximum benefit in a form of fighting chemistry.
50. Bar-On Cohen, "Globalization of the War on Violence," 269.
51. See Benoît Gaudin, "La codification des pratiques martiales: Une approche socio-historique," *Actes de la recherche en sciences sociales* 179 (2009); Johan Heilbron, "Dans la cage: Genèse et dynamique des 'combats ultimes,'" *Actes de la recherche en sciences sociales* 179 (2009).
52. For images from the *SS Pentcho*, see the United States Holocaust Memorial Museum's online collections.
53. For more information about these instructors and the history of krav maga and kapap, see Noah Gross's article, "Krav Maga History Interview," on your-krav-maga-expert.com.
54. David Ben-Gurion envisioned a "People's Army" and chose compulsory military service as the primary tool for building the Jewish nation and allowing for social cohesion, integration, and solidarity. The choice to enlist women was made partly in response to a lack of men of military age, but also because military service was seen as the only patriotic matrix capable of producing a national community. The army was where one learned Hebrew and Jewish culture and history, alongside training in weapons and military discipline. In practice, behind this facade of inclusion, the Israeli army produced a norm of hegemonic masculinity by normalizing practices and constructing a system of meaning and values that resulted in "spontaneous consent to the patriarchal status quo." Orna Sasson-Levy, "Constructing Identities at the Margins: Masculinities and Citizenship in the Israeli Army," *Sociological Quarterly* 43, no. 3 (2002): 374. Sasson-Levy cites Renate Holub as a source for "spontaneous consent": Renate Holub, *Antonio Gramsci Beyond Marxism and Postmodernism* (Routledge, 1992), 6.
55. For more about these exclusively male units, see Martin Van Creveld, "Armed but Not Dangerous: Women in the Israeli

Forces," *War in History* 7, no. 1 (2000): 374. In this article, the author points out that women were excluded from all combat units following a traumatic event in December 1947, when a mixed unit of the Palmach was ambushed and decimated. The bodies of the fighters were found several days later, horribly mutilated. Cited in Vincent Joly, "Note sur les femmes et la féminisation de l'armée dans quelques revues d'histoire militaire," *Clio* 20 (2004). The Israeli army is officially gender inclusive, but although women receive military training, it is not the same as the men's. Most women are assigned to administrative roles, and only a minority become commanders (despite the existence of a special unit, the Hen, or Heil Nashim, the women's corps, that existed from 1949 to 2001). For an overview of this issue, see Ilaria Simonetti, "Le service militaire et la condition des femmes en Israël," *Bulletin du Centre de recherches français à Jérusalem* 17 (2006). [Simonetti also briefly deals with these issues in an English text: Ilaria Simonetti, "Women's Violence and Gender Relations in the Israeli Defence Forces," *Gender and Conflict: Embodiments, Discourses, and Symbolic Practices*, ed. Georg Frerks, Annelou Ypeij, and Reinhilde Sotiria König (Routledge, 2014), 71.—Trans.]

56 In regard to "society of security," see Michel Foucault, "La sécurité et l'État," *Dits et écrits: 1954–1988*, vol. 3 (Gallimard/Quarto, 1994), text no. 213: "Societies of security, in their current form, are tolerant of a whole range of different and varied behaviors, even deviant ones and ones that are antagonistic to each other; as long as, of course, these fall within certain boundaries, such that things, people, and behaviors considered unnecessary and dangerous are eliminated."

57 Krav maga, as it emerged in civilian society, had a small number of precepts: "Do not hurt yourself," "Remain modest" (meaning no needless fights, no overreactions, always control your emotions and affects, and train yourself mentally), "Act decisively" (make the right move at the right time at the right spot, using every advantage presented by the situation and your own resources), "Become as effective as possible" (allowing you not to have to kill). Eight [six?] principles summarize krav maga's martial foundation: avoid being hurt and always analyze risk, which is the essence of self-defense; use the martial body's natural reflexes and movements (never adopt an unnatural level of technical sophistication that takes time to embody or learn to execute properly); react correctly (staying balanced, adapting to the "environment," while defending by attacking); always strike at vulnerable and debilitating points (reducing the energy and time taken by the

fight); use any available object; and do not follow any rules (no technical, deontological, or sporting restrictions). See Imi Sde-Or (Lichtenfeld) and Eyal Yanilov, *Krav maga: How to Defend Yourself Against Armed Assault* (Dekel Publishing House, 2001), 3–4. See also Gavin De Becker, *The Gift of Fear and Other Survival Signals That Protect Us from Violence* (Delta, 1997). My thanks to Emmanuel Renault for having pointed me to this reference and for our correspondence on martial arts. We have used 1964 as the year Lichtenfeld left the army, but Izhac Grinberg, another historian of krav maga, claims that it was in 1963. See his article "History of Krav Maga," on kravmagainstitute.com.

58 Mathieu Rigouste, *La Domination policière* (La Fabrique, 2012), 211.

59 Regarding defensive passivity, Patrick Bruneteaux mentions that in the case of policing in metropolitan France, such techniques also seek to avoid charging so as not to escalate the situation. See Patrick Bruneteaux, *Maintenir l'ordre* (Presses de Sciences-po, 1996), 173, 225. See also David Dufresne, *Maintien de l'ordre* (Hachette, 2007). For self-restraint techniques, see Bruneteaux, *Maintenir l'ordre*, 105.

60 Lesley J. Wood, *Crisis and Control: The Militarization of Protest Policing* (Pluto Press, 2014).

61 In France, the widespread use of plainclothes police units (known as the BAC) and their sudden interventions in working-class neighborhoods has created a climate of fear and insecurity. For the BAC, any act of resistance or opposition is just a chance to *react*. " 'Fear is unavoidable,' says Christophe, a four-year veteran of the Seine-Saint-Denis region's BAC. 'Even with experience, you never know what you're going to run into ... You could get ambushed and hit with a paving stone from up in a building, or a cinder block, a piece of sidewalk, anything some of these people can get their hands on!' " Rigouste, *La Domination policière*, 168. This new dominant virility adds to the appeal of combat sports, self-defense, and any "realistic," "no rules" martial practice, which have become a *defensive hexis*.

62 Michel Foucault, "La sécurité et l'État."

The State, or the Non-Monopoly on Legitimate Defense

1 Thomas Hobbes, *Leviathan*, ed. Richard Tuck (Cambridge University Press, 1996), 91.

2 Ibid., 87.
3 "The notions of Right and Wrong, Justice and Injustice have there no place. Where there is no common Power, there is no Law: where no Law, no Injustice ... It is consequent also to the same condition, that there be no Propriety, no Dominion, no *Mine* and *Thine* distinct." Ibid., 90.
4 Ibid., 88–9.
5 Ibid., 92. "And from this diffidence of one another, there is no way for any man to secure himselfe, so reasonable, as Anticipation; that is, by force, or wiles, to master the persons of all men he can, so long, till he see no other power great enough to endanger him: And this is no more than his own conservation requireth, and is generally allowed." Ibid., 87–8.
6 Pierre-François Moreau perfectly describes the problem of the humanity of humans at play here. Despite the common sentiment *homo homini lupus* (Each man is a wolf to man), Hobbes's state of nature is different in every way from animality, from nature; this does not mean that humans are above nature, since for Hobbes all things are bodies and everything can be explained by the motion of bodies. Hobbes's Man "is a natural being that produces unnatural effects, and we might say that all his thinking is an effort to grasp this inescapable paradox." Pierre-François Moreau, *Hobbes: Philosophie, science et religion* (PUF, 1989), 44. See also ibid., 54–5.
7 Thomas Hobbes, *On the Citizen*, trans. Richard Tuck and Michael Silverthorne (Cambridge University Press, 2003), 39.
8 Ibid., 103.
9 Ibid., 103–4.
10 "Slavery, for all who look to Enlightenment Europe and revolutionary America as the source of their most cherished political values, is not the peculiar institution but the embarrassing institution." Orlando Patterson, *Slavery and Social Death: A Comparative Study* (Harvard University Press, 1982), ix. See also Eleni Varikas, "L'institution embarrassante," *Raisons politiques* 11 (2003).
11 Thomas Hobbes, *Leviathan*, 89.
12 John Locke, *Two Treatises of Government*, ed. Peter Laslett (Cambridge University Press, 2003), 269.
13 Ibid., 271.
14 Ibid., 287–8.
15 There is then a natural right of coalition among property owners against any "noxious creature" (ibid., 390). It draws on Locke's principle that self-preservation should always also involve preservation of the human species (ibid., 381–2): "every Man has a

Power to punish the Crime, to prevent it being committed again, by the Right he has of Preserving all Mankind." Ibid., 274. "Mankind" is clearly defined here as the community of those who own their person and what they have appropriated. The *others*, who have contravened the laws of nature by violating others' property, exclude themselves from humanity and become literally no longer *worthy of preservation*.

16 Ibid., 274.

17 "To have a body" presumes a relationship of property to your self, and therefore to be yourself is essentially a process of identifying this self as your own. To turn in on yourself or return to yourself then becomes a return home. On the question of consciousness and personal identity, see John Locke, *An Essay Concerning Human Understanding* (Penguin Classics, 1998), chap. 27. I would like to thank Bertrand Guillarme for the several years of friendly debates and discussions that contributed greatly to my views on this subject.

18 The goal of the community being the preservation of each and all. On this point, see John Locke, *Two Treatises of Government*, chap. 9 and 11.

19 It was not until the beginning of the nineteenth century that a dedicated police force was created in England. The Metropolitan Police Service, known as Scotland Yard after its first headquarters, was founded in 1829.

20 On the right to bear arms for all Protestants: "That the Subjects which are Protestants may have Arms for their Defence suitable to their Conditions and as allowed by Law." 1689 Bill of Rights, available on legislation.gov.uk. On the connection between the right to self-defense and natural rights, see William Blackstone, "On the Absolute Rights of Individuals," *Commentaries on the Laws of England* (1765–69).

21 Until the mid-eighteenth century, all costs associated with the justice system were to be paid by citizens. In 1752, a law was adopted to set aside a reserve fund to contribute to the costs for parties to a matter, but it was far from sufficient. The situation in France was comparable; see Michel Foucault, "14 February 1973," *The Punitive Society: Lectures at the Collège de France 1972–1973*, trans. Graham Burchell (Palgrave MacMillan, 2015), 121.

22 Craig B. Little and Christopher P. Sheffield, "Frontiers and Criminal Justice: English Private Prosecution Societies and American Vigilantism in the Eighteenth and Nineteenth Centuries," *American Sociological Review* 48, no. 6 (1983): 797.

23 A straight line can be drawn between the emergence of private police forces and the exponential growth in our time of the market for defending economic sites, where guards and other agents hired for security and surveillance are working-class men, the majority of whom are racialized. See Frédéric Péroumel, "Le monde précaire et illégitime des agents de sécurité," *Actes de recherche en sciences sociales* 5, no. 175 (2008).

24 Little and Sheffield, "Frontiers and Criminal Justice," 800.

25 Ibid., 801.

26 In his January 17, 1973, lecture at the Collège de France, Michel Foucault discusses a 1764 text by Guillaume-François Le Trosne, *Mémoire sur les vagabonds et sur les mendiants* [Reflections on vagabonds and beggars]. It is a political economy text dealing with delinquency as it emerged during a process of forcing individuals to work. Le Trosne takes aim at vagabonds in particular, whom he considers the source of all the theft faced by farmers. He advocates for armed self-defense by the farming community to supplement the mounted police. Foucault, *The Punitive Society*, 45–52.

27 Ibid., 131.

28 "As law, emanates from the people, written or not, [and is] nothing [but] certain rules of action by which a people agree to be governed, the unanimous decision among the people to put a man to death for the crime of murder, rendered the act legal." *The Niles Register*, cited in William C. Culberson, *Vigilantism: Political History of Private Power in America* (Greenwood Press, 1990, 5).

29 Benedict Anderson, *Imagined Communities: Reflecting on the Origin and Spread of Nationalism* (Verso, 2006), 6.

30 The term "frontier" is borrowed from French and refers to the myth of the Frontier. It evokes stories of the pioneers' glorious progress through the Great West, a vast territory to "explore" and "civilize." The frontier was the beyond, slowly being erased by the settlers' steps. In 1890, the United States Census Bureau officially did away with the idea of frontier, as they considered that all of the territory to the Pacific Ocean had been acquired: the nation was thus a continent. In 1893, in a talk entitled "The Significance of the Frontier in American History," the historian Frederick Jackson Turner presented a mythic narrative for American nationalism. His "frontier thesis" is an effort at describing an aspect of the typical American temperament. The westward expansion, carried out by generations of pioneers, produced a new kind of citizen, capable of taming the wilderness and forging their own autonomy and independence.

"Alone" against nature, confronting previously unknown challenges, they were able to develop the ability and wherewithal to defend themselves and to survive. "The New Frontier" is frequently referenced in political discourse, whether referring to "the conquest of space," "the war on poverty," or "the march toward peace." (For a notable example, see John F. Kennedy's acceptance speech to the National Democratic Convention on July 15, 1960.)

31 See Howard Zinn, *A People's History of the United States* (Harper Perennial Modern Classics, 2010).

32 "A well-regulated Militia, being necessary to the security of a free State, the right of the people to keep and bear Arms, shall not be infringed."

33 "A 1927 federal law forbade the United States Postal Service (but not private carriers) from transporting weapons; a law from 1934 imposed a heavy tax on certain kinds of weapons, such as submachine guns and sawed-off shotguns; and another in 1938 imposed licensing for gunsmiths. The most important law, the 1968 *Gun Control Act* regulates trade ... and forbids access to weapons for certain sections of the population (the mentally disabled, criminals, minors). In 1993, the Brady law mandated mental health and criminal screening for potential buyers ... These laws might seem coherent and relatively thorough. Unfortunately, many of their provisions don't go far enough, making them useless." Didier Combeau, "Les Américains et leurs armes: Droit inaliénable ou maladie du corps social?," *Revue française d'études américaines* 93 (2002): 101.

34 Regarding the extension of the right to bear arms to former slaves, the Supreme Court's 1857 ruling in *Dred Scott v. Sandford* upheld laws depriving individuals of "the Black race," whether free or enslaved, of the right to bear arms on the ground that this right is reserved exclusively for "American citizens." After the Civil War, most Southern states enacted measures, collectively referred to as the Black Codes, based on this decision, trampling the Fourteenth and Fifteenth Amendments. Regarding the ability of the states to regulate individual liberty, the *United States v. Miller* decision in 1939 returned to the question of militias and seemed to reach an unprecedented conclusion: it states that there are certain kinds of weapons that are not necessary for "the preservation or efficiency of a well-regulated militia." In other words, the decision means the right to armed legitimate defense is restricted to citizen militias. However, it leaves the door open to contradictory interpretations and does not present a fundamental challenge to the freedom of individuals and states to enact permissive legislation in

regard to personal weapons. This decision followed on a 1934 law adopted after a bloody episode in the context of Prohibition, known as the Saint Valentine's Day Massacre: on February 14, 1929, a violent clash occurred between Irish and Italian gangs (involving Al Capone on one side and Bugs Moran on the other), in which the use of automatic weapons and sawed-off shotguns led to seven deaths.

35 For more on this debate, see Robert E. Shallope, "The Ideological Origins of the Second Amendment," *Journal of American History* 69 (1982); Lawrence Delbert Cress, "An Armed Community: The Origins and Meaning of the Right to Bear Arms," *Journal of American History* 71, no. 1 (1984); Michael A. Bellesiles, "The Origins of Gun Culture in the United States, 1760–1865," *Journal of American History* 83, no. 2 (1996); Don Higginbotham, "The Federalized Militia Debate: A Neglected Aspect of Second Amendment Scholarship," *William and Mary Quarterly* 55, no. 1 (1998); Saul Cornell and Nathan Kozuskanich, eds., *The Second Amendment on Trial: Critical Essays on* District of Columbia v. Heller (University of Massachusetts Press, 2013).

36 See Hubert Howe Bancroft, *Popular Tribunals* (History Co., 1887), 27. In this text, the author bases his argument for "the illegal administration of justice by the people," or vigilantism, on two principles: the sovereignty of the people and the right to revolution.

37 Alexandre Barde (1811–63). "The Attakapas" originally referred to a Native American people, given this name by the Spanish in reference to their supposed cannibalism. The Attakapa nation was decimated and exterminated by infectious diseases spread by Europeans throughout the eighteenth century, and the name "Attakapas" came to simply refer to their territory—the southwest of modern-day Louisiana.

38 The first American vigilance committee is considered to have emerged in South Carolina—then a colony of British North America—in the 1760s, calling themselves "regulators." This name referred to the ongoing War of Regulation, which took place in North Carolina between 1765 and 1771 and pitted the working classes against the colonial elite (big landowners) and the corrupt local administration. This event is considered one of the major struggles of the American Revolution. Against this backdrop, between 1766 and 1769, a group of small landowners in South Carolina established themselves as a regulator against those they considered thieves, poachers, and bandits. See Ray Abrahams, *Vigilant Citizens: Vigilantism and the States* (Polity, 1998).

39 Richard Maxwell Brown, *Strain of Violence: Historical Studies of American Violence and Vigilantism* (Oxford University Press, 1975), 134.
40 "Courage, probity, and honor had sprouted from the ground and blossomed like orange trees in the tropics, and the crosses atop the humble clock towers of the villages across the Attakapas must have been proud that their shadows fell only on lands and souls ripe for a social life in the footsteps of Christ . . . Even the Negros themselves knew not theft." Alexandre Barde, *Histoire des comités de vigilance des Attakapas* (Imprimerie de Meshacébé et de l'Avant-Coureur, 1861), 8–9.
41 Ibid., 12.
42 Ibid., 15.
43 Ibid., 23.
44 Ibid. See also p. 208.
45 Ibid., 24.
46 Ibid., 27–8.
47 Ibid., 44.
48 Ibid., 28. Lawyers were excluded, along with the principle of contradiction itself: *audiator et altera pars* (let the other side also be heard).
49 Alexandre Barde frequently cites the French Revolution as a legendary time of vigilantism.
50 Ibid., 32. Vigilantism has more in common with military justice than civilian. Regarding the hunt for bandits and people "who need to be wiped out," see ibid., 29.
51 Giambattista Vico, *The New Science*, trans. Thomas Goddard Bergin and Max Harold Fisch (Cornell University Press, 1948), 320.
52 Grégoire Chamayou, "Le jour des représailles: Théories de la vengeance et de la révolution au XIXe siècle," in *Faire justice soi-même: Études sur la vengeance*, ed. Jean-Claude Bourdin (Presses universitaires de Rennes, 2010), 159.
53 G. W. F. Hegel, *Philosophy of Right*, trans. S. W. Dyde (Batoche Books, 2001), §350, 269. See also §93. I am following Grégoire Chamayou's argument here.
54 G. W. F. Hegel, *The Philosophy of History*, trans. J. Sibree (Prometheus Books, 1991), 311.
55 Ibid., 45.

White Justice

1 William D. Carrigan, *The Making of a Lynching Culture: Violence and Vigilantism in Central Texas 1836–1916* (University of Illinois Press, 2006); Frederick Douglass, "Lynch Law in the South," *North American Review* 155, no. 428 (1892): 17–24.
2 James Allan, ed., *Without Sanctuary: Lynching Photography in America* (Twin Palms, 2000). See the associated website, withoutsanctuary.org. See also Amy Louise Wood, *Lynching and Spectacle: Witnessing Racial Violence in America* (University of North Carolina, 2009).
3 The archives of anti-lynching organizations show that out of a hundred cases of lynching, in half, the police actively turned the detainee over to the crowd, and they turned a blind eye in 90 percent of the remaining cases. Jacquelyn Dowd Hall, *Revolt Against Chivalry: Jesse Daniel Ames and the Women's Campaign Against Lynching* (Columbia University Press, 1993), 139.
4 In 1935, the painter Joe Jones displayed one of his paintings during an opening in New York City. Titled *American Justice* (or *White Justice*), it denounced the atrocities committed by the KKK. The painting depicts a nocturnal scene; in the foreground is the sprawled corpse of an African American woman who has been raped and hung, and behind her are her masked executioners. A dog howls beside the woman, and in the background, a house is in flames.
5 Jacquelyn Dowd Hall notes that in the majority of cases, the crowds were mobilized and directed by groups of notables, made up of respectable citizens, representatives of the religious or civic establishment, and businessmen. In the same vein, lynchings in rural areas were usually directed by planters, especially in the summer months when the Black laborers' work in the fields was at its most exhausting, and the terror they inspired made possible other forms of coerced productivity. "Now is the season," proclaimed an editorial in a Georgia newspaper denounced by the ASWPL (Association of Southern Women for the Prevention of Lynching) in the January 13–14, 1936, issue of their paper. Cited by Dowd Hall, *Revolt Against Chivalry*, 140.
6 Ibid., 141.
7 In the 1920s, 95 percent of lynchings occurred in the southern United States. During the same period, the percentage of white victims dropped from 32 percent to 9 percent. Ibid., 133. One of the first large statistical analyses of lynching was carried out by Ida B. Wells (1862–1931) in 1895 and published under the title *Red Record: Tabulated Statistics and Alleged Causes of Lynchings*

in the United States. Wells was a feminist, abolitionist, teacher, journalist, and one of the leading figures of the movement against lynching. For an overview of Wells's work, see Ida B. Wells-Barnett, *On Lynchings* (Humanity Books, 2002); and Paula J. Giddings, *A Sword Among Lions: Ida B. Wells and the Campaign Against Lynching* (Harper Paperbacks, 2009).

8   Ida B. Wells, *Southern Horrors: Lynch Law in All Its Phases* (The New York Age Print, 1892). The text is available online on archive.org.

9   Women also knowingly lied, whether by accusing men of rape or assault and thereby condemning them to death, or by failing to refute the accusation. The case of Emmett Till is a revealing example. In 2007, fifty years after the events in question, Carolyn Bryant acknowledged that she had lied during the trial of the murderers of Emmett Till. Bryant had claimed that Till, a fourteen-year-old African American teenager, had physically and verbally assaulted her in a Mississippi grocery store, causing her to fear for her life. On August 28, 1955, Emmett Till's horribly mutilated body was found in a river. The murderers, Carolyn Bryant's husband, Roy Bryant, and her half brother, were acquitted at trial on September 12 by a jury made up of twelve white men. This killing became a major focus for the movement against lynching and for civil rights in the United States, notably because Emmett Till's mother had insisted that her son's casket be left open during his funeral. The photos of the teenager's body spread across the country and around the world and provoked an international mobilization against American racism. In 1960, Aimé Césaire dedicated a poem in his book *Ferrements* to the memory of Emmett Till, and in 1962, Bob Dylan wrote "The Death of Emmett Till," which Joan Baez later performed. See Timothy B. Tyson, *The Blood of Emmett Till* (Simon & Schuster, 2017).

10 Wells, *Southern Horrors: Lynch Law*, chap. 6, "Self-Help."

11 See Crystal Nicole Feimster, *Southern Horrors: Women and the Politics of Rape and Lynching* (Harvard University Press, 2009), 62.

12 During the WCTU's Texas campaign, its leader, Helen Stoddard, defended her desire to raise the age of consent using a reference to young Black girls that could not have been clearer: "As I pass along the streets of our cities and see the mulatto children, I think the colored girl needs protection, and more than that, the Anglo-Saxon man needs the constraint of this law to help him take measure of the dignity and the sacred heritage he possesses for having been born in the dominant race." Ibid., 72. Locally, the WCTU was one of the rare organizations that allowed Black women to

join, and it sought to encourage the safety and morality of households; however, this amounted to a means of social, racial, and sexual control of the poorest classes. The campaign around the age of consent for females occurred alongside the WCTU's struggles against alcoholism (and in support of prohibition), against prostitution (which the organization defined as a consequence of the sexual violence faced by the lower classes), and for what they termed "family values," which included African American families and legitimate mixed-race children. The movement worked to advance a specific dominant form of femininity, defined in terms of the values of white motherhood, and it failed to break from the racist portrayals of Black femininity rooted in the slavery era.

13 The first demonstrations Rebecca L. Felton organized in the 1880s followed the sentencing by an Atlanta judge of a young African American woman named Adaline Maddox to five years of hard labor for the theft of fifty cents. The large majority of prisoners sentenced to hard labor were Black teenagers who were almost exclusively in for minor offenses, and they frequently died from abuse and mistreatment (ibid., 64).

14 Ibid., 71.

15 Georgia did not raise the age of female sexual consent from ten to fourteen years of age until 1918. In 1897, Felton gave a famous speech, "Woman on the Farm," which was reprinted in several Southern newspapers. In it, she dismisses the idea that Black men have a propensity toward rape and argues that all rapes of women are the fault of white men for failing to provide sufficient legal protection and social rights to their women. She denounces the instrumentalization of the Black electorate by white men who trick the African American man by making him believe "he is a man and your brother," because this also makes Black men think they have an equal claim to white women. Her conclusion is thus that if white men do not accept responsibility, consider the morality of their actions and policies, and give rights to women, they will have to continue lynching in order to maintain the illusion and deflect blame from their own corruption and immorality. She closed her speech by saying, "Lynch, a thousand times a week if necessary." This phrase was extracted from her speech and was widely circulated throughout the South as a front-page newspaper headline: "Lynch 1,000 weekly, Declares Mrs. Felton." See Feimster, *Southern Horrors: Women and the Politics of Rape and Lynching*, 127.

16 Philip Alexander Bruce played an important role in the development of this racist myth, providing the theoretical backbone. Philip Alexander Bruce, *The Plantation Negro as a Free Man:*

Observations on His Character, Condition, and Prospects in Virginia (Putnam's Sons, 1889). The number of lynchings of African American men increased significantly starting in the 1890s, making the practice of lynching into a veritable racist technology of execution. Beyond the fact that this myth created a form of gendered xenophobia (in the literal sense, as white women developed a fear of Black men), Diane Miller Sommerville provides a detailed analysis of the way this racist representation of Black men was spread, how it was incorporated into Southern feminist spaces, and the various ways the women in them took it up. Diane Miller Sommerville, *Rape and Race in the Nineteenth Century South* (University of North Carolina Press, 2004).

17 See Glenda Gilmore, *Gender and Jim Crow: Women and the Politics of White Supremacy in North Carolina 1896–1920* (University of North Carolina Press, 1996).

18 Dowd Hall, *Revolt Against Chivalry*, 79.

19 "Nobody in this section of the country believes the old threadbare lie that Negro men rape white women." Wells, *Southern Horrors: Lynch Law*, chap. 1, "The Offense."

20 The Woman's Era Club was founded in 1892 by Josephine St. Pierre Ruffin (1842–1924). Ruffin's family was from Martinique on her father's side, and she created the first newspaper written by and intended for African American women in 1894, *The Woman's Era*, and in 1895 she organized the various associations of Black women into a national federation.

21 Feimster, *Southern Horrors: Women and the Politics of Rape and Lynching*, 110.

22 Waco was considered both a modern and moderate city at that time compared with other cities in the South, largely due to the presence of an established and educated Black middle class and of legislation forbidding lynchings in the state of Texas.

23 W. E. B. Du Bois, "Waco Horror," *Crisis* 12, no. 3 (1986): section 6. The full article is available online in the University of Massachusetts's digital archive, Credo. From 1885 to 1916, the NAACP recorded 2,843 lynchings.

24 Dowd Hall, *Revolt Against Chivalry*, 164.

25 Ibid.

26 *The Nation*, cited in Ibid.

27 See Elizabeth Fox-Genovese, *Within the Plantation Household: Black and White Women of the Old South* (University of North Carolina Press, 1988).

28 For more on this point, see the African American writer Pauline Hopkins's novel *Contending Forces* (Oxford University Press, 1991).

29 From a speech by Florida Ruffin, the daughter of Josephine St. Pierre Ruffin. Cited in Feimster, *Southern Horrors: Women and the Politics of Rape and Lynching*, 108.
30 Wendy Brown, *States of Injury: Power and Freedom in Late Modernity* (Princeton University Press, 1995), 170.
31 Gayatri Chakravorty Spivak, *Can the Subaltern Speak? Reflections on the History of an Idea* (Columbia University Press, 2010), 72.
32 Leila Ahmed, *Women and Gender in Islam: Historical Roots of a Modern Debate* (Yale University Press, 1992). See also Karima Ramdani, "Femmes modernes et de traditions musulmanes: Traduction de la modernité coloniale dans les rhétoriques féministes anticolonialistes," *Comment s'en sortir?* 1 (2015).
33 "I was taken back when I first came across the assertion in Brigadier General [at Abu Ghraib] Janis Karpinski's memoir that she sees herself as part of a generation that led a feminist revolution within the military." Coco Fusco, *A Field Guide for Female Interrogators* (Seven Stories Press, 2008), 61.
34 On this issue, see Judith Butler, *Precarious Life* (Verso, 2004); and *Frames of War: When Is Life Grievable?* (Verso, 2009). On the use of sexuality—notably the obsession with sodomy in the forms of torture used by American soldiers, see Judith Butler, *Humain inhumain: Le travail critique des normes*, trans. Jérôme Vidal and Christine Vivier (Éditions Amsterdam, 2005), 150.
35 Coco Fusco draws on the narrative of Sergeant Kayla Williams, who participated in interrogations in the Mosul detention center: "The male interrogators on hand brought in a prisoner and removed his clothes, and then instructed her to 'mock his manhood,' 'ridicule his genitals,' and 'remind him that he is being humiliated in the presence of a blond American female.'" Fusco, *A Field Guide for Female Interrogators*, 44–5. In addition to the words, the women soldiers used provocative clothing, makeup, and high heels, as well as "many forms of sexually aggressive behavior in booths, ranging from touching themselves and removing their clothing, to touching the prisoners." Ibid., 46.
36 "Technologies of gender" is a phrase borrowed from Teresa De Lauretis, *Technologies of Gender: Essays on Theory, Film, and Fiction* (Indiana University Press, 1987).

Self-Defense: Power to the People!

1 Amiri Baraka, *Arm Yourself or Harm Yourself: A One Act Play* (Jihad Publications, 1967). Baraka (formerly known as Everett

LeRoi Jones, 1934–2014) was among the fiercest critics within the 1960s artistic and cultural world of the integrationist and pacifist currents in the civil rights movement. His revolutionary poetry called for violence, as this was the only way to struggle against the injustice of white America. His works include *Black Art* (1965), which became the manifesto of the Black Arts Literary Movement. See Jerry Gafio Watts, *Amiri Baraka: The Politics and Art of a Black Intellectual* (New York University Press, 2001).

2 Ida B. Wells, *Southern Horrors: Lynch Law in All Its Phases* (The New York Age Print, 1892), chap. 6.

3 Marcus Garvey, "Soldiers of Ethiopia," *Negro World*, October 11, 1919. Cited in Theodore G. Vincent, ed., *Voices of a Black Nation: Political Journalism in the Harlem Renaissance* (Ramparts Press, 1973), 139.

4 W. E. B. Du Bois, "Introduction," *An Appeal to the World!* (National Association for the Advancement of Colored People, 1947), 12. The petition was accompanied by a report by Leslie S. Perry for the NAACP, and excerpts from it were used in the international press. For instance, a section is available in Leslie S. Perry, "Facts About Jim Crow," *Fourth International* 7, no. 9 (1947). This quotation is discussed in Timothy B. Tyson, *Radio Free Dixie: Robert F. Williams and the Roots of Black Power* (University of North Carolina Press, 1999), 51–2.

5 Tyson, *Radio Free Dixie*, 52. Walter White, a white journalist and intellectual involved in the NAACP who was one of the initiators of the Harlem Renaissance, described nations "pleased to have documentary proof that the United States did not practice what it preached about freedom and democracy." Ibid.

6 Ibid.

7 Despite the Supreme Court's historic 1954 ruling in *Brown v. Board of Education*, some Southern states retained segregationist structures, following Mississippi's lead. The success of the Montgomery bus boycott in Alabama led to protests by white people and to shows of force by the KKK and other white supremacist groups, along with an increase in the intensity of their violent acts. In Charleston, South Carolina, a demonstration of between 12,000 and 15,000 white people made the September 21, 1956, edition of the *News and Courier*, and in Monroe, North Carolina, there were hundreds of cross burnings and demonstrations by the KKK, described in the *Monroe Enquirer*'s March 17, 1958, edition. Timothy B. Tyson, "Introduction: Robert F. Williams, Black Power and the Roots of the African American Freedom Struggle," in Robert F. Williams, *Negroes with Guns* (Wayne State University Press, 1988), xviii–xix.

8   Ibid.
9   For "fighting unit," see Julian Mayfield, "Challenge to Negro Leadership: The Case of Robert Williams," *Commentary*, April 1961, 298. Cited in Tyson, "Introduction," xix. Regarding military veterans: when he returned from the front, Bernie Montgomery, a childhood friend of Williams and a fellow veteran, killed his white employer during an altercation over his weekly pay being withheld. Montgomery evaded the KKK but was eventually captured by police. He was tried for murder and executed in the gas chamber of Raleigh's Central Prison. While his remains were on the way to Monroe to be returned to his family for the funeral, the KKK made it known that Montgomery's body belonged to them and that they were going to come reclaim it to display it in town. A number of Black militants, including Robert F. Williams, decided to organize and wait for the group of Klansmen to arrive at the morgue. Williams and his comrades had been members of the National Rifle Association for many years, since this controversial organization has historically been open to veterans and reservists, which allowed them to train. Regarding the second KKK, the organization is usually seen as having two periods. The first period began with its founding in 1865 and ran until 1877, when the group was banned (and other groups took its place, such as the White League). The second period was heavily inspired by the successful film *The Birth of a Nation* (directed by D. W. Griffith and released in 1915), in turn based on a novel by Thomas Dixon (*The Clansman*, 1906). The KKK spread rapidly in this period, claiming to have 10 million members in 1924, and it enjoyed the obvious support of Washington. However, in 1928 it was once again outlawed. After the Second World War, it tried to regain its position, but its influence was limited to the Southern states.
10 Notably, Roy Wilkins, an anticommunist NAACP leader, opposed organizing around the Kissing Case. He would go on to become one of the most prominent opponents of the Black Power movement.
11 Williams was accused of kidnapping, and, considered a dangerous criminal, he was forced to flee to Cuba in 1961. He spent four years there with his family, during which time he developed a model of Black internationalism for global revolution that brought together Black nationalism and anti-imperialism. In Havana, he founded Radio Free Dixie, which ran from 1961 to 1965. It mostly played music but also broadcast speeches, notably during the Watts rebellion, when Williams called for insurrection. Williams continued inspiring revolutionaries in the United States,

notably the Revolutionary Action Movement (RAM), formed in 1961 by students in Ohio already involved in civil rights organizations. Among them were Donald Freeman, Max Stanford, and Wanda Marshall, who would go on to publish the journals *Black America* and *RAM Speaks*. Their activities were largely centered on the university: at Fisk in 1964, RAM organized the first conference of African American students on Black nationalism, and the theoretical work of its members was very influential, notably for Bobby Seale, one of the founders of the Black Panther Party for Self-Defense. See Robin D. G. Kelley and Betsy Esch, "Black Like Mao: Red China and the Black Revolution," in *The New Black Renaissance: The Souls Anthology of Critical African-American Studies*, ed. Manning Marable (Routledge, 2005), 39.

12 Du Bois's position on self-defense is similar to that of Ida B. Wells. In 1906, while the white population of Atlanta was in the streets demonstrating, Du Bois wrote, "If a white mob had stepped on the campus where I lived I would without hesitation have sprayed their guts over the grass." See W. E. B. Du Bois, *The Autobiography of W. E. B. Du Bois: A Soliloquy on Viewing My Life from the First Decade to the Last* (International Publishers Co., 1968), 286. In 1961, encouraged by Robert F. Williams, Du Bois added his signature to the text "Cuba: A Declaration of Conscience by Afro-Americans," which appeared in the *Baltimore Afro-American* on April 22 and 29, and in the *New York Post* on April 25: "Because we have known oppression, because we have suffered more than other Americans, because we are still fighting for our own liberation from tyranny, we Afro-Americans have the right and the duty to raise our voices in protest against the forces of oppression that now seek to crush a free people linked to us by bonds of blood and a common heritage." The declaration was also signed by Amiri Baraka, Julian Mayfield, Maya Angelou, and Du Bois's partner, Shirley Graham. See also Tyson, *Radio Free Dixie*, 242.

13 The commissioner of the Board of Corrections and Training added conditions to the release of the children on January 2, 1959. Because the boys had been found guilty, their behavior must never be "unruly, disobedient to parents, and wayward." Ibid., 125. This form of conditional release essentially meant social control for life, and it also affected the children's mothers, as they were held responsible for the so-called wrongs for which their children had been imprisoned. While saying that the boys' time in the youth correctional facility had allowed them to make progress and improve their behavior, the commissioner added that their families needed to continue that work: "Local welfare

personnel ... must establish that [the families] will not neglect [the boys] and will give reasonable protection, guidance, and home care for [the children].'" Ibid. The children were finally freed a month after the commissioner made this comment: "I hope that the mothers of these two boys will meet their responsibilities as mothers." Ibid., 135.

14 Situations of this kind are a constant in accounts of the period. Denying the attack makes defensive actions seem like the initial attack.
15 Williams, *Negroes with Guns*, 9.
16 Ibid., 9–10.
17 Ibid., 17.
18 Ibid., 26.
19 Ibid.
20 Ibid., 72.
21 Robert F. Williams, "Revolution Without Violence?" *The Crusader: Monthly Newsletter* 5, no. 2 (1964).
22 Williams, *Negroes with Guns*, 82.
23 Ibid.
24 "White racist brutality." Christopher B. Strain, *Pure Fire: Self-Defense as Activism in the Civil Rights Era* (University of Georgia Press, 2005), 65. "Something as fundamental as racist oppression." Williams, *Negroes with Guns*, 72.
25 "The Montgomery bus boycott was perhaps the most successful example of completely pacifist action. But we must remember that in Montgomery where there are Negroes riding in the front of buses, there are Negroes who are starving." Ibid., 77.
26 Williams's reference points are the struggle against anti-Semitic pogroms and Nazism, the struggle of the Vietnamese against imperialism, the struggle of African nations against colonialism, and the Cuban struggle.
27 Following his exile in Cuba, Williams traveled to China at Mao Zedong's invitation.
28 Representatives were present from the following organizations: Stokely Carmichael for the Student Nonviolent Coordinating Committee (the SNCC, founded in 1960); Martin Luther King for the Southern Christian Leadership Conference (SCLC) and the Mississippi Freedom Democratic Party (MFDP); Floyd McKissick and James Farmer for the Congress of Racial Equality (CORE, an interracial group created in 1947); the Medical Committee for Human Rights (MCHR); and finally, the controversial Deacons for Defense and Justice, a self-defense group formed in Louisiana in 1964 to protect activists in groups like CORE from the KKK and who would provide protection for the march.

29 "What we are going to start saying now is Black Power."
30 On this point, see Strain, *Pure Fire*, 116.
31 Malcolm X, interview by Kenneth B. Clark, "Malcolm X," *The Negro Protest* (Beacon Press, 1963), 26.
32 In the Schomberg Center for Research in Black Culture in New York City, there exists an archive of photographs of nonviolent resistance training held by the SCLC and other groups. In it, there are photos of seated activists enduring hot cigarette ashes thrown onto their necks or faces. For more on nonviolence, see Hourya Benthouhami-Molino, *Le dépôt des armes: Non-violence et désobéissance civile* (PUF, 2015).
33 Robert F. Williams, cited in Tyson, *Radio Free Dixie*, 149.
34 "The oppressor must be harassed until his doom. He must have no peace by day or by night." Huey P. Newton, "In Defense of Self-Defense 1: June 20, 1967," *To Die for the People* (Vintage Books, 1972), 84.
35 One of the party's first actions was to challenge changes to the laws around bearing arms in California, which were an attempt to cripple African American self-defense movements. "The Black Panther Party for Self-Defense calls upon the American people in general and the Black people in particular to take careful note of the racist California Legislature, which is now considering legislation aimed at keeping the Black people disarmed and powerless at the very same time that racist police agencies throughout the country are intensifying the terror, brutality, murder and repression of Black people." Huey P. Newton, "In Defense of Self-Defense: Executive Mandate Number One," *The Black Panther*, June 2, 1967, in Philip S. Foner, ed., *The Black Panthers Speak* (Haymarket Books, 2014), 40.
36 Bobby Seale, "Bobby Seale Explains Panther Politics: An Interview," *Guardian*, February 1970, in Foner, *The Black Panthers Speak*, 86.
37 California made it illegal to carry weapons in public spaces in 1969.
38 Simon Wendt, "The Roots of Black Power? Armed Resistance and the Radicalization of the Civil Rights Movement," in *The Black Power Movement: Rethinking the Civil Rights–Black Power Era*, ed. Peniel E. Joseph (Routledge, 2006), 158–9.
39 "When Black people send a representative, he is somewhat absurd because he represents no political power. He does not represent land power because we do not own any land. He does not represent economic or industrial power because Black people do not own the means of production. The only way he can become political is to represent what is commonly called a military

power—which the Black Panther Party for Self-Defense calls Self-Defense Power. Black people can develop Self-Defense Power by arming themselves from house to house, block to block, community to community, throughout the nation. Then we will choose a political representative and he will state to the power structure the desires of the Black masses." Huey P. Newton, "Functional Definition of Politics," *The Black Panther*, January 17, 1969. For a related discussion, see Strain, *Pure Fire*, 163–4.

40 Wendt, 158, 163.
41 Regarding "civil war": "It is our belief that the Black people in America are the only people who can free the world, loosen the yoke of colonialism, and destroy the war machine. Black people who are within the machine can cause it to malfunction. They can, because of their intimacy with the mechanism, destroy the engine that is enslaving the world. America will not be able to fight every Black country in the world and fight a civil war at the same time. It is militarily impossible to do both of these things at once." Newton, *To Die for the People*, 83. Regarding "social war": "The racist dog oppressors fear the armed people; they fear most of all Black people armed with weapons and the ideology of the Black Panther Party for Self-Defense. An unarmed people are slaves or are subject to slavery at any given moment. If a government is not afraid of the people, it will arm the people against foreign aggression. Black people are held captive in the midst of their oppressors. There is a world of difference between thirty million unarmed submissive Black people and thirty million Black people armed with freedom, guns, and the strategic methods of liberation." Ibid., 85. Regarding "war of liberation," Huey P. Newton cites "Brother Mao Tse-tung." Ibid., 86.
42 Strain, *Pure Fire*, 167.
43 Some critics of the Black Panthers accused them of being essentially a racist militia. Bobby Seale addressed this in his interview with the *Guardian*. Foner, *The Black Panthers Speak*, 85.
44 This critique was also made by voices outside the organization. For instance, Angela Davis pointed out (in the context of protesting the wrongful arrest of Huey Newton) that calls for self-defense or to take up arms are great for firing up a crowd or getting cheers at meetings, but "the gaping void was a clear-cut line of action spelling out the way to organize masses of people in struggle in order to guarantee that Huey Newton would be set free." Angela Davis, *An Autobiography* (International Publishers, 1988), 169.
45 Sarah Webster Fabio, "Free by Any Means Necessary," in Foner, *The Black Panthers Speak*, 20.

46 The FBI's COINTELPRO program was officially established in 1956 to eradicate, infiltrate, and discredit the Communist Party USA, as well as to surveil the leaders of Black organizations considered to be infested with communists. These included the Southern Christian Leadership Conference (founded in 1957), Martin Luther King Jr., and the Socialist Workers' Party (founded in 1961). The FBI was implicated in the murder of Malcolm X, and the agency's attacks, infiltration, and persecution continued with the Black Hate program, aimed at the Student Nonviolent Coordinating Committee, the Deacons for Defense and Justice, and the Congress of Racial Equality. In late 1968, FBI director J. Edgar Hoover declared, "The Black Panther Party is the single greatest threat to the internal security of the United States," and said that 1969 would be its last year of existence. Elaine Brown, *A Taste of Power: A Black Woman's Story* (Anchor Books, 1994), 156. On December 4, 1969, Fred Hampton was murdered by the Chicago police and the FBI. Hampton was born in Monroe in 1948 and became a militant with the Black Panther Party in 1968, where he quickly evolved into a major intellectual and political figure. He contributed to the development of the party's social revolutionary politics and worked to form a broad coalition of movements on the radical left, in particular the Rainbow Coalition in Chicago, which brought together leftists from student, socialist, and feminist currents with white, Black, and Hispanic revolutionaries. The FBI designated Hampton a charismatic leader who needed to be killed. They used an undercover agent who had been hired by the party to be his bodyguard in order to get close to him before killing him in the early morning on December 4. Hampton was shot several times in the head while he slept beside his partner, eight months pregnant, who was charged, along with the other militants present in the house at the time, of attempting to murder a police officer.

47 Women militants were in fact mostly assigned to positions involving the party's social projects.

48 Elaine Brown was an early member of the Black Panther Party for Self-Defense, having joined in 1968. In 1971, she joined the party's central committee as the minister of information, replacing Eldridge Cleaver, and served as president from 1974 to 1977.

49 Brown describes how already in the party's first year of existence, there were between fifty and a hundred new recruits at their Wednesday night meetings: "The party was popular, especially among gang members and young girls who lived on the streets. It was admirable and 'tough,' they felt, to be a Panther. There was the uniform: black leather jackets and berets. There were the

guns. There was the manhood and the respect to be claimed. There was the heroic image of the leadership. Most of those who came were men. Many did not return. They were driven away by the discipline and the reading. There were, however, those like me who signed on for the duration." See Brown, *A Taste of Power*, 137.

50 "Armed Black Brothers in Richmond Community," *Black Panther*, April 25, 1967. Reproduced in Foner, *The Black Panthers Speak*, 11.

51 Ibid., 12.

52 Brown, *A Taste of Power*, 137. Specifically, she is referring to Vietnam.

53 Brown, *A Taste of Power*, 444. These pages, in which Elaine Brown describes her decision to leave the party, are particularly tragic. Regina Davis, an activist in charge of the Black Panther Party's school, was attacked by some Brothers, suffering a broken jaw, because of an argument with a male activist who was not doing the work at the school he had been hired to do. Huey Newton himself authorized this disciplinary measure, and in a phone call, Brown criticized him for making a decision that meant suicide for the party: "Just put the Brothers in line and keep this thing alive. I'm not just talking about Regina. I'm talking about all the women. They're critical. And all of them are scared." Ibid., 446.

54 "His desire to be white—i.e., to be a man." Frantz Fanon, *Black Skin, White Masks*, trans. Richard Philcox (Grove Press, 2008), 190.

55 Davis, 167. Discussions about the need to reconceptualize Marxism with a more central focus on racism had been ongoing for some time. See W. E. B. Du Bois, "Marxism and the Negro Problem," *Crisis*, May 1933. In Vincent, *Voices of a Black Nation*, 2010.

56 Frances Beal used the term "counterrevolutionary" in one of the major texts in African American feminism. See Frances Beal, "Double Jeopardy: To Be Black and Female," *Black Women's Manifesto* (The Third World Women's Alliance, 1970), 22.

57 The publication of Daniel P. Moynihan's text *The Negro Family* in 1965 breathed new life into the idea that Black matriarchy was the cause of the violence and criminality carried out by boys who had been abandoned by their "castrated" fathers, which was in turn the cause of social service deficits. Moynihan was a Harvard professor and a liberal intellectual who worked for the Kennedy administration, but he came to represent the influential neoconservative movement and became Richard Nixon's right hand on social issues. Daniel P. Moynihan, *The Negro Family: The Case*

for National Action (Office of Policy Planning and Research, US Department of Labor, 1965).

58 "We had much to make up for by being gentle in the face of our own humiliation, by being soft-spoken (ideally to the point that our voices could not be heard at all), by being beautiful (whatever that was), by being submissive—how often that word was shoved at me in poems and in songs as something to strive for." Michele Wallace, "Anger in Isolation: A Black Feminist's Search for Sisterhood," in *Words of Fire: An Anthology of African-American Feminist Thought*, ed. Beverly Guy-Sheftall (New York Press, 1995), 222.

59 For mimicry within colonial relations, see Homi Bhabha, *The Location of Culture* (Routledge, 1994), 85. In regard to being vulgar, a perfect example is the stigmatization of the language of the ghetto, notably the use of the term "motherfucker." This is a way of masking the social and structural violence of the racist justice system and police. See Bobby Seale's interview with the *Guardian*, in Foner, *The Black Panthers Speak*, 87. For "original," see Judith Butler, *Gender Trouble* (Routledge, 2007), 43.

60 Bobby Seale interview in Foner, *The Black Panthers Speak*, 86–7.

61 For "ideological sign," see Valentin Voloshinov, *Marxism and the Philosophy of Language*, trans. Ladislav Matejka and I. R. Titunik (Harvard University Press, 1986), 9. "Thus, various different classes will use one and the same language. As a result, differently oriented accents intersect in every ideological sign. Sign becomes an arena of the class struggle . . . This social *multiaccentuality* of the ideological sign is a very crucial aspect . . . The very same thing that makes the ideological sign vital and mutable is also, however, that which makes it a refracting and distorting medium. The ruling class strives to impart a supraclass, eternal character to the ideological sign to extinguish or drive inward the struggle between social value judgments which occurs in it, to make the sign uniaccentual . . . In the ordinary conditions of life, the contradiction embedded in every ideological sign cannot emerge fully because the ideological sign in an established, dominant ideology is always somewhat reactionary and tries, as it were, to stabilize the preceding factor in the dialectical flux of the social generative process, so accentuating yesterday's truth so as to make it appear today's." Ibid., 23–4.

62 See Hortense Spillers, "Mama's Baby, Papa's Maybe: An American Grammar Book," *Diacritics* 17, no. 2 (1987); and Patricia Hill Collins, *Black Feminist Thought* (Routledge, 2000).

Self-Defense and Safety

1 The GLF was created just a few days after Stonewall in New York, and its name was chosen in reference to the National Liberation Front of South Vietnam.
2 Christina B. Hanhardt, *Safe Space: Gay Neighborhood History and the Politics of Violence* (Duke University Press, 2013), 87.
3 See *The Combahee River Collective Statement*, first released in 1977 and widely available online, for instance at blackpast.org.
4 In March and April 1979, six Black women were murdered in the same area of Boston. A march was organized in April, and following it, the Combahee River Collective, including one of its cofounders, Barbara Smith, released a text denouncing the general indifference surrounding the murders. It also challenged the failure to recognize their sexist and racist character and the structural violence racialized women face that makes them more vulnerable. The text is a manifesto for feminist self-defense, providing women with resources to protect themselves at a time when the authorities were encouraging them to stay home or to go out accompanied by a man. In May, the number of victims rose to twelve.
5 Carl Wittman, *A Gay Manifesto* (The Red Butterfly, 1970). Available online from the Gay Homeland Foundation.
6 Hanhardt, *Safe Space*, 96.
7 Ibid., 73–5.
8 "Once in the cities, erotic populations tend to nucleate and to occupy some regular, visible territory ... Gay pioneers occupied neighborhoods that were centrally located but run-down. Consequently, they border poor neighborhoods. Gays, especially low-income gays, end up competing with other low-income groups for the limited supply of cheap and moderate housing. In San Francisco, competition for low-cost housing has exacerbated both racism and homophobia and is one source of the epidemic of street violence against homosexuals ... Poor gay renters are visible in low-income neighborhoods; multimillionaire contractors are not. The specter of the 'homosexual invasion' is a convenient scapegoat which deflects attention from the banks, the planning commission, the political establishment, and the big developers. In San Francisco, the well-being of the gay community has become embroiled in the high-stakes politics of urban real estate." Gayle S. Rubin, *Deviations: A Gayle S. Rubin Reader* (Duke University Press, 2011), 167–8.
9 Hanhardt, *Safe Space*, 102.

10 Concretely, there were also calls for there to be more gays and lesbian in the police force and to raise awareness among police of homophobic violence. Ibid., 104.
11 Ibid.
12 Ibid., 105. See also Manuel Castells, *The City and the Grassroots: A Cross-Cultural Theory of Urban Social Movements* (University of California Press, 1983), 97–172.
13 See Loïc Wacquant, *Punishing the Poor* (Duke University Press, 2009).
14 Regarding "lives worth living," see Judith Butler, *Frames of War: When Is Life Grievable?* (Verso, 2009), 22; and Judith Butler, *Precarious Life* (Verso, 2004).
15 As Sara Ahmed writes, "We can reflect on the *ontology of insecurity* within the constitution of the political: it *must be* presumed that things are not secure, in and of themselves, in order to justify the imperative *to make things secure*." Sara Ahmed, *The Cultural Politics of Emotion* (Routledge, 2004), 76.
16 In reference to the systematic hyperfocus on homophobic aggression carried out by teenage delinquents or gangs.
17 Black, Indigenous, and Hispanic lesbians made up the activist groups and mobilized communities that did the most to build a radical movement against the violence by police (and prisons) inherent to the intrinsically racist and heterosexist capitalist system. Through this, they also worked to do away with the language of fear, including (or especially) by criticizing and abandoning its supposedly positive or empowering iterations, like "No more fear," "Fear is changing sides," and "We aren't scared." See Hanhardt, *Safe Space*, 132.
18 Newton, *To Die for the People*, 152.
19 Ibid.
20 Ibid.
21 "Some problems we share as women, some we do not. You fear your children will grow up to join the patriarchy and testify against you, we fear our children will be dragged from a car and shot down in the street, and you will turn your backs upon the reasons they are dying." Audre Lorde, *Sister Outsider* (Persephone Press, 1982) in *Zami, Sister Outsider, Undersong* (Quality Paperback Book Club, 1993), 119.
22 From an interview published in the July 1974 issue of *The Tide*. Quoted in Hanhardt, *Safe Space*, 150.
23 Ibid., 152.
24 Alyson M. Cole and Kyoo Lee, "Safe," *Women's Studies Quarterly* 39, no. 1/2 (2011).
25 Wendy Brown, *States of Injury: Power and Freedom in Late Modernity* (Princeton University Press, 1995), 52.

26 June Jordan, "Notes Towards a Model of Resistance," in *Some of Us Did Not Die: New and Selected Essays* (Basic/Civitas Books, 2003), 78. June Jordan (1936–2002) was a contemporary Caribbean American (her parents migrated from Jamaica) poet and essayist. As an activist, she was a prominent member of the Black Power and lesbian feminist movements.
27 Ibid., 79.
28 Ibid.
29 Ibid., 80.
30 Ibid.
31 Ibid.
32 June Jordan, "I Am Seeking an Attitude," in *Some of Us Did Not Die*, 100.
33 Let's not forget that in the real world, catcalling is mostly negative: "You're ugly!" "Fat ass!" etc.
34 For an analysis of the game, see Thea Lim, "Genderlicious: What Do You Think of *Hey Baby!?*," Bitch Media, August 4, 2011, bitchmedia.org.
35 Some other initiatives responding to street harassment include: (i) Holla Back New York, which is an LGBTIQ collective that has since expanded to several other cities in North America, and whose goal is to film or photograph harassers and post their images on the group's blog. The site is also a trove of practical and theoretical information for the struggle against heterosexism: hollabacknyc.blogspot.com. (ii) *Femme de la rue* is a documentary film by Sofie Peeters about sexual harassment in Brussels; there is also Rob Bliss's film starring Shoshana Roberts, *Ten Hours of Walking in NYC as a Woman*. Both are available on YouTube. (iii) In Egypt, there is the HarassMap collective, whose work is on harassmap.org, and also the short video by Tinne Van Loon and Colette Ghunim called *Creepers on an Egyptian Bridge*, from September 2015. (iv) In January 2015, Everlast (a martial arts equipment company) released a video showing men being tricked into catcalling their own mothers. (v) In Mexico, the feminist collective Las Morras films routine scenes of street harassment and their resistance to the constant calls. Their videos are widely available online, including on YouTube.
36 Concerning contemporary feminist thinking on self-defense, most feminist approaches to violence understand the use of violence as politically aporetic. There are three main series of arguments. The first is essentialist and argues that nonviolence is consubstantial with femininity—however, this position amounts to an approach based on the shared history of pacifist and

feminist movements. The second series of arguments sees the use of violence as mimetism, and therefore as a form of collaboration with patriarchy. The third series is the most pragmatic, warning about the danger involved in resorting to violence, especially considering how women are resigned to ignorance and inexperience of the matter, but also because violence will trigger far more violence in reprisal. Broadly speaking, the two intellectual traditions that see feminist self-defense (and by extension the use of defensive violence) as substantially legitimate are contractualism and anarchism.

37 Judith Halberstam, "Imagined Violence/Queer Violence: Representation, Rage, and Resistance," *Social Text* 37 (1993): 187–202.

38 See Donna Haraway, "A Cyborg Manifesto: Science, Technology, and Socialist Feminism in the Late Twentieth Century," in *Manifestly Haraway* (University of Minnesota Press, 2016).

39 See Amanda Denis Phillips, "Gamer Trouble: The Dynamics of Difference in Video Games" (PhD diss., University of California Santa Barbara, 2014); and Bernard Perron and Mark J. P. Wolf, eds., *Video Game Reader 2* (Routledge, 2009).

40 Regarding "empowerment," see Marie-Hélène Bacqué and Carole Biewener, *L'Empowerment: une pratique émancipatrice* (La Découverte, 2013).

41 See Carole Pateman, *The Sexual Contract* (Stanford University Press, 1988).

Reprisals

1 One need look no further than how commonplace contemporary portrayals of radical powerlessness are. Poster campaigns about famine, leprosy, or violence against women plaster subway stations in every big city in western Europe at appointed times, constituting the most prosaic expression of a gendered and racialized semiology. Lepers, battered women, starving children from Ethiopia, Somalia, or South Sudan are all defenseless figures that the population should take into consideration ethically. Some of the rhetoric about public policy to prevent or combat social injustice and inequality, whether nationally or internationally, makes use of the register of compassionate protection.

2 [The name of this office in French is *le secrétariat d'État chargé de la Famille et de la Solidarité*. These portfolios are part of the Ministry of Health and change with each government. —Trans.]

3 See Pauline Delage, *Violences conjugales: Du combat féministe à la cause publique* (Presses de Science-po, 2017).
4 Prevention and awareness-raising are not quite the same, in that campaigns aimed at prevention are rarer than those that seek to "raise awareness," and they also show the political will to combat violence. As a comparison, the municipal government of Paris supported a 2008 campaign not framed around prevention but around combatting violence against women in the city. It featured images of activists from various feminist organizations (ASFAD, CFCV, Femmes Solidaires, GAMS, MFPF, NPNS) forming something like a human chain of solidarity. For instance, one poster by an organization showed an activist holding the hand of a woman whose arm alone was visible. The imagery is quite different, since it evokes the idea of feminist solidarity among women in the struggle against the violence they experience, which allows that violence to be reframed in terms of relations of power and domination. Pauline Delage provides an analysis of the activities of feminist collectives in the struggle against violence against women. Among other examples, she cites the charter of the Fédération Nationale Solidarité Femmes (National Federation of Feminist Solidarity) adopted at their general assembly on May 28 and 29, 2011: "The member organizations of the FNSF share a feminist political analysis of the violence that is wielded against women . . . The Fédération Nationale Solidarité Femmes (FNSF) condemns and commits to struggle against intimate partner violence and all forms of violence against women. The struggle against violence against women is shared by all feminist organizations, including the Fédération. This violence includes rape, incest, workplace sexual harassment, prostitution, and sexual mutilation, and combatting it is part of the broader movement to transform the relationship between men and women to be one of equality." See Pauline Delage, "Des héritages sans testament: L'appropriation différentielle des idées féministes dans la lutte contre la violence conjugale en France et aux États-Unis," *Politix* 109 (2015): 27.
5 Regarding the issue of mobilizing emotions through public actions and the politicization of causes, see Sandrine LeFranc and Lilian Mathieu, eds., *Mobilisations des victimes* (Presses universitaires de Rennes, 2009).
6 Roland Barthes, *Camera Lucida: Reflections on Photography*, trans. Richard Howard (Hill and Wang, 1981), 9. *Camera Lucida* is a text about photography, but it is also a text about the death of Barthes's mother and grieving. See "the wakening of intractable reality," p. 119.
7 Ibid., 14.

8   This is a characteristic of journalistic or advertising photography: "They come from the world to me without my asking; they are only 'images,' their mode of appearance is heterogenous." Ibid., 16.
9   Drawing on Sartre, Barthes writes that the people in a photograph "drift between the shores of perception, between sign and image, without ever approaching either." Ibid., 20.
10 Ibid., 41.
11 Barthes gives journalistic and pornographic photography as examples.
12 "In these images, no punctum: a certain shock—the literal can traumatize—but no disturbance; the photo can 'shout,' not wound... I glance through them, I don't recall them; no detail (in some corner) ever interrupts my reading: I am interested in them (as I am interested in the world), I do not love them." Ibid.
13 Ibid., 53.
14 Ibid., 91.
15 See Jacqueline Rose, *Sexuality in the Field of Vision* (Verso, 1986); and Linda Williams, *Hard Core: Power, Pleasure, and the "Frenzy of the Visible"* (University of California Press, 1989). As Rutvica Andrijasevic has shown in her analysis of the International Organization for Migration's campaigns: "The production of femininity through representational strategies of victimization and eroticization seems to be intrinsically bound to the female body as a spectacle." Rutvica Andrijasevic, "Beautiful Dead Bodies: Gender, Migration, and Representation in Anti-Trafficking Campaigns," *Feminist Review* 86, no. 1 (2007): 39.
16 "The display of suffering and beautiful victims positions the woman's body as the object of the (male) gaze and mobilizes erotic ways of looking that disclose a voyeuristic eroticization and fetishist fascination with a severed/captive female body. The representation of violence is thus itself violent." Ibid., 42. Susan Sontag's work on images of the suffering of others inspired us, although she is dealing with war photography and not staged photos, as is the case here. Susan Sontag, *Regarding the Pain of Others* (Picador, 2004).
17 "Narratives can make us understand. Photographs do something else: they haunt us." Sontag, *Regarding the Pain of Others*, 89.
18 Helen Zahavi, *The Weekend* (Donald I. Fine Inc., 1991). [Citations refer to the US edition of Helen Zahavi's book, which was titled *The Weekend*. The author's original title, *Dirty Weekend*, is employed in the body of the text. —Trans.]
19 Ibid, 2.
20 Ibid, 11.

21 See Denise Riley, *Am I That Name? Feminism and the Category of Women in History*, University of Minnesota Press, 1988, 6.
22 Zahavi, *The Weekend*, 2.
23 "'Ask not what I want from you. Ask rather what you can get from me. I don't take. I give. I'm a very giving person. I'm going to give you what you deserve.'

'If you call again, I'll report you.'

'Only if I call again? You're enjoying it this time then. I knew you would. I knew you would enjoy it. I know what you'd enjoy. I want you to stand in front of the light, facing the wall, so you're in profile. Then I want you to touch yourself. I want you to do that for me now and then I want—'

She slammed down the phone. She slammed down the phone and slumped in the chair and felt the fear turning and the nausea rising." Ibid., 10–11.
24 "They had everything, and they knew they had everything, and it seemed only right that they had everything." Ibid., 146.
25 Regarding the prologue: "This is the day her story starts. What went before ... was just the prologue." Ibid., 22. Regarding "What it is like to be a woman": "What is it like to be a bat?" is the title of a famous article by the philosopher Thomas Nagel in which he revisits a classic problem in the philosophy of knowledge using an experimental situation to analyze the limits of how experience is situated. Not only can we never know what it is like to be a bat, but no supposedly objective observer could claim to reconstruct a bat's lived experience, even though it is possible to determine certain structural traits or properties. In Nagel's example, what makes the bat unknowable—or, more specifically, what makes its perspective unique—is not its individuality. Rather, any being's singular perspective on the world (which make up the phenomenal world that scientists claim is an abstraction) is specific, but it is also a constituent part of intersubjectivity. This means that we cannot know what it means to be a bat because we don't belong to this species, but the experiences of each "I," although unique (in that they are intimate, singular experiences), are commensurable. Nagel's text can be read much more politically: relations of power, and the symbolic representations that contribute to their reproduction, produce frameworks of intelligibility. They serve as phenomenal borders, barriers between the species, and make it impossible to understand how life is experienced or the world is understood from a different point of view. See Thomas Nagel, "What Is It Like to Be a Bat?" *The Philosophical Review* 83 (1974).

26 "I am going to hurt you. If you tell the police, I will kill you. But if you don't, I'll only hurt you. It will happen soon. I will come into your home and I will hurt you. I want you to imagine what I'm going to do. I want you to picture in your mind the different ways I can give you pain. Think of the worst thing I can do to you, and think of me doing it." Zahavi, *The Weekend*, 20.
27 Ibid., 33.
28 Ibid., 48.
29 Ibid., 22.
30 Walking down the street, she spots a sign that reads: "Iranian Clairvoyant Services. Unlock your hidden powers. The key is within." Ibid.
31 Ibid., 31
32 Ibid., 35.
33 "You're unlucky because the rules have changed, and nobody let you know." Ibid., 115.
34 "Even Bella, even brittle little Bella, can lift a hammer. Even she can hold it in her hands, and swing it high, and bring it down. The crunch of metal on bone was a fairly unusual sound . . . The foundations of his world were being shaken so fiercely that he hardly remembered to scream, and for one ghastly moment she thought he might be going into a state of catatonic shock, which would have denied her the human interaction she valued so highly." Ibid., 58.
35 This very short time frame makes clear that daily violence is not latent but crass—it is high-intensity, and the smallest thing can trigger it.
36 Ibid., 167.
37 Ibid., 108, 134, 147, 133, 183.
38 "Within two days, she would have learned that you mustn't wait too long before you do it . . . Women like her can't afford to wait. Brittle-boned women aren't built to absorb blows. You can't wait too long, if you're Bella . . . Women like her have to do it and run. Women like her can't sit and wait. No one will save them if they just sit and wait." Ibid., 41. "If you hear them say they're sorry, don't believe it. They're never sorry and it wouldn't make a difference if they were." Ibid., 60. "She has to make them understand that she'll chop off the hand that would harm her . . . But she can't tell them. To tell them is to warn them, and to warn them is to arm them." Ibid., 119. "A rape-scream doesn't bring anyone." Ibid., 168. "The thing about the knife, the thing you must remember, if you think you'd like a knife: it's only as strong as the hand that holds it. And if the hand isn't strong, it must be quick. She has to quickly slide it in him, here, there and everywhere. She has

39 In an article published in 1983, "To Be and Be Seen: The Politics of Reality," the feminist philosopher Marilyn Frye describes what she terms the phallocratic scheme: "The phallocratic scheme does not admit women as authors of perception, as seers ... The hypothesis that we are seeing from a different point of view, and hence simply seeing something he cannot see, is not available to a man, is not in his repertoire, so long as his total conception of the situation includes a conception of women as not authoritative perceivers like himself, that is, so long as he does not count women as men. And no wonder such a man finds women incomprehensible." See Marilyn Frye, *The Politics of Reality: Essays in Feminist* Theory (The Crossing Press, 1983), 165–6. "to slash him where she can, before he reaches out and takes the wrist that bears the hand that holds the knife, and snaps it like a twig." Ibid., 185.

40 Zahavi, *The Weekend*, 162–3.
41 The hunting metaphor recurs several times, for instance on p. 178.
42 Ibid., 74.
43 "It must be tough when you're Tim. If you're an ordinary, honest-to-goodness, salt-of-the-earth sort of guy, who likes swilling beer with the boys and swapping tales of random conquest. If you find a silent woman to feed your fantasy, and you stroke your heavy scrotum as you whisper dank obscenities down the line. If you trail her in the street, and you watch her shrivel up, and it makes you feel like a man. And you don't question it, you don't doubt it, you don't think twice about it. You've got a cock and the cock is king. Then suddenly, horribly, disgustingly, she opens her filthy mouth and she whispers filthy words. It's not meant to be like this. You don't dream of it like this. You're not even sure if you want it, if it's going to be like this. The lousy bitch. The lousy, stinking, prick-tease bitch, they're all the same." Ibid., 45–6.
44 "Not all have given up the battle." Simone de Beauvoir, *The Second Sex*, trans. H. M. Parshley (Jonathan Cape, 1953), 23.
45 Zahavi, *The Weekend*, 41.
46 Ibid., 147.
47 See Patricia Paperman and Sandra Laugier, eds., *Le Souci des autres: Éthique et politique du care* (Éditions de l'École des hautes études en sciences sociales, 2005); and Marie Gareau and Alice Le Goff, *Care, justice et dépendance: Introduction aux théories du care* (PUF, 2010).
48 See Pascale Molinier, "Quel est le bon témoin du care?," in *Qu'est-ce que le care? Souci des autres, sensibilité, responsabilité,*

ed. Pascale Molinier, Sandra Laugier, and Patricia Paperman (Payot, 2009).
49 For "radical anxiety," see Grégoire Chamayou, *Manhunts: A Philosophical History* (Princeton University Press, 2012), 59.
50 "The maintenance of phallocratic reality requires that the attention of women be focused on men and men's projects." Frye, *The Politics of Reality*, 172.
51 Marilyn Frye observes that the etymology of the English and Spanish word "real" involves expressions connected to "royal," or that pertain to the king. "Real property is that which is proper to the king . . . He sees what is proper to him. To be real is to be visible to the king." Ibid., 155.
52 For "modest witness," see Donna Haraway, "ModestWitness@SecondMillenium," in *Modest_Witness@Second_Millenium. FemaleMan_Meets_OncoMouse: Feminism and Technoscience* (Routledge, 1997).
53 See Miranda Fricker, *Epistemic Injustice: Power and the Ethics of Knowing* (Oxford University Press, 2009); and Ian James Kidd, José Medina, and Gaile Pohlaus Jr., eds., *The Routledge Handbook of Epistemic Injustice* (Routledge, 2017).
54 See Robert N. Proctor and Londa Schiebinger, *Agnotology: The Making and Unmaking of Ignorance* (Stanford University Press, 2008).
55 See Charles Mills, "White Ignorance," in *Race and Epistemologies of Ignorance*, ed. Shannon Sullivan and Nancy Tuana (SUNY Press, 2007).
56 The end result of this knowledge is to capture, tire out, or kill prey that is isolated, cornered, or considered particularly vulnerable (or, on the contrary, whose quality makes for a better trophy or yield). Additionally, hunting allows for many different goals: domestication, use and exploitation, exhibition and display, domination, eradication, and extermination. In a hunt, there are no belligerent parties (who would be respected as such), and there are no enemies rightly speaking. There are only prey, whose *lives do not matter* and are not worth sparing, preserving, or even living.
57 Gilles Deleuze, "Michel Tournier and the World Without Others," in *The Logic of Sense*, trans. Mark Lester (Athlone Press, 1990), 305. Deleuze is citing Michel Tournier, *Friday, or, The Other Island*, trans. N. Denny (Penguin, 1973).
58 Deleuze, "Michel Tournier," 307.
59 Ibid.
60 Neighborhood Watch is an organization founded in the late 1960s in the United States (drawing explicitly on organized vigilantism

from the colonial period) whose goal was to supplement the police by demonstrating concern for anything unusual or that threatened the security of their neighborhood. In France, this model was imported under the name *Voisins vigilants* in the mid-2000s.

61 Lizette Alvarez, "Justice Department Investigation Is Sought in Florida Teenager's Shooting Death," *New York Times*, March 16, 2012.

62 Ibid.